CONFLICTED BOUNDARIES IN
WISDOM AND APOCALYPTICISM

Society of Biblical Literature

Symposium Series

Christopher R. Matthews,
Editor

Number 35

CONFLICTED BOUNDARIES IN
WISDOM AND APOCALYPTICISM

CONFLICTED BOUNDARIES IN WISDOM AND APOCALYPTICISM

Edited by
Benjamin G. Wright III and Lawrence M. Wills

Society of Biblical Literature
Atlanta

CONFLICTED BOUNDARIES IN WISDOM AND APOCALYPTICISM

Copyright © 2005 by the Society of Biblical Literature

All rights reserved. No part of this work may be reproduced or transmitted in any form or by any means, electronic or mechanical, including photocopying and recording, or by means of any information storage or retrieval system, except as may be expressly permitted by the 1976 Copyright Act or in writing from the publisher. Requests for permission should be addressed in writing to the Rights and Permissions Office, Society of Biblical Literature, 825 Houston Mill Road, Atlanta, GA 30329 USA.

Cover photo of Pesher Habakkuk, Qumran, courtesy of the D. Samuel and Jeane H. Gottesman Center for Biblical Manuscripts, The Israel Museum, Jerusalem.

Cover photo of the leaf of Papyrus 46 containing 2 Cor 11:33–12:9 courtesy of the Papyrology Collection, Graduate Library, University of Michigan.

Library of Congress Cataloging-in-Publication Data

Conflicted boundaries in wisdom and apocalypticism / edited by Benjamin G. Wright, III, and Lawrence M. Wills.
      p. cm. — (Society of Biblical Literature symposium series ; no. 35)
  Includes bibliographical references and index.
  ISBN-13: 978-1-58983-184-1 (paper binding : alk. paper)
  ISBN-10: 1-58983-184-5 (paper binding : alk. paper)
  1. Apocalyptic literature—History and criticism. 2. Apocryphal books—Criticism, interpretation, etc. 3. Wisdom—Religious aspects—Judaism. 4. Wisdom—Religious aspects—Christianity. 5. Bible. N.T.—Criticism, interpretation, etc. I. Wills, Lawrence M. (Lawrence Mitchell), 1954– II. Wright, Benjamin G. (Benjamin Givens) III. Series: Symposium series (Society of Biblical Literature) ; no. 35.
  BS646.C658 2005
  220'.046—dc22
                                                                          2005017070

13 12 11 10 09 08 07 06 05   5 4 3 2 1

Printed in the United States of America on acid-free, recycled paper conforming to ANSI/NISO Z39.48-1992 (R1997) and ISO 9706:1994 standards for paper permanence.

Contents

Abbreviations vii

Introduction
Benjamin G. Wright III and Lawrence M. Wills 1

Part 1: Issues and Outlook

Wisdom and Apocalypticism in Early Judaism: Some Points
for Discussion
George W. E. Nickelsburg 17

Response to George Nickelsburg, "Wisdom and Apocalypticism
in Early Judaism"
Sarah J. Tanzer 39

Response to Sarah Tanzer
George W. E. Nickelsburg 51

Part 2: Wisdom and Apocalypticism in Early Judaism

Wisdom, Apocalypticism, and the Pedagogical Ethos of 4QInstruction
Matthew J. Goff 57

The *Psalms of Solomon* and the Ideology of Rule
Rodney A. Werline 69

Putting the Puzzle Together: Some Suggestions concerning
the Social Location of the Wisdom of Ben Sira
Benjamin G. Wright III 89

Israel at the Mercy of Demonic Powers: An Enochic Interpretation
of Postexilic Imperialism
Patrick A. Tiller 113

The Politics of Cultural Production in Second Temple Judea:
Historical Context and Political-Religious Relations of the
Scribes Who Produced 1 *Enoch*, Sirach, and Daniel
Richard A. Horsley 123

PART 3: WISDOM AND APOCALYPTICISM IN EARLY CHRISTIANITY

"Who Is Wise and Understanding among You?" (James 3:13):
An Analysis of Wisdom, Eschatology, and Apocalypticism
in the Letter of James
Patrick J. Hartin 149

The Rich and the Poor in James: An Apocalyptic Ethic
Patrick A. Tiller 169

City Visions, Feminine Figures, and Economic Critique:
A Sapiential *Topos* in the Apocalypse
Barbara R. Rossing 181

"The *Basileia* of Jesus Is on the Wood": The *Epistle of Barnabas*
and the Ideology of Rule
Ellen Bradshaw Aitken 197

Select Bibliography 215

Contributors 221

Index of Ancient Literature 223

Index of Modern Authors 237

ABBREVIATIONS

All abbreviations not in this list, including those of ancient texts, can be found in Patrick H. Alexander et al., *The SBL Handbook of Style* (Peabody, Mass.: Hendrickson, 1999).

AB	Anchor Bible
ABD	*Anchor Bible Dictionary*. Edited by D. N. Freedman. 6 vols. New York: Doubleday, 1992.
ABRL	Anchor Bible Reference Library
ANRW	*Aufstieg und Niedergang der römischen Welt: Geschichte und Kultur Roms im Spiegel der neueren Forschung*. Edited by H. Temporini and W. Haase. Berlin: de Gruyter, 1972–.
ANTZ	Arbeiten zur neutestamentlichen Theologie und Zeitgeschichte
BETL	Bibliotheca ephemeridum theologicarum lovaniensium
Bib	*Biblica*
BZAW	Beihefte zur Zeitschrift für die alttestamentliche Wissenschaft
CBQ	*Catholic Biblical Quarterly*
CBQMS	Catholic Biblical Quarterly Monograph Series
CNT	Commentaire de Nouveau Testament
ConBOT	Coniectanea biblica: Old Testament Series
DJD	Discoveries in the Judean Desert
DSD	*Dead Sea Discoveries*
DSS	Dead Sea Scrolls
DTT	*Dansk teologisk tidsskrift*
HR	*History of Religions*
HTR	*Harvard Theological Review*
HTS	Harvard Theological Studies
HUCA	*Hebrew Union College Annual*
HvTSt	*Hervormde teologiese studies*
IB	*Interpreter's Bible*. Edited by G. A. Buttrick et al. 12 vols. New York: Abingdon, 1951–1957.
IDBSup	*Interpreter's Dictionary of the Bible: Supplementary Volume*. Edited by K. Crim. Nashville: Abingdon, 1976.
Int	*Interpretation*

JBL	*Journal of Biblical Literature*
JJS	*Journal of Jewish Studies*
JRS	*Journal of Roman Studies*
JSJSup	Journal for the Study of Judaism Supplement Series
JSNTSup	Journal for the Study of the New Testament Supplement Series
JSOT	*Journal for the Study of the Old Testament*
JSOTSup	Journal for the Study of the Old Testament Supplement Series
JSP	*Journal for the Study of the Pseudepigrapha*
JSPSup	Journal for the Study of the Pseudepigrapha Supplement Series
JTS	*Journal of Theological Studies*
LXX	Septuagint
NIGTC	New International Greek Testament Commentary
NovT	*Novum Testamentum*
NovTSup	Supplements to Novum Testamentum
NRSV	New Revised Standard Version
NTOA	Novum Testamentum et Orbis Antiquus
NTS	*New Testament Studies*
OTP	*Old Testament Pseudepigrapha*. Edited by J. H. Charlesworth. 2 vols. New York: Doubleday, 1983–1985.
PEQ	*Palestine Exploration Quarterly*
RevQ	*Revue de Qumran*
RB	*Revue Biblique*
RSV	Revised Standard Version
SBL	Society of Biblical Literature
SBLEJL	Society of Biblical Literature Early Judaism and Its Literature
SBLSP	Society of Biblical Literature Seminar Papers
SBT	Studies in Biblical Theology
SC	Sources chrétiennes. Paris: Cerf, 1943–.
SJLA	Studies in Judaism in Late Antiquity
SR	*Studies in Religion*
STDJ	*Studies on the Texts of the Desert of Judah*
SUNT	Studien zur Umwelt des Neuen Testaments
SVTP	Studia in Veteris Testamenti pseudepigraphica
TDNT	*Theological Dictionary of the New Testament*. Edited by G. Kittel and G. Fredrich. Translated by G. W. Bromiley. 10 vols. Grand Rapids: Eerdmans, 1964–1976.
VC	*Vigiliae Christianae*
VT	*Vetus Testamentum*
VTSup	Supplements to Vetus Testamentum
WUNT	Wissenschaftliche Untersuchungen zum Neuen Testament

INTRODUCTION

Benjamin G. Wright III and Lawrence M. Wills

For ten years now, the Wisdom and Apocalypticism Group has tried to bring together categories that are too often kept separate in the Society of Biblical Literature: wisdom *and* apocalypticism; ancient Judaism *and* early Christianity; historical studies, literary studies, *and* sociological analysis; analysis on the objects of study (ancient texts) *and* reflection on the subjects who study them (scholars). This Symposium volume originated from a desire to present some of the results of the work of this Group. Our primary aim is to highlight the issues and questions connected with the problem of the relationship between wisdom and apocalypticism in early Jewish and Christian literature. The papers presented here all explore, but frequently in different ways, how these scholarly constructions do or do not reflect what we see in these literatures. Like the Group from which they derive, all are concerned in one way or another to scrutinize the ambiguities of the division that scholars have traditionally seen between wisdom and apocalyptic literature.

Whereas a number of older studies suggested that there were indeed connections between wisdom and apocalypticism, they most frequently constructed some genetic relationship between the two. So, for example, Gerhard von Rad argued that apocalyptic literature actually had its roots in wisdom.[1] By and large, scholars have not accepted von Rad's arguments without modification, and the notion that wisdom and apocalyptic represent fundamentally different categories, whether in literary genre or worldview, has persisted into current scholarship. These papers, whether explicitly or implicitly, explore and challenge that generally held view.

In 1994, a number of scholars from the fields of New Testament and Second Temple Judaism within the SBL inaugurated the Wisdom and Apocalypticism in Early Judaism and Early Christianity Consultation (which later was renewed as a Group), because, after several decades of influential studies of wisdom and apocalypticism treated separately and some far-reaching contributions that addressed the relationship between

---

1. Gerhard von Rad, *Wisdom in Israel* (trans. J. D. Martin; London: SCM, 1972).

wisdom and apocalypticism, the Group's founders believed that the concepts of these two modes of discourse had become reified in scholarly conversation and differentiated as fundamentally different kinds of language. This Consultation took up the task of reexamining the social context of wisdom and apocalypticism and rethinking the overly rigid boundaries that had been erected between them. The Group differed from others within the SBL, and indeed other discussions of these topics outside of the Society, by intentionally shifting much of the focus to the social context and by opening up the parameters of what would be discussed. As the first sentence in this introduction indicates, the Group took a *both-and* approach to the problem. Since the perceived gulf between wisdom *and* apocalypticism is still very much part of scholarly discourse, both wisdom *and* apocalyptic texts were included, and, more to the point, texts that had typically been analyzed as *either* wisdom *or* apocalyptic were considered in terms of how they engaged *both* modes of discourse. In addition, the Group examined *both* Jewish *and* Christian texts, and a longer time span was discussed than is usually the case in these types of scholarly meetings. In order to expand the parameters, the steering committee invited participants with specialties in Hebrew Bible, Second Temple Judaism, and New Testament (and frequently scholars from other related fields) who approached these literatures from different methodological points of view. As a part of this agenda, questions of class and political context were self-consciously introduced to try to gain some purchase on the elusive sociological contexts of the texts.

The Group operated from the beginning with several methodological goals at the forefront, and the editors selected the papers contained in this volume primarily for the ways that they illustrate how the Group pursued those goals.[2] First, we wanted to problematize the categories of wisdom and apocalypticism, which had become so deeply embedded in scholarly constructions of ancient Judaism and Christianity. Indeed, from the very first meeting of the Group the problem of how scholars had reified these constructions was apparent. The issues at stake seemed akin to the Zen Buddhist warning about fingers pointing at the moon: the finger can properly direct the viewer's gaze, but woe to the person who confuses the finger for the moon. Practically all of the papers in this volume address this fundamental difficulty in some way or another. Second, the Group struggled with the basic awareness (1) that human

---

2. A full listing of all the papers presented to the Group and the names of respondents can be found as an appendix to this introduction. As one can see simply from scanning the list, the discussions in the Group produced quite a number of distinguished papers, many of which have been published elsewhere. (These publication data are included here.)

beings in real social contexts produce texts and (2) that reconstructing those social worlds from the texts is fraught with what seem at times to be insurmountable obstacles. Yet, one of the methods of getting at the relationship between wisdom and apocalyptic would be, if possible, (1) to identify those who wrote these texts, (2) to locate their position(s) in the landscapes of Second Temple Judaism and early Christianity, and (3) to investigate how they might relate, if they do at all. The papers collected in this volume take this problem as fundamental to the task of the Group, and social context constitutes a central theme of the papers as a whole. Third, because we were trying to break down categories that had traditionally been kept apart, the Group felt the need to arrive at a more accurate description of these modes of discourse. The presentations given to the Group over its history thus far have been characterized by a multiplicity of approaches, including genre analysis, rhetoric and discourse analysis, thematic analysis, and examination of worldviews. Again, a number of the papers printed here utilize these approaches.

This volume collects papers presented to the Group between the years 1994 and 2002 that, taken together, give a good indication of the results and progress of the Group's work. They analyze a variety of Jewish and Christian texts, Daniel, Sirach, the Enoch corpus, *Psalms of Solomon*, 4QInstruction, James, Revelation, and the *Epistle of Barnabas*, in an attempt to carry through these methodological goals. They also highlight the many questions that remain to be explored. While as a working Group we are convinced that we have made tremendous progress in the first decade of the Group's existence, there is a definite what-next factor in this entire collection. Much work remains to be done in pursuit of the methodological goals outlined here, and many other questions undoubtedly will arise in the continued course of our investigations. Thus, this Symposium volume and the papers contained in it provide a sense of the state of the question in the Group's work thus far and the prospects for future discussion. What the Group has accomplished successfully, as this volume demonstrates, is to show that wisdom and apocalypticism *are indeed* related both in many of their literary aspects and in their social contexts. As the following brief summaries of the papers in this volume reveal, the categories of wisdom and apocalypticism are well on their way to being fundamentally rethought.

In the first session of the Wisdom and Apocalypticism Group in 1994, George W. E. Nickelsburg presented a paper that introduced many of the issues that the Group would investigate over the next ten years ("Wisdom and Apocalypticism in Early Judaism: Some Points for Discussion"). In this presentation he reviews the history of investigation of wisdom and apocalypticism, and argues that there remains in the field a lack of clarity about "the nature and interrelationship of the wisdom, prophetic, and eschatological components in Jewish apocalyptic writings." Nickelsburg highlights two problems that have been constitutive for the work of the Group and for the publication of the present collection: (1) the terms "wisdom" and "apocalyptic" have become too narrowly reified into separate and mutually exclusive concepts, and (2) the social world and roles of the authors are not clearly described. In an attempt to evoke possible strategies to address both of these problems, he argues that texts usually considered sapiential on one hand or apocalyptic on the other were both produced by "wisdom circles" that were changing quickly in the Greco-Roman period. He surveys texts that are generally considered sapiential (and finds eschatological elements), texts that are generally considered apocalyptic (and finds sapiential elements), and texts that "complicate the categories:" Wisdom of Solomon and the Qumran scrolls. He then proceeds to a discussion of the social settings of their composition and plots possible means of investigating them that would avoid the pitfalls of a rigid distinction of the genres and of the social locations and roles of their authors.

One of the responses to the 1994 presentation, by Sarah J. Tanzer, is reprinted here.[3] While agreeing with the overall program that Nickelsburg was charting, Tanzer raises a number of questions about how the investigation might proceed. Where Nickelsburg focuses mainly on the problems inherent in defining apocalyptic genres, Tanzer turns more to the problems of defining wisdom texts. Although she agrees that the overlap of sapiential and apocalyptic texts is important, the clarification of the designation "wisdom text" would aid in the discussion of the range of texts listed by Nickelsburg. Further, though Nickelsburg speaks of the more precise designation of social location and roles of a number of authors, Tanzer notes that a close analysis of individual texts may uncover more precise clues (an approach, as it turned out, that some of the other essays exemplify). Nickelsburg, in a two-volume engagement with his scholarly work, published a response to Tanzer's response, which is also reprinted here. He points to the possibility of finding the mysterious ingredient that defines wisdom in the theme of active searching. Wisdom is not just known; it is sought out. In addition, wisdom texts say much about whether God's role will be found as the source of wisdom. These texts

---

3. The version reprinted here is the updated response published in the two-volume tribute to Nickelsburg, "Response to 'Wisdom and Apocalypticism in Early Judaism': Some Points for Discussion," in *George W. E. Nickelsburg in Perspective: An Ongoing Dialogue of Learning* (ed. J. Neusner and A. J. Avery-Peck; 2 vols.; Leiden: Brill, 2003), 1:288–99. Nickelsburg's response to Tanzer mentioned below was also published in that volume, "Response to Sarah Tanzer," 1:300–303.

differ in their assertion of where one would go to seek out wisdom: reliable experience, nature, dreams, revealed wisdom. Nickelsburg concludes with a restatement of some of the suggestions for how best to proceed in the study of sapiential and apocalyptic texts.

The following papers were presented to the Group with many of the questions in mind that had been raised by Nickelsburg and Tanzer. In "Wisdom, Apocalypticism, and the Pedagogical Ethos of 4QInstruction," Matthew Goff analyzes 4QInstruction as a text from a wisdom genre that has been developed under the influence of the Qumran sect's interest in revealed wisdom and apocalyptic worldview. By bringing wisdom, revealed wisdom, and apocalypticism together in a single text, 4QInstruction is an important continuation of what Hans-Peter Müller and John J. Collins saw in the book of Daniel, that is, mantic wisdom as an intermediary link between wisdom and apocalypticism.[4] Although 4QInstruction takes the form of instructional proverbs addressed to the *mebin* ("understanding one"), it also emphasizes special knowledge of the *raz nihyeh*, "the mystery that is to be." Although *raz*, or mystery, occurs in Daniel and 1 Enoch, *raz nihyeh* is found only at Qumran, and almost exclusively in this text. Further, it is used in a more specific way. Whereas Daniel and *1 Enoch* are written as apocalypses describing the content of the mystery and *future* consequences (even though they may be understood as *present* to the time of the reader), 4QInstruction assumes knowledge of the mystery and urges its proper contemplation: "Wisdom is a two-step process: revelation then contemplation." (One is reminded of Nickelsburg's identification of the essence of wisdom as active searching. Compare also Hartin's view below on the nature of wisdom.) Thus 4QInstruction links a number of aspects of form and content that connect the full range of discourse from practical wisdom and knowledge of creation to revealed wisdom and apocalyptic determinism.

Rodney A. Werline argues that scholarly assumptions about the nature of apocalypticism have affected the interpretation of *Psalms of Solomon* ("The *Psalms of Solomon* and the Ideology of Rule"). References to messianic deliverance have caused this text to be lumped with apocalypses, and vague theological motifs are used to associate it with Pharisees or Essenes. Werline attempts to shift the focus from traditional categories to a more political and sociological investigation. *Psalms of Solomon* relies on Deuteronomic theology to explain the fall of

---

4. Hans-Peter Müller, "Magisch-mantische Weisheit und die Gestalt Daniels," *UF* 1 (1969): 79–94; idem, "Mantische Weisheit und Apokalyptik," in *Congress Volume: Uppsala, 1971* (VTSup 22; Leiden: Brill, 1972), 268–93; and John J. Collins, "The Court-Tales in Daniel and the Development of Apocalyptic," *JBL* 94 (1975): 218–34.

the Hasmonean rulers and the success of the Roman rulers, but there is also the remarkable statement that even the Hasmonean rulers rose to power as a punishment of the people (*Pss. Sol.* 17). Thus, this text critiques both Roman and Hasmonean rule of Judea, while the "pious" look forward to a messianic king in the line of David who will rid Judea of both Roman and false Jewish kings. The pious, who will be reconstituted as the people of Israel, are like disenfranchised scribes; the messiah, in fact, is described as a scribal king. The *Psalms of Solomon* are not written as apocalypses but are similar instead to many of the psalms of the Hebrew Bible. Further, in contrast to the typical apocalyptic view, the fall of Israel is not a result of determinism, but rather, human choice in righting the situation is presumed. A similarity to apocalypticism can be found in the social location of the authors, however. Dissident scribes probably composed Dan 7–12, parts of *1 Enoch*, and *Psalms of Solomon*, for example. The imposition of the category of apocalypticism is thus less valuable than the investigation of the social location of the authors.

In "Putting the Puzzle Together: Some Suggestions concerning the Social Location of the Wisdom of Ben Sira," Benjamin G. Wright III turns specifically to the social location of some of the authors of wisdom and apocalyptic texts. Ben Sira supports the Jerusalem temple and the priesthood and seems to respond to criticisms of them found in the apocalyptic texts Book of the Watchers, Astronomical Book (*1 En.* 6–36 and 72–82, respectively) and the *Aramaic Levi Document*. It is possible, Wright suggests, that the authors of these texts were roughly contemporary and in direct or indirect dialogue with each other. A number of issues are addressed in both Ben Sira and the apocalyptic texts—revelation (both mysteries and dreams), creation, judgment, calendar, and the integrity of the Jerusalem priests—but opposing positions are taken. The apocalyptic texts, for instance, advocate a solar-based calendar, while Ben Sira demythologizes the sun and plays up the moon as regulating the times and seasons. Similarly, the apocalyptic texts condemn the practices of the Jerusalem priests, particularly what their authors considered illegitimate marriages, while Ben Sira is generally positive toward priests. In particular, Sirach, unlike the other texts, supports the restriction of the priesthood to descendants of Aaron. As to social location, then, Wright argues that Ben Sira is "a scribe, with strong priestly connections," while the other texts are a form of "counter wisdom" that arises from alienated scribes.

In "Israel at the Mercy of Demonic Powers: An Enochic Interpretation of Postexilic Imperialism," Patrick A. Tiller analyzes the allegory found in the Animal Apocalypse section of *1 Enoch*. The Animal Apocalypse (*1 En.* 83–90) is influenced by biblical texts such as Jer 25, Ezek 34, and Zech 11, but also by earlier apocalyptic traditions in the Enochic tradition, especially the Book of the Watchers. The latter influence is usually ignored in scholarly discussions, but it is important because it demonstrates an Enochic tradition lasting over several centuries that is not simply based on new interpretations of biblical texts. Further, the political nature of the allegory is often overlooked. The history of imperial rule of Judea is critiqued in the Animal Apocalypse, but also condemned are the high priests and temple authority as a whole. It may even be said that the scribes who produced the Animal Apocalypse looked forward to the eschatological restoration of a purified community under God, but were not interested in establishing one party or another in the temple. Purification of the temple does not seem to play a part in the Animal Apocalypse. This article thus stresses the use and reuse of apocalyptic traditions by alienated scribes who did not envision a renewed temple, but a purified community of scribes.

In an attempt to go beyond the usual vague statements about the "movements" that produced apocalyptic texts such as Daniel and *1 Enoch*, Richard A. Horsley looks to clues within the texts to identify the political allegiances of the authors in regard to the Judean politics of the period ("The Politics of Cultural Production in Second Temple Judea: Historical Context and Political-Religious Relations of the Scribes Who Produced *1 Enoch*, Sirach, and Daniel"). The authors of *1 Enoch* and Daniel and wisdom texts such as Sirach arise from circles of literate scribes, asserts Horsley, and would not have been identified with nonelites. Rather, they were retainers of one or another political faction among the elite, who were in turn in league with (or opposed to) one of the foreign empires. Horsley first analyzes Sirach, and notes his support of the temple priestly establishment and the imperial rule of the Seleucids. Daniel and the early parts of *1 Enoch*, on the other hand, condemn the foreign imperial rule and the temple establishment as well. What the authors of Sirach, Daniel, and *1 Enoch* have in common is that as scribes, they are all retainers of the different rival factions of the ruling aristocrats, and all share a repertoire of sapiential learning. They differ, however, in their attitude toward the Seleucid rulers and the temple. Ultimately, the political situations of the authors is more telling for the function of the text than a purely literary or theological analysis would reveal.

According to Patrick J. Hartin, wisdom texts generally address two areas: ethical admonitions and reflection on the nature of wisdom. Hartin analyzes the Epistle of James with regard to these two areas ("'Who Is Wise and Understanding among You?' [James 3:13]: An Analysis of Wisdom, Eschatology, and Apocalypticism in the Epistle of James"). In both the ethical admonitions and the reflection on the nature of wisdom, James presumes an eschatological version of the ideal of the wise person. Yet in both of these areas James does not make use of fully realized apocalyptic motifs, but an eschatological concern pervades the letter that moves beyond that which is found, for instance, in the prophets. James may even distance himself from the use of some apocalyptic motifs, such as a detailed scene of judgment and punishment. Hartin concludes with a description of similarities between James and *1 Enoch*. But relative to *1 Enoch*, James retains more interest in actions in the present than vindications and punishments in the future. James and *1 Enoch*, then, are not to be seen as texts drawn from the diametrically opposed categories of wisdom and apocalypticism, but rather, they and other texts bring together wisdom, prophecy, apocalypticism, and eschatology. In the case of James, as with Q, "the wisdom tradition functions as the dominant tradition bringing the others together."

A second contribution of Patrick A. Tiller, "The Rich and Poor in James: An Apocalyptic Ethic," was presented to the Wisdom and Apocalypticism Group two years after Hartin's paper and is in explicit dialogue with it (and others from the session). He agrees with Hartin's conclusions about the coexistence of wisdom, prophecy, eschatology, and apocalyptic in James but presses further the question of the attitude toward rich and poor in the epistle. James condemns the rich and advances a strong preferential option for the poor. Tiller investigates the background of the designation "the poor," and finds it in a number of different kinds of discourse in the Hebrew Bible: Deuteronomy, the prophets, but more proximately, in some psalms, Job, and Ben Sira. In addition, it is used in a similar way in *1 Enoch*, and Tiller notes that the "humble poor" in some psalms is utilized also in *Psalms of Solomon*. What is distinctive in this use is the "identification of poverty and piety," which James sees in the context of apocalyptic developments. (Tiller emphasizes this swing toward an apocalyptic worldview slightly more than does Hartin.) An apocalyptic view of reality is reflected in the division of the cosmos into above and below, God and this world, God and the devil, and desire (which leads to sin) and the word of truth (which leads to birth).

The book of Revelation, which is the source of our term "apocalypse," would seem at first to be very distant from any associations with wisdom. It is normally compared with prophetic texts and Jewish apocalypses, but Barbara R. Rossing, in "City Visions and Economic Critique: Transformations of a Sapiential *Topos* in the Apocalypse," argues that wisdom traditions are also important in its composition. The representation of Babylon and New Jerusalem as two women between which the audience must choose is based on a common *topos* found in Jewish wisdom texts and Greek philosophy. But John's application is not strictly "wisdom." It is transferred by John of Patmos from the realm of wisdom and personal morality to the realm of political and economic critique. This use is in keeping with the goals of some apocalypses, but the raw material is from the world of wisdom and moral persuasion. Just as several of the essays analyze a wisdom text to find apocalyptic elements, Rossing analyzes an apocalypse to find wisdom elements. But in all of these papers a neat distinction of wisdom and apocalypticism is problematized.

Ellen Bradshaw Aitken analyzes the *Epistle of Barnabas* and finds within it a connection between ethics, ritual processes, the interpretation of scripture, and knowledge of past, present, and future ("'The *Basileia* of Jesus Is on the Wood': The *Epistle of Barnabas* and the Ideology of Rule"). Here baptism is identified with Jesus' suffering and death on the cross, and the ritual of baptism itself is described as a process by which people enter the reign of Jesus and rule (κυριεύω). This dramatic ritual transformation is set in a context of eschatological dualism: the evil one rules the present age, but members of the covenant of Jesus have escaped this reign and entered into another. The social situation of *Barnabas* is illuminated by the fact that the author imposes sharp boundaries with Judaism. The apocalyptic framework is couched, however, in a context of sapiential instruction of "wisdom, understanding, knowledge (ἐπιστήμη), and gnosis." Thus sapiential wisdom is connected with special knowledge and ritual processes for those within the community, and the proper interpretation of biblical passages.

This collection of essays thus pushes the discussion in a number of directions, but in each article one can find a contribution to an important rethinking of the scholarly constructions that dominate the field. Ultimately, to understand any one of the ancient texts usually labeled as sapiential or apocalyptic, one must come to terms with the social context of the production of all of these texts and with their interrelations. In addition to the contributors to this volume, who advance the discussion in varied and important ways, we wish to thank SBL Symposium Series editor Chris Matthews, not only for accepting this volume for publication, but also for his advice concerning the content and structuring of the volume. In addition, we are grateful to SBL's Editorial Director Bob Buller and Managing Editor Leigh Andersen for their sage counsel and prompt responses in the production of this volume.

APPENDIX TO INTRODUCTION: WISDOM AND APOCALYPTICISM IN EARLY JUDAISM AND EARLY CHRISTIANITY
(Papers and Respondents: 1994–2004)

1994

George W. E. Nickelsburg, "Some Theses on the Interrelationship of Wisdom and Apocalyptic Traditions in Early Judaism" [1994 Seminar Papers, 715–32; J. Neusner and A. J. Avery-Peck, eds., *George W. E.*

Nickelsburg in Perspective: An Ongoing Dialogue of Learning (JSJSup 80; 2 vols.; Leiden: Brill, 2003), 1:267–87]

Respondents: John J. Collins; Sarah J. Tanzer [*George W. E. Nickelsburg in Perspective*, 1:288–99]

Richard A. Horsley, "Wisdom Justified by All Her Children: Examining Allegedly Disparate Traditions in Q" [1994 Seminar Papers, 733–51]

Respondents: Arland Jacobson; Robert Doran

1995

Randal A. Argall, "Reflections on *1 Enoch* and *Sirach*: A Comparative and Conceptual Analysis of the Themes of Revelation, Creation, and Judgment" [1995 Seminar Papers, 337–51]

Respondent: Patrick A. Tiller

E. Elizabeth Johnson, "The Function of Apocalyptic and Wisdom Traditions in Romans 9–11: Rethinking the Questions" [1995 Seminar Papers, 352–61]

Respondent: Robert Jewett

Torleif Elgvin, "Wisdom and Eschatology in an Early Essene Writing (4Q416–418)" [1995 Seminar Papers, 440–63]

Respondent: Daniel J. Harrington

1996 [Joint Session with Sociology of the Literature of the Second Temple Period Group]

Jack T. Sanders, "When Sacred Canopies Collide: The Reception of the Torah of Moses in Light of the Wisdom Literature of the Second Temple Period" [*JSJ* 32 (2001): 121–36]

Respondents: John M. Halligan, "Competing Coordinates in the Berger Parallax"

George W. E. Nickelsburg, "The Enochic Alternative to Deuteronomic Torah" [A compressed version of "Enochic Wisdom: An Alternative to the Mosaic Torah?" in *HESED VE-EMET: Studies in Honor of Ernest S. Frerichs* (ed. J. Magness and S. Gitin; BJS 320; Atlanta: Scholars Press, 1988), 123–32]

Daniel J. Harrington, "Two Early Jewish Approaches to Wisdom: Sirach and Qumran Sapiential Text A" [1996 Seminar Papers, 123–32]

Benjamin G. Wright III, "Putting the Puzzle Together: Some Suggestions concerning the Social Location of the Wisdom of Jesus Ben Sira" [1996 Seminar Papers, 133–49]

Respondent: Lester L. Grabbe

Patrick J. Hartin, "'Who Is Wise and Understanding among You?' (James 3:13): An Analysis of Wisdom, Eschatology and Apocalypticism in the Epistle of James" [1996 Seminar Papers, 483–503; *Hervormde Teologiese Studies* 53 (1997): 969–99]

Matt A. Jackson-McCabe, "A Letter to the Twelve Tribes in the Diaspora: Wisdom and 'Apocalyptic Eschatology' in James" [1996 Seminar Papers, 504–17]

Respondent: Jon L. Berquist

1997

Carol Newsom, "You May Already Be a Winner: Rewards and Punishments in Serekh Ha-Yahad"

Sarah J. Tanzer, "Rewards and Punishments in the Hodayot"

John J. Collins, "The Reward of Piety: Retribution in the Wisdom of Solomon"

Respondent: John Kampen

John S. Kloppenborg, "Reward and Punishment in Matthew's Sermon"

Robert A. Kraft, "Whence and Wherefore? Forms and Functions of the Two Ways Traditions" [published in revised form as "Early Developments of the 'Two-Ways Tradition(s),' in Retrospect" in R. A. Argall et al., *For a Later Generation: The Transformation of Tradition in Israel, Early Judaism and Early Christianity* (Harrisburg, Pa.: Trinity Press International, 2000), 136–43]

Respondent: Anthony J. Saldarini

1998

Benjamin G. Wright III, "The Discourse of Riches and Poverty in Ben Sira" [1998 Seminar Papers, 2:559–78; published in revised form with Claudia V. Camp as "'Who Has Been Tested by Gold and Found Perfect?' Ben Sira's Discourse of Riches and Poverty," *Henoch* 23 (2001): 153–74]

George W. E. Nickelsburg, "Revisiting the Rich and the Poor in 1 Enoch and the Gospel According to Luke" [1998 Seminar Papers, 2:579–605; Neusner and Avery-Peck, *Nickelsburg in Perspective*, 547–71]

Catherine M. Murphy, "The Disposition of Wealth in the Damascus Document Tradition" [material included in her book, *Wealth in the Dead Sea Scrolls and in the Qumran Community* (STDJ 40; Leiden: Brill, 2002)]

Respondents: Claudia V. Camp; Michael A. Knibb

Ronald A. Piper, "Issues of Poverty and Wealth in the Sayings Source Q"

Patrick A. Tiller, "'You Have Dishonored the Poor': The Apocalyptic Wisdom of James" [1998 Seminar Papers, 2:909–20]

Barbara R. Rossing, "City Visions and Economic Critique: A Sapiential Topos in the Apocalypse"

Respondent: Richard A. Horsley

1999

Erich S. Gruen, "Seleucid Royal Theology" [1999 Seminar Papers, 24–53]

Mark R. Kurtz, "The Social Construction of Judea in the Greek Period" [1999 Seminar Papers, 54–76]

Benjamin G. Wright III, "'Put All the Nations in Fear of You': Ben Sira and the Problem of Foreign Rule" [1999 Seminar Papers, 77–93]

Robert Doran, "Independence or Co-existence: The Responses of 1 and 2 Maccabees to Seleucid Hegemony" [1999 Seminar Papers, 94–103]

Respondent: George W. E. Nickelsburg

Patrick A. Tiller, "Israel at the Mercy of Demonic Powers: An Enochic Interpretation of Post-Exilic Imperialism"

Matthias Henze, "The Ideology of Rule in the Narrative Frame of Daniel (Dan 1–6)" [1999 Seminar Papers, 527–39]

Daniel J. Harrington, "The Ideology of Rule in Daniel 7–12" [1999 Seminar Papers, 540–51]

Respondents: Randal A. Argall; John Kampen

2000

Rodney A. Werline, "The Psalms of Solomon and the Ideology of Rule" [2000 Seminar Papers, 774–95]

Neil Elliot, "The 'Patience of the Jews': Sapiential and Apocalyptic Strategies of Resistance and Accommodation"

Steven J. Friesen, "Dreams of Destruction: Revelation 13 and Symbolic Resistance"

Ellen Bradshaw Aitken, "'The *Basileia* of Jesus Is on the Wood': The *Epistle of Barnabas* and the Ideology of Rule"

Respondents: Adela Yarbro Collins; Simon F. R. Price

Rollin A. Ramsaran, "Resisting Imperial Domination and Influence: Paul's Apocalyptic Rhetoric in 1 Corinthians" [in *Paul and the Roman Imperial Order* (ed. R. A. Horsley; Harrisburg, Pa.: Trinity Press International, 2004), 89–102]

E. Elizabeth Johnson, "Apocalypticism and the Roman Imperial Order in 1 Corinthians"

Demetrius K. Williams, "Paul's Anti-Imperial Rhetoric of the Cross" [2000 Seminar Papers, 796–823]

James M. Scott, "The Apocalyptic Framework of Paul's Apostolic Ministry of World Reconciliation"

Respondents: Ray Pickett; Martinus C. de Boer

2001
Richard A. Horsley, "The Politics of Production in Second Temple Judah"

Panelists: Benjamin G. Wright III, Carol Newsom, George W. E. Nickelsburg, and Lawrence M. Wills

2002 [All papers are available electronically on the Society of Biblical Literature website at: www.sbl-site.org/seminarpapers/]
Lawrence M. Wills, "Wisdom and Instruction in Matthew"

Aaron Milavec, "Apprenticeship in the Way of Wisdom within the Apocalyptic-Oriented Didache Communities"

Ellen Bradshaw Aitken, "Wily, Wise, and Worldly: Instruction and the Formation of Character in the Epistle to the Hebrews"

Respondents: Christine M. Thomas; Jonathan A. Draper

Benjamin G. Wright III, "Wisdom and Instruction in Ben Sira and *1 Enoch*" [published in significantly revised form as "Wisdom, Instruction and Social Location in Ben Sira and *1 Enoch*," in *Things Revealed:*

Studies in Early Jewish and Christian Literature in Honor of Michael E. Stone (ed. E. G. Chazon et al.; JSJSup 89; Leiden: Brill, 2004), 105–21]

Yonder M. Gillihan, "Astral Knowledge and the General's Authority in Greco-Roman Military Manuals"

Matthew J. Goff, "Wisdom, Apocalypticism, and the Pedagogical Ethos of 4QInstruction" [material included in his book, *The Worldly and Heavenly Wisdom of 4QInstruction* (STDJ 50; Leiden: Brill, 2004)]

Respondents: George W. E. Nickelsburg; John Kampen

2003 [All papers are available electronically on the Society of Biblical Literature website at: www.sbl-site.org/seminarpapers/]

Claudia V. Camp, "Ben Sira and the Making of the Bible"

Rollin A. Ramsaran, "Composition, Performance, and Prophecy in 1 Corinthians"

Whitney Shiner, "Sounding the Eschatological Alarm: Chapter Thirteen in the Performance"

Adela Yarbro Collins, "Composition and Performance in Mark 13"

Respondents: George W. E. Nickelsburg; Lawrence M. Wills

2004 [All the papers, except for Eibert J. C. Tigchelaar's, are available electronically on the Society of Biblical Literature website at: www.sbl-site.org/seminarpapers/]

George W. E. Nickelsburg, "The Study of Apocalypticism from H. H. Rowley to the Society of Biblical Literature"

David M. Carr, "Wisdom and Apocalyptic: Different Types of Educational/Enculturational Literature"

Respondents: Sarah J. Tanzer; Patrick A. Tiller

Eibert J. C. Tigchelaar, "'How Can You Say?' and 'Do Not Say!' Reprimand and Instruction—Forms and Styles in 4QInstruction"

Timothy Jay Johnson, "Job as Proto-apocalypse: A Fresh Proposal for Job's Governing Genre"

R. Glenn Wooden, "Changing Perceptions of Daniel: Reading Daniel 4 and 5 in Context."

Sabrina Inowlocki, "From Apocalypticism to Wisdom: The Transformation of Aseneth's Speech"

Respondent: Robert Doran

Part 1:
Issues and Outlook

WISDOM AND APOCALYPTICISM IN EARLY JUDAISM:
SOME POINTS FOR DISCUSSION

George W. E. Nickelsburg

1. INTRODUCTION

A renewed interest in the description, definition, and categorization of apocalypticism has been a major preoccupation for scholars of early Judaism during the past two and a half decades.[1] Catalyzed by the discovery and analysis of the Qumran Scrolls and spurred on by the pioneering monograph of Klaus Koch, the discussion of apocalypticism has been advanced by such persons as Paul D. Hanson, Michael E. Stone, John J. Collins, and other scholars who have worked on the problem in general or on certain apocalypses in particular. So radical have been the shifts in emphasis and method and in the primary materials discussed, that some of the giants who dominated the discussion in the late nineteenth and early twentieth centuries (R. H. Charles, Hermann Gunkel, and Paul Volz) would find the current discussion of apocalypticism as much alien territory as they often found the apocalypses themselves. Because apocalyptic literature holds such a central place in the study of Israelite religion in the Greco-Roman period, a revolution in the understanding and assessment of this literature was bound to have a ripple effect in the broader discussion of the history of Israelite religion. And so it has, as one can see by reviewing the burgeoning literature on early Judaism.

Ripples, however, do not always follow their predetermined path, either because they meet with counterforces or because they run up against the inertia of stationary objects. For reasons too complex to analyze here, much New Testament scholarship has had a love-hate, attraction-avoidance relationship with the modern study of early Judaism—

---

1. See Paul D. Hanson, "Apocalyptic Literature," in *The Hebrew Bible and Its Modern Interpreters* (ed. D. A. Knight and G. M. Tucker; SBLBMI 1; Philadelphia: Fortress, 1985), 465–88; John J. Collins, "Apocalyptic Literature," in *Early Judaism and its Modern Interpreters* (ed. R. A. Kraft and G. W. E. Nickelsburg; SBLBMI 2; Philadelphia: Fortress, 1986), 345–70.

drawing deeply from it at times and blissfully ignoring or even actively resisting it at other times. Perhaps the two places where the ripples have most often been diverted or blocked have been in discussions of Torah and in the use of the term "apocalyptic." My interest here is with the latter, specifically, the manner in which this adjective-become-noun is sometimes used with little or no concern for the discussion during the past two decades and no evident knowledge that *much in that discussion remains unresolved and unclarified.*

2. THE PRESENT PROJECT

Two related objectives have been set for a new SBL Consultation on Wisdom and Apocalyptic in Early Judaism and Early Christianity. The initiators of the consultation believe that the achievement of these objectives will require the full five-year term of an SBL seminar, and we would like to structure the consultation sessions this year and next year in order to shape such a scenario.

The first objective is some clarification of the nature and interrelationship of the wisdom, prophetic, and eschatological components in Jewish apocalyptic writings. Like the study of Jewish apocalypticism, the discussion of Israelite wisdom literature has made substantial advances over the past decades.[2] Within this first objective, two developments are especially significant for our present concern. The first is the increasing frequency with which works like Sirach and the Wisdom of Solomon are discussed in connection with the wisdom literature of the Hebrew Bible.[3] The second is a recognition of wisdom elements in apocalyptic literature, as well as a debate about their origin, function, and importance. During the first half of the life of our projected seminar, we propose to look at the apocalyptic literature with a view toward identifying wisdom elements and their relationship to analogous elements in post-biblical Jewish sapiential literature, including, possibly, some of the texts from Qumran. Our second proposed objective is to shed light on some relevant New Testament texts, such as "Q" and the Epistle of James. Is it appropriate to ascribe wisdom and apocalyptic elements in Q to separate sources and separate communities? What might our study of the Jewish texts tell us

---

2. See James L. Crenshaw, "The Wisdom Literature," in Knight and Tucker, *Hebrew Bible*, 369–407; Burton L. Mack and Roland E. Murphy, "Wisdom Literature," in Kraft and Nickelsburg, *Early Judaism*, 371–410.

3. Gerhard von Rad, *Wisdom in Israel* (trans. J. D. Martin; Philadelphia: Westminster, 1972); James L. Crenshaw, *Old Testament Wisdom: An Introduction* (Atlanta: John Knox, 1981).

about the coexistence of sapiential and eschatological elements in Q and in James?

Two considerations will guide our discussion of the Jewish and Christian material. The first is some serious reflection on the way in which the study of our primary sources has tended to distill, abstract, and often reify terms like "wisdom" and "apocalyptic" without recognizing that the abstraction is the result of a (necessary) process of historical reconstruction. The second is a concerted effort to reconstruct aspects of the social and cultural realities that gave rise to and are reflected in the relevant primary sources: the institutions, offices, roles, and functions that resulted in the Jewish sapiential and apocalyptic literature and made use of it. These two considerations, in turn, have immediate implications for our understanding of the rise of Christianity, the genetics and functions of its literature, and perhaps our reconstructions of the career of Jesus of Nazareth. The program for the initial session of the consultation will provide entree into the two segments of the life of the projected seminar. The present paper offers for discussion in the first part of the session some observations about wisdom and apocalypticism in early Judaism. The second half of the session will consider the paper of Richard Horsley, entitled "Wisdom Justified by All Her Children: Examining Allegedly Disparate Traditions in Q," a review and evaluation of the discussion of Q as it relates to the topic of the consultation.

The relationships between wisdom and apocalypticism and the implications that these might have on the current discussion of Q have already been taken up in an article by John J. Collins, which focuses on "generic compatibility."[4] The present project was conceived with no knowledge of the Collins article, yet both his article and mine have reached similar conclusions: Jewish wisdom and apocalypticism cannot be cleanly separated from one another. Our conclusions are also complementary; he focuses on genre and on distinctions within the sapiential literature whereas I have attempted a more detailed comparison of a broader range of sapiential and apocalyptic texts with less concern for generic matters as such. Collins concludes that a posited dichotomy between wisdom and apocalypticism must be used with caution in the analysis of Q. Considerations of space, a companion paper on the Q discussion, and the prospect of a multi-year seminar have led me to omit any explicit discussion of relevant New Testament texts, but in general, I am wary of the wisdom/apocalytpic dichotomy that has become an

---

4. John J. Collins, "Wisdom, Apocalypticism, and Generic Compatibility," in *In Search of Wisdom: Essays in Memory of John G. Gammie* (ed. L. G. Perdue et al.; Philadelphia: Westminster John Knox, 1993), 165–85.

important part of the Q discussion. It is my hope that the extended discussion of our topic will bring some clarity to the issues.

The thesis of this paper is that the entities usually defined as sapiential and apocalyptic often cannot be cleanly separated from one another because both are the products of wisdom circles that are becoming increasingly diverse in the Greco-Roman period. Thus, apocalyptic texts contain elements that are at home in wisdom literature, and wisdom texts reflect growing interest in eschatology. Moreover, claims to revelation, inspiration, or divine enlightenment can be found in both "sets" of texts. Our subject matter is complex and the issues are often not clear. The presentation in this paper is intended only to be suggestive—to present briefly *some* issues for discussion, some pointers toward an agenda.

3. Some Established Findings or Points of Consensus

The renewed discussion of apocalypticism that began in the early 1970s has produced some important results; in some cases they have found wide consensus. It is useful to distinguish between three terms: the literary genre "apocalypse"; the "apocalyptic eschatology" found in such documents and, according to some scholars,[5] in texts antecedent to the apocalypses; and "apocalypticism," "the symbolic universe in which an apocalyptic movement codifies its identity and interpretation of reality."[6]

In order to be semantically meaningful, the terms "apocalyptic" and "apocalypticism" should designate entities for which revelation is a significant component. In this respect, it makes a great deal of sense to begin a study of apocalypticism with an analysis of texts that are widely agreed to be apocalypses, such as *1 Enoch, Daniel, the Apocalypse of Abraham, 4 Ezra, 2* and *3 Baruch,* and the book of Revelation.[7] While all of these texts contain, in part or as a whole, revelations of a hidden past or future and/or of hidden parts of the cosmos mediated through a revealer figure, they vary widely in their specific content and emphases.[8] For example:

---

5. E.g., Paul D. Hanson, *The Dawn of Apocalyptic* (Philadelphia: Fortress, 1975); idem, "Apocalypticism," *IDBSup*, 28–34.

6. Hanson, "Apocalypticism," 29–30.

7. Klaus Koch, *The Rediscovery of Apocalyptic* (SBT 2/22; Naperville, Ill.: Allenson, 1972), 23.

8. John J. Collins, "Jewish Apocalypses," *Semeia* 14 (1979): 21–59.

♦ *1 Enoch* is a complex text attributed to a pre-Mosaic sage, which contains mythic narratives about the primordial past, a prophetic call based on a heavenly ascent, guided tours of the cosmos interpreted by angels, detailed torah about the movement of the heavenly bodies, dream visions about the future of human history, and discourses composed of ethical admonitions and prophetic exhortations.

♦ In the book of Daniel, the narrative section consists of a cycle of legends about the wisdom and faithful conduct of Jewish sages in exile. Revelation comes through dream visions and their interpretation, through inspired sages.

♦ The *Apocalypse of Abraham* combines legend (Abraham's rejection of idolatry), an ascent to the divine throne, and visions about the shape of the cosmos and (mainly) the future of Israel.

♦ The contemporary apocalypses *4 Ezra* and *2 Baruch* claim to base their information on auditions and visions about the future of Israel, mediated or interpreted by angels. *4 Ezra* in particular eschews the notion that one can know the kind of cosmic secrets revealed in *1 Enoch*,[9] and both *4 Ezra* and *2 Baruch* understand wisdom in terms of the Mosaic Torah and its post-prophetic interpretation by scribes and sages.

In short, even when we tie the notion of apocalypticism to texts that are formally apocalypses, we find wide diversity in the content of what is revealed and the form through which it is mediated. *We must use the generic terms with caution and the recognition that we do not know exactly what we are talking about.*

It has long been recognized that Jewish apocalyptic texts are rooted, in part, in Israel's prophetic tradition. The throne visions in *1 En.* 12–16, Dan 7, and the *Apocalypse of Abraham* recall Isa 6, 2 Kgs 22, and Ezek 1–2. *1 Enoch* roots the sage's authority as a revealer in a prophetic call scene that draws heavily on Ezek 1–2 and prepares Enoch to be preacher against the sins of the watchers. Although Dan 7 is not a call scene, the seer describes the heavenly tribunal taking action against the rebellious kingdoms and kings of the earth. Both within and outside the framework of dream visions about the future, apocalyptic texts from *1 Enoch* to *2 Baruch* have an eschatological focus and emphasis that has much in common with the biblical prophetic texts. The discussion of apocalyptic literature has also recognized that these texts draw on the language, genres, and motifs of Israel's wisdom literature. Even if von Rad

---

9. Michael E. Stone, "Lists of Revealed Things in the Apocalyptic Literature," in *Magnalia Dei: The Mighty Acts of God: Essays on the Bible and Archaeology in Memory of G. Ernest Wright* (ed. F. M. Cross et al.; Garden City, N.Y.: Doubleday, 1976), 414–52.

overemphasized this point,[10] scholars have continued to discuss the sapiential elements in apocalyptic texts.[11] In short, a careful study of Jewish apocalypses from 1 Enoch to the post-70 texts places us in a religious and intellectual world that is strongly reminiscent of the prophetic and sapiential corpuses of the Hebrew Bible. The texts also reflect the influence of ancient Near Eastern myth and Mesopotamian mantic wisdom,[12] but that is not our concern at present.

4. Some Points for a Discussion of the Jewish Literature and Its Settings

Working from the findings of a generation of scholarship and my own investigation especially of *1 Enoch*, I suggest that it is worthwhile to discuss the following issues, observations, and theses about the sapiential and apocalyptic literatures, their possible social settings, and the modern discussion of these bodies of literature.

4.1. Jewish Literature

4.1.1. Wisdom Literature: Its Interest in Prophecy and Claims to Inspiration
Although Israelite wisdom texts like Tobit, Sirach, and Baruch hold the Mosaic Torah in high regard and contain much (proverbial) instruction about (sometimes Torah-related) human conduct, they also have a high regard for the *prophetic* tradition, including its concern about future events, and they place the sage, scribe, or teacher in the role of an inspired spokesman of God and interpreter of Torah and prophets.

4.1.1.1. The Book of Tobit
The righteousness of Tobit and his family is tied to the Mosaic Torah, and Israel's exile is due to the people's apostasy from the Torah.

---

10. Collins, "Apocalyptic Literature," 355.
11. Jonathan Z. Smith, "Wisdom and Apocalyptic," in *Religious Syncretism in Antiquity: Essays in Conversation with Geo Widengren* (ed. B. A. Pearson; Series on Formative Contemporary Thinkers 1; Missoula, Mont.: Scholars Press, 1975), 131–56, repr. in Smith, *Map Is Not Territory: Studies in the History of Religion* (SJLA 23; Leiden: Brill, 1978), 67–87; R. A. Coughenour, "The Woe Oracles in Ethiopic Enoch," *JSJ* 9 (1978): 192–97; idem, "The Wisdom Stance of Enoch's Redactor," *JSJ* 13 (1982): 47–55; Randal A. Argall, 1 Enoch and *Sirach: A Comparative Literary and Conceptual Analysis of the Themes of Revelation, Creation and Judgment* (SBLEJL 8; Atlanta: Scholars Press, 1995).
12. John J. Collins, *The Apocalyptic Vision of Daniel* (HSM 16; Missoula, Mont.: Scholars Press, 1977).

Although Tobit is not a sage, as such, he speaks in proverbs, some of which are tied to the concerns of the Torah. His function as a court official is reminiscent of the sage Daniel and his colleagues, and his association with Ahikar recalls the heavily proverbial content of *The Story of Ahikar*. Nonetheless, the book of Tobit ends with a look toward the future. The Zion hymn in chapter 13 draws on the tradition of Second and Third Isaiah. Tobit predicts the time when the words of the prophets will be fulfilled in detail, and his scenario for the future in chapter 14 is reminiscent of *1 Enoch's* periodized Apocalypse of Weeks.[13] Tobit is the recipient of revelation when Raphael discloses his identity as one of the seven holy ones in the divine throne room, and Tobit's predictions presume a certainty about the future that, while tied to prophecy, functions as new revelation.

4.1.1.2. The Wisdom of Ben Sira

For Ben Sira, the Torah is the repository of heavenly wisdom, which the sage, inspired by God, expounds like prophecy (ch. 24). Wisdom instruction—both the exposition of Torah and practical advice—is the primary content of Ben Sira's book. Nonetheless, Ben Sira's fascination with the prophets is evident in chapters 44–50, which feature Moses, Samuel, Nathan, Elijah, Isaiah, Jeremiah, Ezekiel, and the Twelve. He also evidences a deep concern about the unfulfilled oracles of the prophets (notably Second and Third Isaiah) and the need that these divine spokesmen be found faithful (36:11–16). Moreover, he employs traditional prophetic literary forms.[14]

4.1.1.3. Baruch

The book of Baruch has important sapiential elements, makes explicit reference to the Mosaic Torah, and speaks in prophetic idiom. The book is attributed to the scribe of Jeremiah. The wisdom poem in chapter 3 is reminiscent of Job 28. In 4:1–9, the Torah is said to be the repository of heavenly Wisdom (cf. Sir 24), and both in these verses and in 3:29–30 the author takes up the idiom of the wisdom material in Deut 30:11–14. In the early chapters, Baruch speaks and acts like a prophet, employing the language of Jeremiah and Ezekiel, as well as the prophetic voice of Moses in Deuteronomy. Israel's exile was predicted by "your servant Moses" (Bar

---

13. George W. E. Nickelsburg, "Tobit and Enoch: Distant Cousins with a Recognizable Resemblance," in *Society of Biblical Literature 1988 Seminar Papers*, (SBLSP 27; Atlanta: Scholars Press, 1988), 341–60.

14. Walter Baumgartner, "Die literarischen Gattungen in der Weisheit des Jesus Sirach," *ZAW* 34 (1914): 161–98.

2:28). The book of Baruch concludes as the author predicts Israel's return from exile (Deut 30:1–5), employing the idiom of Second and Third Isaiah (Bar 4:9–5:9).

To summarize, in various ways, the authors of Tobit, Sirach, and Baruch focus on the importance of the Mosaic Torah, employ the idiom of the wisdom texts of the Hebrew Bible, and evidence high respect for the predictions of Israel's prophets, either referring to them explicitly or speaking in the language of their writings. While we might debate whether these authors have an eschatological emphasis, they do operate with a teleology that anticipates a time when the prophetic oracles will reach their goal or fulfillment.

4.1.2. Apocalyptic Literature: Its Focus on Revelation and Use of Wisdom Elements

Although the heavy emphasis on prediction has led scholars to see the apocalypticists as successors to the prophets, at many points these apocalyptic texts speak in the idiom, motifs, and forms of Israelite wisdom literature. The variety in these texts, which span four hundred years (300 B.C.E. to 100 C.E.), is especially evident in their attitudes toward the Mosaic Torah, their relationship to the prophets, and the emphasis that they place on the newness or derivative character of the revelation that they present.

4.1.2.1. 1 Enoch

The collection known as *1 Enoch* is especially remarkable for its wisdom components.[15] The content itself is described as "wisdom" (5:6; 37:1; 92:1; 93:10). The heart of the opening oracle is an appeal to observe the created world (2:1–5:4). Much of the content of Enoch's journeys is paralleled in wisdom texts like Job.[16] The two-ways instruction that runs through chapters 91 and 94–105 (e.g., 91:3–4, 18–19; 94:1–4; 99:10; 105:2) speaks the wisdom vocabulary of Proverbs, Tobit, and Sirach. The relationship of Enoch's wisdom to the Mosaic Torah is ambiguous. His revelations preceded those of Moses by millennia. At least in the Animal Vision, the giving of the Torah is deleted from the account of the Sinai experience (89:28–35). Instruction focuses on cosmology and, where it deals with ethical issues (chs. 92–105), it parallels the concerns of the

---

15. Coughenour, "Woe Oracles"; idem, "Wisdom Stance"; Argall, 1 Enoch *and Sirach*, which, to my knowledge was the first systematic attempt to compare in detail a sapiential text and an apocalyptic text. At many points my discussion here is indebted to his work.

16. Michael E. Stone, "The Book of Enoch and Judaism in the Third Century," *CBQ* 50 (1978): 479–92.

prophets and the wisdom corpus,[17] though not ignoring "the commandments of the Most High" (99:10). Especially striking is the use of the wisdom myth in 81:1–82:4, where, in contrast to Sir 24 and Bar 4:1, it is Enoch's books rather than the Mosaic Torah that are the earthly repository of heavenly wisdom.[18] Enoch's relationship to the prophets is also ambiguous. His use of prophetic forms is evident in the opening oracle of salvation and judgment (chs. 1–5), which employs the vocabulary of the Balaam oracle and language reminiscent of Third Isaiah. Enoch's ascent to heaven is cast in the form of a prophetic call vision (chs. 12–16). The woes, exhortations, and predictions of the future in chapters 92–105 also recall prophetic usage.[19] Nonetheless, the prophets are never cited, and the long recitation of Israel's history in the Animal Vision barely alludes to them (89:51–53). As with the Mosaic Torah, here Enoch's primordial prophecy long precedes the voice of the prophets.

4.1.2.2. The Book of Daniel

The book of Daniel offers a narrower spectrum of wisdom components when compared to 1 *Enoch*. Its chief feature is the mantic wisdom that dominates the stories in chapters 1–6 and runs through the visions in chapters 7–11. Daniel and his colleagues are skilled interpreters of dreams and visions, greatly exceeding the capabilities of their Babylonian counterparts. Lacking in Daniel are the many sapiential literary forms found in 1 *Enoch*, the Enochic books' heavy emphasis on cosmology, and any equation between wisdom and Torah, even if the piety of Daniel and his friends relates to *kashrut* and the avoidance of idolatry. Daniel's relationship to the prophetic corpus has two aspects. The last vision draws on the prophecies of Isaiah,[20] though it does not cite them. Alongside this use of prophetic material, which parallels 1 *Enoch*'s approach, is the explicit concern with the fulfillment of Jeremiah's prophecy in 9:2, 24.

4.1.2.3. 2 Baruch

In 2 *Baruch*, an extensive apocalypse from around the year 100 C.E., wisdom is especially equated with the Torah (51:1–10). Although Baruch is the scribe mentioned in Jeremiah, he is the recipient of dream visions and, like the prophets, of the word of the Lord (1:1; 10:1). Different from

---

17. George W. E. Nickelsburg, "The Apocalyptic Message of 1 *Enoch* 92–105," *CBQ* 39 (1977): 309–28.
18. Argall, 1 *Enoch and Sirach*, 91–98.
19. Nickelsburg, "Apocalyptic Message."
20. H. L. Ginsberg, "The Oldest Interpretation of the Suffering Servant," *VT* 3 (1953): 400–404.

Daniel, his interpretation of dream visions derives not from innate wisdom, but from conversation with God or an angel (e.g., chs. 41–42, 55). Nonetheless, the use of prayer to trigger these interpretive conversations is reminiscent of Daniel 9 and Sir 39:5–8, and some of the wisdom vocabulary in these prayers is noteworthy (38:1–4; 54:1, 13).

4.1.2.4. 4 Ezra

For Baruch's contemporary, the author of *4 Ezra*, wisdom is less tied to Torah than to the understanding of eschatological secrets, and though Ezra is inspired to rewrite the Torah (14:1–26), similar inspiration results in Ezra's dictation of the twenty-four secret books (14:37–48). *First Enoch's* strong interest in cosmological wisdom, however, appears to be the object of polemic in *4 Ezra*.[21] Finally, the literary form of both *2 Baruch* and *4 Ezra*, with their argumentative dialogues between the sage and God over the issue of theodicy, are reminiscent of the book of Job.

4.1.3. *Different Emphases in Wisdom and Apocalyptic Texts*

Our survey has identified ways in which texts that are usually categorized as sapiential can equate wisdom with Torah and also transmit elements of the prophetic tradition, and how they can even make claims of revelation or inspiration. Conversely, we have noted wisdom components in the apocalyptic texts, with wisdom and Torah being equated especially in *2 Baruch*. The prophetic element, especially noteworthy in the many strata of *1 Enoch*, is to some extent retained in the ongoing interest in eschatology.

In short, both sapiential and apocalyptic texts display a number of common elements: wisdom forms; an interest in Torah and prophets; prediction of future events; ethical admonitions; and claims of revelation. Of course, there are many variations among the texts in each group. Nonetheless, in the paragraphs that follow, I shall suggest some differences in nuance and emphasis that might help us to distinguish the one group from the other. In making these generalizations, however, I shall also indicate some exceptions and qualifications, which reflect the complexity in the historical development of sapiential and apocalyptic literature.

4.1.3.1. Dualism

Some apocalypses are strongly dualistic in their orientation. For example, *1 Enoch* is marked by a spatial dualism between earth and

---

21. Stone,"Lists."

heaven, or the inhabited world and the recesses of the cosmos inaccessible to humanity; a temporal dualism between the present time and the eschatological future, and, perhaps, the primordial past; an ontological dualism between humans and a vast world of good and, especially, evil spirits.[22] The book of Daniel reflects the same general viewpoint.

Exception 1: The book of Tobit posits a heavenly throne room from which emissaries are sent to earth to do battle with a world of evil spirits who inflict illness on human beings.[23]

Exception 2: Although *4 Ezra* and *2 Baruch* have a strong eschatological emphasis, neither focuses on a heaven/earth dichotomy or the activity of evil spirits.

4.1.3.2. Eschatology

Although wisdom texts such as Tobit, Sirach, and Baruch work with prophetic eschatological themes, eschatology is more dominant in most of the texts that we describe as apocalypses.

Qualification 1: For some apocalypses such as *2 Enoch* and *3 Baruch,* eschatology focuses more on the fate of the individual than on a general conclusion to history.[24]

Qualification 2: 1 Enoch is striking for the diversity with which it deals with eschatology. Little space is devoted to periodized reviews of history. The judgment is rooted in creation, where the places of reward and punishment are located (chs. 17–36). Reward and punishment are referred to in woes and exhortations typical of the prophetic tradition (chs. 92–105).

4.1.3.3. New or Derived Revelation

The claims of revelation in the wisdom literature tend to be tied to traditional texts, namely, the Mosaic Torah and the prophets. The authors of apocalyptic texts, while they actually draw heavily on the Torah and the prophets, present new revelations, although they attribute them variously to pre-Mosaic authors (Enoch and Abraham), Moses himself, and post-Mosaic figures (Daniel, Ezra and Baruch). The sources of these new

---

22. George W. E. Nickelsburg, "The Apocalyptic Construction of Reality of *1 Enoch,*" in *Mysteries and Revelations: Apocalyptic Studies since the Uppsala Colloquium* (ed. J. J. Collins and J. H. Charlesworth; JSPSup 9; Sheffield: Sheffield Academic Press, 1991), 51–64.
23. Nickelsburg, "Tobit and Enoch."
24. John J. Collins, *The Apocalyptic Imagination* (New York: Crossroad, 1984), 198–201.

revelations are said to be cosmic journeys and dream visions, interpreted by angels

Exception: On occasion, the association with scripture is explicit in apocalyptic texts: Daniel obtains an explicit interpretation of Jeremiah, albeit from an angel. Both *Jubilees* and the *Testament of Moses* are expanded versions of parts of the Pentateuch, which, however, are said to be part of a revelation to the author of the biblical text.

4.1.4. Texts That Complicate the Categories

4.1.4.1. The Wisdom of Solomon

Its attribution to the author of the book of Proverbs and Qoheleth, its frequent references to wisdom, and its use of the literary form of the proverb situate the Wisdom of Solomon within the tradition of sapiential literature. Other characteristics of the work suggest close analogies with apocalyptic thought,[25] even if they are expressed in ways that seem closely related to Greek philosophy. The story of the righteous one in chapters 2 and 5 is dominated by eschatology. In this context immortality is an important conception, but the description of the judgment in chapter 5 reflects a Jewish apocalyptic tradition attested also in *1 En.* 62–63.[26] The cosmic dualism that governs the story also suggests Platonic thought, while reflecting Jewish apocalyptic cosmology. Moreover, the form of the story of the persecuted and exalted righteous one recalls the genre attested both in the wisdom tradition of Gen 39 and the stories included in chapters 3 and 6 of the apocalyptic book of Daniel. Finally, wisdom for this author involves revelation of divine mysteries and an understanding of the secrets of the heavenly realm, unknown to the ungodly (2:22–3:4).

An intriguing aspect of the Wisdom of Solomon is its parallels to *1 Enoch*.[27] Enoch is the epitome of the righteous person (4:10–15). In addition to the judgment scene in chapter 5, which is paralleled in *1 En.* 62–63, the general form of argumentation in chapters 2–5 is reminiscent of *1 En.* 102:4–104:8.[28] It appears, therefore, that the first part of the Wisdom of Solomon is a Hellenizing and philosophizing version of Jewish apocalyptic

---

25. John J. Collins, "Cosmos and Salvation: Jewish Wisdom and Apocalyptic in the Hellenistic Age," *HR* 17 (1977): 121–42.

26. George W. E. Nickelsburg, *Resurrection, Immortality, and Eternal Life in Intertestamental Judaism* (HTS 26; Cambridge: Harvard University Press, 1972), 70–78.

27. C. Larcher, *Études sur le livre de la Sagesse* (Paris: Gabalda, 1983), 106–12.

28. Nickelsburg, *Resurrection*, 128–29.

tradition. The transformation is possible because of the perceived compatibility of the alternate forms of expression.

The interest in prophetic tradition, which we have observed in both sapiential and apocalyptic writings, is present also in the Wisdom of Solomon. The story of the persecution and exaltation of the righteous one in chapters 2 and 5 is a traditional, rewritten form of Isa 52–53,[29] set in part in the context of other material drawn from Third Isaiah. Like other texts in the apocalyptic tradition, the author reshapes rather than quotes the prophetic prototype. Strikingly, the prophetic figure in the Deutero-Isaianic text looks like the sages in Gen 39–45 and Dan 3 and 6.

4.1.4.2. The Qumran Scrolls

The Qumran Scrolls are a treasure trove and a mine field for students of apocalyptic literature. Although no apocalypse has been identified as originating at Qumran, the Scrolls contain many motifs characteristic of apocalyptic literature. The *Community Rule* (1QS) offers an example of the complexity of the situation, attesting both sapiential and apocalyptic conceptions and characteristics. 1QS 3:13–4:26 is a section of two-ways teaching with many analogies in sapiential literature.[30] A major difference from these wisdom texts, however, is the pronounced dualism that governs the section. Human works are functions of the good and evil spirits. The section concludes with reference to an eschatological confrontation between the two spirits and an eschatological purifying of the earth (4:18–26), both with analogies in apocalyptic literature.[31]

Although the two-ways section lacks the revelatory component necessary for our definition of apocalyptic literature, 1QS 11:3–9 is startling for its saturation with language and conceptions at home in accounts of visionary experiences recorded by the apocalypticists: revelation in the form of enlightening and seeing; the mystery to come; the fount of righteousness; knowledge hidden from humans; the dwelling place of glory; standing in the presence of the holy ones, the sons of heaven. Thus while 1QS is not generically an apocalypse and should not be defined as apocalyptic in a technical sense, its dualism, eschatology and use of apocalyptic conceptions indicate that the authors of this wisdom and legal text worked within an apocalyptic orbit.

---

29. Ibid., 70–78.
30. Ibid., 156–64.
31. Ibid., 158; see, in addition, *1 En.* 10:11–11:2.

4.2. Institutions and Social Settings

Since texts are products of persons and communities, the discussion of apocalyptic and sapiential material should include an attempt to reconstruct the institutions, social settings, and functions that gave rise to this literature and made use of it. Such a focus may also help us to avoid the elusive abstraction that sometimes attends the history of ideas.

4.2.1. Figures and Functions in the Texts

A brief survey of some of the texts surveyed above may enable us to identify types of figures who were involved in the generating and use of sapiential and apocalyptic literature and some of their roles or functions.

4.2.1.1. The Wisdom of Ben Sira

Among all our texts, the Wisdom of Ben Sira is the only one attributed to a named historical figure; hence, it may be useful to start in his "non-fictional" world with his own self-description. Ben Sira's title, according to 38:24, is "scribe" (γραμματεύς). Here and elsewhere his work involves not only the ability to write, but also divinely given "wisdom" (σοφία). The prologue of the book, written by Ben Sira's grandson and translator, and three passages in the book describe his activity. According to the prologue (7–13), Ben Sira read and studied the Torah, the Prophets, and the other books of the fathers and then wrote his book for the purpose of instruction and wisdom (παιδεία and σοφία). The third-person singular self-description in 39:1–11 also refers to the study of "the Torah of the Most High," "the wisdom of the ancients," which includes proverbs and parables, and "prophecy" (vv. 1–3). The use of "ponder" (διανοέομαι) with reference to the Torah, "occupy oneself with" (ἀσχολέω) of the prophets, and "seek out" (ἐκζητέω, twice) of wisdom indicates a thorough, ongoing scholarly process, one that excludes the possibility of another occupation (38:24). This daily activity is preceded by prayer, which, the Lord willing, results in the scribe's being filled with "the spirit of understanding" (πνεύμα συνέσεως) that enables him to pour forth words of wisdom (σοφία), rightly direct "counsel" and "knowledge" (βουλή and ἐπιστήμη) (cf. Isa 11:2–3, of the king's inspired wisdom for judgment), ponder "secrets" (ἀπόκρυφα), and "make the instruction of his teaching shine forth" (ἐκφάνει παιδείαν διδασκαλίας αὐτοῦ). In 24:27, 32–34, Ben Sira speaks again of his teaching activity as enlightenment, analogous to inspired prophecy, which extends the life-giving power of Torah's wisdom, preserving it in Ben Sira's book. In 51:21–29 the wording suggests that his teaching activity has a specific locus, in his "house of instruction" (οἶκος παιδείας). In addition, 39:4 describes the scribe as a traveling scholar, who presents his knowledge before rulers and in foreign lands.

Thus, Ben Sira the scribe is a *scholar* of the Torah, the Prophets, and the wisdom texts, who is also a *teacher*. The form of his teaching, to judge from his book, is not halakic exposition of the Torah, but proverbial. A text like 3:1–16 suggests a kind of homiletical exposition on the implications of the Torah, and the form of many of his proverbs embodies the notion that obedience and disobedience result in divine blessing or judgment.[32] Taken as a whole, the body of his teaching has a strong ethical and admonitory character, rather than being directed simply to the transmission of knowledge.

4.2.1.2. 1 Enoch

A discussion of the real-life figures behind 1 *Enoch* is difficult because of the pseudepigraphic character of the text. But a few observations are possible, first with reference to Enoch. The authors' term is "scribe" (12:3; 92:1) and "scribe of righteousness" or "scribe of truth" (γραμματεύς τῆς δικαιοσύνης [12:4], γραμματεύς τῆς ἀληθείας [15:1]). Most basically, the scribal designation relates to his alleged writing of the Enochic corpus, whose character as book is emphasized in 81:6–82:3, 100:6, and 104:12–13. In addition, his writing and reading of the Watchers' petition in 12:3–13:7, which has an analogy in Ezra 9–10, places him in the role of a religious mediator, if not, strictly speaking, a priest. Like Ben Sira, the fictional Enoch presents his books as the embodiment of life-giving heavenly wisdom, intended for "all the generations of eternity" (82:1-4; cf. Sir 24:33). Though he does not call his instruction "prophecy," he repeatedly speaks in the idiom and forms of the biblical prophets (see above, 4.1.1), and though the text does not cite them, it knows them well.

If we move from the fictional world of the primordial sage to the real world of the authors, we find figures who parallel Enoch the scribe. In 98:9 and 99:10 they are "the wise" (φρόνιμοι), and their "words" are heard and, to judge from 98:15 (where their opponents are mentioned as writing books), they write their words in books that are read. Thus the fictional Enoch has real life counterparts, known as "the wise" and functioning as scribes. They are, in fact, the persons who compose and utter the prophetic woes that run through chapters 94–103. In this respect they parallel Enoch's role as God's spokesman of doom against the wicked. The form of much of the material in chapters 94–105 is typical of sapiential literature (e.g., two-ways sayings), but a passage like 99:2 (Greek) suggests that they are also engaged in halakic disputes about the proper

---

32. Argall, 1 Enoch *and Sirach*, 220–47.

interpretation of divine law.³³ Much of the content in *1 Enoch* relates to the rewards and punishment that will come to those who obey or disobey Enochic Torah. In addition, Stone has rightly seen behind the cosmology of the journey accounts in chapters 17–36 the activity of learned scholars,³⁴ and there are remarkable parallels between *1 Enoch* and the Wisdom of Ben Sira in this respect.³⁵ However, it needs to be emphasized that the authors of *1 En.* 17–19 and 20–36 have put their cosmological wisdom at the disposal of their eschatological message.³⁶

4.2.1.3. The Book of Daniel

Different from Sirach and *1 Enoch*, the book of Daniel places little emphasis on the role of the scribe. Daniel is alleged to have written down the visions in chapters 7–12, but even in 12:9 this is not explicit; in all of Daniel's visions the emphasis is on his receipt of, or participation in the visions, the interpretations that he heard, and his undefined transmission of them. The chief quality of Daniel and his friends, apart from their faithfulness to their God (1:17), is their wisdom as inspired interpreters of dream visions, similar to, but vastly superior to their Babylonian counterparts.³⁷ Different from Enoch, who received and recounts visions, these persons belong to a professional class of interpreters. In addition, though they are not interpreters of the Torah, both the three youths and Daniel are God's spokesmen, preaching, on the basis of revealed information, against the arrogance of Nebuchadnezzar and Belshazzar and announcing God's judgment. The role is prophetic, even if they are not called prophets.

A hint of the real world of Daniel's authors appears in 12:3 in the reference to the *maskilim*, who "cause many to be righteous." The teaching role of these wisdom figures may be suggested in the claim that they will "shine" (*yazhiru*) like the firmament, perhaps an allusion to the metaphor of teaching as enlightenment (cf. Sir 24:27, 32; 39:8; cf. *1 En.* 5:8 Greek; 1QH 12[4]:5–6, 27). The teaching role is explicit in the statement that they cause many to be righteous. Striking in 12:3 is the author's use of Isa 52:13 and 53:10; the prophetic Servant of that text is identified with the wise

---

33. George W. E. Nickelsburg, "The Epistle of Enoch and the Qumran Literature," *JSS* 33 (1982): 334–43 = *Essays in Honour of Yigael Yadin* (ed. G. Vermes and J. Neusner; Totowa, N.J.: published for the Oxford Centre for Postgraduate Studies by Allanheld, Osmun, 1983).

34. Stone, "Book of Enoch."

35. Argall, 1 Enoch *and* Sirach, 99–164.

36. George W. E. Nickelsburg, *Jewish Literature between the Bible and the Mishnah* (2nd ed.; Philadelphia: Fortress, 2005), 51–52.

37. Although Ben Sira is suspicious of dream interpretation (34:1–8), his description of the sage who travels to foreign courts (39:4) is reminiscent of the stories in Dan 1–6.

teachers of the Maccabean period. In view of the issues at stake in chapters 1–6 (observance of *kashrut* and rejection of idolatry) and in the Maccabean period, these teachers are rightly seen as teachers of the Torah, encouraging other Jews to stand fast in righteous conduct.

4.2.1.4. The Wisdom of Solomon

The protagonist in Wis 2 and 5 is not only a righteous person, but one who, inspired by the knowledge given by God (2:13) and privy to divine secrets (2:22), speaks against the sins of the godless (2:12), claiming to be God's son or servant (2:13). Combining motifs in Dan 1–6 and 12:3, he is the righteous and wise spokesman of God, persecuted and exalted, and he is described in the language of Isa 52–53. Once again, the prophet-like figure emerges as a wise man. The role of scribe or writer is implied in the book only in Solomon's authorship of the book. The real author, of course, is an expositor of Torah and prophets, who speaks in the idiom of Israelite wisdom and Greek philosophy.

4.2.1.5. The Qumran Texts

The Qumran texts provide many hints about their authors and their roles. The sapiential and eschatological instruction in 1QS 3:13–4:26 is for the *maskil* to use in teaching the community (3:13). The *Damascus Document* describes a plurality of sages (*ḥkmym*) and persons of perception (*nbwnym*) who are led by one who "searches" (*drš*) the Torah (CD 6:2–11). A continued process of Torah study is reflected in 1QS 8:12–16, and 1QS 5:7–9 makes it clear that the community's definitive interpretation is revealed. The author of 1QH 12[4]:5–5:4 describes himself as an enlightened teacher of the Torah, cast in the image of Second Isaiah's Servant,[38] who stands in opposition to a cadre of false interpreters and seers (cf. *1 En.* 98:8–99:10).[39] The Teacher of Righteousness (cf. Enoch, the scribe of righteousness) is both an expounder of the Torah and an inspired interpreter of the prophets (CD 1:10–12; 1QpHab 6:1–5). In addition to the study of the Torah and the prophets, the sapiential ambience of Qumranic activity (Ben Sira's third area of activity) is evident not just in the term *maskil*, but in the language and conceptions of texts like 1QS 11 and 1QH 9(1).

4.2.1.6. 2 Baruch and 4 Ezra

I note only briefly that the alleged authors of two post-70 apocalypses, Ezra and Baruch, although they speak like prophets at times, are both scribes. Their activity, moreover, involves the receipt and transmission of

---

38. Nickelsburg, *Jewish Literature*, 134.
39. Nickelsburg, "Epistle of Enoch," 334–43.

revelation. Ezra's function is to reconstitute the Torah, while Baruch makes heavy allusion to the wise interpreters of the law who will follow him as community leaders (ch. 77).[40] Thus, again, we are led toward scribes as prophetic successors with responsibility for teaching Torah and interest in eschatology.

4.2.2. Synthesizing Our Information: Developments in Israelite Wisdom Circles

Our review of texts has pointed us toward a related set of figures with specific roles or functions. Of course, it is not possible to equate all of these types of figures with one another, but I shall risk framing a hypothesis about the situation in the fourth to the second century B.C.E. In the Greco-Roman period, the study of the Torah and the collection and study of prophetic oracles became a major occupation among "scribes" and "the wise." Although these persons worked with the vocabulary and conceptions of the proverbial wisdom tradition, they were interpreters of the Mosaic Torah and understood themselves to be the heirs of the prophets.[41] Theirs was a learned profession, dedicated to "searching" (Heb. *daraš*) ancient texts for new meanings.[42] As such, they were scholars and teachers. However, standing in the train of the prophets, they also played the role of preachers, though precisely in what settings is not clear. Through their interpretation of Torah *and* prophets, a new thing was coming into being. While some of the prophets surely knew some of the Mosaic traditions and could speak in a sapiential idiom, "the wise" framed their ethical instruction with reference to the *Torah,* in the genres used by *the prophets,* and in *wisdom* idiom. In addition, their sensitivity to the realities of their historical circumstances led them increasingly to employ the language and historical scheme of Deut 28–32 and the eschatological scenarios of the prophets, notably Second and Third Isaiah, to describe problem and solution. There was clearly a close relationship between these interpreters of the tradition and the "apocalypticists," those who claimed that the new teaching they presented was *revelation* apart from the Torah and the prophets. This is attested in the manifold similarities evident in their common use of the literary forms and vocabulary of the wisdom tradition and the titles "the wise" and "scribe," their

---

40. Gwendolyn B. Sayler, *Have the Promises Failed? A Literary Analysis of* 2 Baruch (SBLDS 72; Chico, Calif.: Scholars Press, 1982).

41. Martin Hengel, *Judaism and Hellenism: Studies in Their Encounter in Palestine during the Early Hellenistic Period* (2 vols.; Philadelphia: Fortress, 1974), 1:134–35.

42. See Smith ("Wisdom and Apocalyptic"), who concludes that apocalypticism is a learned, scribal phenomenon.

keen de facto interest in both the Torah and the prophets, and their focus on the future resolution of present troubles.

As we compare the sapiential and apocalyptic literatures, we shall *not* discover that Ben Sira and the authors of *1 Enoch* and Daniel were really clones of one another. Indeed they had some serious points of disagreement. Nonetheless, they appear to be different species of the same genus, and as is often the case, one argues most heatedly with those most similar to oneself, or those using different methods to draw divergent and sometimes conflicting conclusions from a common starting point. The activity of interpreting the Torah had its own variations, developing alternatively into halakic refinement and sapiential instruction. The former may well reflect the belief that the circumstances of the nation or one's community reflected the covenantal curses and required careful searching of the Torah to determine precisely how it was to be obeyed (*Jub.* 23:17; CD 1).

In discussing the social settings in which the wise did their exposition and admonition, we need to consider the issue of community and community setting. Here caution is important, because diversity is likely. The detailed evidence that we have about the Qumran community is helpful but can send us in wrong directions. Some of the apocalyptic texts in *1 Enoch* do suggest a sectarian setting,[43] though of what sort is unclear. Closed groups can be the function of halakic disputes, but *1 Enoch* breaks the mold with its openness to outsiders (indeed, Gentiles, it would appear). Daniel is an apocalypse that suggests an open, non-sectarian setting with anyone in Hellenizing Israel as the potential object of the author's admonition.

The spectrum of allusions in the sapiential and apocalyptic literature suggest many possibilities for consideration as one thinks of concrete settings: school (of what sort); synagogue (with what meaning); temple court; closed conventicles; the open market place. All of this requires hard work with Jewish and non-Jewish texts, as well as epigraphic and archeological evidence, using the tools of philology, literary criticism, and social scientific methods, and keeping an open mind that is not bound to traditional categories and conclusions.

4.2.3. Two Cautions about Compartmentalization

4.2.3.1. Confusing Functions with Institutions and Offices

Although I wish to avoid the notion that everyone was like everyone else, it seems important to emphasize that the differentiation of

---

43. Nickelsburg, "Epistle of Enoch."

functions need not indicate a corresponding differentiation in offices and institutions. We need not suppose that first century teachers of the Torah and the prophets were professors of the academic study of religion, who might never take to the pulpit or the soap box. Indeed, texts as different as *1 Enoch,* the Wisdom of Ben Sira, and certain Qumranic texts referring to the Teacher of Righteousness seem to indicate that sages of very different dispositions engaged in analogous (though not totally identical) sets of functions. It would be worthwhile to set up a table or grid in which one could plot: text, titles or self-designations, functions, and settings.

4.2.3.2. Confusing Scholarly Terminology and Historical Reality

The history of scholarship indicates that we have sometimes confused our scholarly abstractions and heuristic categories with flesh and blood realities in the ancient culture that we study. Terms such as *sapiential, apocalyptic,* and *eschatological* are useful and, indeed, necessary, but they must be seen for what they are: windows into another world, means for trying to understand that to which we do not have first-hand access. It is imperative that the means not be construed as the end, or the window confused with the landscape.

The history of scholarship also attests the ways in which our categories have become hermetically sealed compartments that give the impression that each refers to, or contains something totally different from the other. Thus "wisdom" or "sapiential" is distinct from "apocalyptic." By focusing intently on one or the other, as the thing itself, we fail to see that in the world from which they have come to us, they were related parts of an organic whole, each with some of the same genes as the other. Having used the terms "wisdom" or "sapiential" and "apocalyptic" in this paper to describe discrete bodies of literature, I have drawn conclusions that suggest that these are flawed categories.

4.2.4. *Thinking Holistically about the Past*

My observations, as rough and flawed as they are, invite us to think holistically about the past. In synchronic terms, we can consider the following:

- ✦ How did the apocalypticism variously attested in the texts we have surveyed relate to broader currents and countercurrents in the circles of the learned successors of the prophets?
- ✦ In what various ways were eschatology and ethics related to each other in the texts of the Greco-Roman period and the activities of those who created and read them?

We also need to think about the crucial diachronic dimension:

- ◆ Can we find a continuum from prophet to sage?
- ◆ Is it really meaningful to use the term "apocalyptic eschatology" to refer both to the prophet Third Isaiah, whose oracle is not an apocalypse, and his successor, the author of *1 En.* 26–27, who cast material from Isa 65–66 into the form of an apocalypse?
- ◆ What were the different nuances in the notions of revelation or inspiration held by the prophets and their various successors?

Above all, I wish to emphasize the need to study text in context. Part of the bind that scholarship has gotten itself into is the result of dealing with texts and our abstract descriptions of them apart from the real worlds that created the texts. In fact, texts are historical artifacts. As we try to understand the functions that they fulfilled and the settings in which they were employed, we may discover that the similarities in texts that *we have decided* belong to different categories are not really all that strange after all, because in the wholeness of life in antiquity they were tied together in ways that we have yet to understand.[44] In short, the problem may not be in the texts, but in the categories and methods that we have used to describe and interpret them.

---

44. In my paper, "Tobit and Enoch," I struggled with the similarities between a sapiential and an apocalyptic text. For further discussion since the original publication of the present paper, see George W. E. Nickelsburg, "The Search for Tobit's Mixed Ancestry: A Historical and Hermeneutical Odyssey," *RevQ* 17 (1996): 339–49 = *Hommage à Józef T. Milik* (ed. F. García Martínez and É. Puech; Paris: Gabalda, 1996), repr. in *George W. E. Nickelsburg in Perspective: An Ongoing Dialogue of Learning* (ed. J. Neusner and A. J. Avery-Peck; 2 vols.; JSJSup 80; Leiden: Brill, 2003), 241–53, together with responses by Robert Doran and me on pages 254–66.

Response to George Nickelsburg, "Wisdom and Apocalypticism in Early Judaism"

Sarah J. Tanzer

George Nickelsburg's 1994 essay, "Wisdom and Apocalypticism in Early Judaism: Some Points for Discussion," defined the problem and tentatively proposed half of the agenda for a new Society of Biblical Literature Consultation (and later a Group) working on Wisdom and Apocalypticism in Early Judaism and Early Christianity.[1] Although I had an opportunity to respond to George's essay when the paper was originally presented, returning to it eight years later I am struck by, first, the impressionistic style of the essay, and yet its clarity of insight into the issues involved in rethinking the interrelationship of wisdom and apocalypticism and the producers of these early Jewish texts; second, how much our SBL group has been guided by the agenda proposed in this essay; and third, the fact that so many of the stumbling blocks still remain in understanding the dynamic interrelationship of Jewish wisdom and apocalyptic literature, the communities and individuals behind these texts, and the ways in which we might learn from the interrelationship of Jewish wisdom and apocalyptic about what we see in some New Testament and early Christian writings.

The core of George's thesis about Jewish texts from the Greco-Roman period is beyond dispute: "that the entities usually defined as sapiential and apocalyptic often cannot be cleanly separated from one another.... Thus, apocalyptic texts contain elements that are at home in wisdom literature, and wisdom texts reflect growing interest in eschatology."[2] Some of the details of his thesis will be discussed

---

1. While George's paper considered the issues from the early Judaism side of things, Richard Horsley made suggestions about the other half of the agenda—looking at issues raised by the study of early Christianity—in his essay, "Wisdom Justified by All Her Children: Examining Allegedly Disparate Traditions in Q," *Society of Biblical Literature 1994 Seminar Papers* (SBLSP 33; Atlanta: Scholars Press, 1994), 733–51.

2. George W. E. Nickelsburg, "Wisdom and Apocalypticism in Early Judaism: Some Points for Discussion," reprinted in this volume. The quotation is from p. 20 above.

below.³ George's "cautions" offered at the end of his essay should not go unnoticed: we have a tendency to confuse scholarly constructs with the realities of the ancient cultural world which we are studying: "Terms such as *sapiential, apocalyptic,* and *eschatological* are useful and, indeed, necessary, but they must be seen for what they are: windows into another world, means for trying to understand that to which we do not have first-hand access. It is imperative that the means not be construed as the end, or the window confused with the landscape"⁴ So too, he cautions us away from setting impermeable boundaries between the categories of wisdom and apocalyptic and advises us to think more holistically about life in antiquity and the producers of these texts: "[O]ur categories have become hermetically sealed compartments that give the impression that each refers to, or contains something totally different from the other.... By focusing intently on one or the other, as the thing itself, we fail to see that in the world from which they have come to us, they were related parts of an organic whole, each with some of the same genes as the other."⁵

What follows includes a more detailed look at George's points for discussion organized around his two larger categories, "Jewish Literature" and "Institutions and Social Settings." While it highlights some of the prescient strengths of his essay as well as offering some of my reservations, its primary purpose is to look at how the conversation has developed in the eight years since, how the work of the Wisdom and Apocalypticism Group relates more broadly to scholarly trends, and to note where we seem no further along and what some of the questions and issues are that remain.

Jewish Literature

George reminds us that over the last three decades we have learned to distinguish the literary genre of apocalypse⁶ from "apocalypticism" or

---

3. A more detailed thesis about the scribes and "wisdom circles" that produced this literature can be found in Nickelsburg, "Wisdom and Apocalypticism," 34–35.
4. Ibid., 36.
5. Ibid.
6. Revelation, mediated by an otherworldly being to a human recipient, dealing with matters which are in principle beyond ordinary human knowledge and involving supernatural powers, a final judgment and eschatological salvation. This definition is drawn from John J. Collins's work, both in "Response to George Nickelsburg" (paper presented at the Annual Meeting of the Society of Biblical Literature, Chicago, 21 November 1994), and in "The Jewish Apocalypses," *Semeia* 14 (1979): 21–59.

an "apocalyptic worldview,"[7] and perhaps very cautiously to speak of apocalyptic movements (such as the Qumran community),[8] even while admitting that the diversity of what is included in these categories belies the thought that these are any more than necessary scholarly constructs.[9]

What needs to be added to George's observations about definitions of apocalypse—apocalyptic worldview—apocalypticism is that there has not been any corresponding discussion around the issues of definitions of wisdom, either as a literary genre or as a worldview, and that while the general character of the category has been thoughtfully described by many, wisdom literature as a literary genre has eluded definition. This too should remind us that genre definitions are scholarly constructs and limited. Complicating the issue of definitions of wisdom is that unlike apocalyptic it has no single large genre (such as an apocalypse), which would make it easily identifiable and from which one could seek a constellation of features that would contribute to defining a worldview. A lot depends on the literary context in which the various broad types and smaller forms of wisdom are found. What has been defined is a literary corpus, including: Proverbs, Qoheleth, Job, Sirach, and the Wisdom of Solomon—with Proverbs typically being considered as the norm when discussing wisdom forms, themes, and language. James Crenshaw in his intelligent study, *Old Testament Wisdom*, states, "However much these literary productions differ from one another, they retain a mysterious ingredient that links them together in a special way."[10] The difficulty comes in attempting to isolate that "mysterious ingredient." All five of these texts are formally, thematically, and linguistically diverse, just as they also differ in their attitudes towards wisdom—her theological connections, her attainability, and her benefits or lack thereof. In fact, Qoheleth and Job are often seen as both related to and yet a critique of the sort of wisdom found in Proverbs. The diversity of these texts is one problem.

---

7. A constellation of elements drawn from apocalypses (typically including, with variations, interest in otherworldly regions, angels and demons, eschatology emphasizing judgment of the dead, and a promise that the faithful would rise for their rewards). Again, so much of the work of Collins has been formative here.

8. John J. Collins has pointed out the dangers inherent in moving from literary works to social movements in "Genre, Ideology and Social Movements in Jewish Apocalypticism," in *Mysteries and Revelations: Apocalyptic Studies since the Uppsala Colloquium* (ed. J. J. Collins and J. H. Charlesworth; JSPSup 9; Sheffield: Sheffield Academic Press, 1991), 11–32.

9. Nickelsburg, "Wisdom and Apocalypticism," 19.

10. James L. Crenshaw, *Old Testament Wisdom: An Introduction* (Atlanta: John Knox, 1981), 17.

On the other hand, this corpus (despite its Hellenistic members) may be too circumscribed to be helpful in describing the evolving and more pervasive character of wisdom in early Judaism as it shows up within different literary genres. This lack of distinctiveness means that wisdom "threatens to become an all-encompassing category. Any form of knowledge that is recognized as good may be dubbed 'wisdom,' and it is difficult to pin down any one literary form that might provide a criterion for identifying material as sapiential."[11] One useful strategy is to look for a constellation of wisdom elements, e.g., smaller forms, themes, and language which are found in the five-member wisdom corpus to assess what makes them distinctive (for example, context in which they are found, the totality of the constellation, etc.) and to evaluate other texts on the basis of clusters of these distinctive features.[12]

John J. Collins identifies five distinct, broad types of wisdom: (1) wisdom sayings; (2) theological wisdom; (3) nature wisdom; (4) mantic wisdom; and (5) higher wisdom through revelation.[13] These typologies of wisdom seem useful, but need more attention than they have so far received and more precision about the scope and features of the literature that fits under each heading. They should be looked into closely both with texts that have been widely acknowledged as wisdom literature and with those texts that challenge the boundaries between apocalyptic and wisdom (such as many of the Qumran texts). It has often been acknowledged that mantic wisdom is very much a part of apocalyptic writings, whereas wisdom sayings are rare in such a context. It is not too difficult

---

11. Collins, "Response," 2. It is difficult to know where one should draw the line. Different scholars have included different texts under the heading "wisdom." George, for example, has included Tobit and Baruch in this category (Nickelsburg, "Wisdom and Apocalypticism," 22–24, 27).

12. Cf. Michael V. Fox, *Proverbs 1–9* (AB 18A; New York: Doubleday, 2000), 17: "No definition of Wisdom literature will identify precisely which works belong and which do not. But we should not think of Wisdom literature as a field that can be marked out and fenced in. Wisdom literature is a *family* of texts. There are clusters of features that characterize it. The more of them a work has, the more clearly it belongs in the family. In fact, in the case of Wisdom literature, the family resemblances are quite distinctive." There is a problem, however, with this issue of distinctiveness, because of the universalism of Israelite wisdom. It means that the forms, themes, and language tend not to be the exclusive property of Wisdom, and so when found by themselves (not in clusters) it would be difficult to argue that they are indicators of a wisdom tradition at work.

13. John J. Collins, "Wisdom, Apocalypticism, and Generic Compatibility," in *In Search of Wisdom: Essays in Memory of John G. Gammie* (ed. L. G. Perdue et al.; Louisville: Westminster John Knox, 1993), 168, where he expands on the threefold typology of James Crenshaw ("Method in Determining Wisdom Influence upon 'Historical' Literature," *JBL* 88 [1969]: 132).

to speculate on the reasons for this. Apocalyptic texts may show a preference for mantic wisdom and higher wisdom through revelation because of their orientation toward the supernatural world and because of their reliance upon revelation as the source of wisdom. However, wisdom sayings, which draw upon human experience and observation, will naturally tend to be less compatible with an apocalyptic worldview. It has also been noted that some wisdom literature in which wisdom sayings predominate actively shuns mantic wisdom.[14] Sirach is one such text that actively rejects the sort of apocalyptic revelation (mantic wisdom) that is found in *1 Enoch*, Daniel, and other apocalyptic texts. The issue is less related to categories and more related to the issue of esoteric vs. exoteric wisdom and the worldviews that underlie this tension. Jon Berquist has noted that: "Both wisdom and apocalyptic seek hidden knowledge. For sages, this knowledge hides within the structure of reality and presents itself eagerly to the observant sage. Knowledge provides solutions to the problems of life. Such knowledge makes itself available to everyone.... Apocalyptists, on the other hand, find a hidden knowledge that limits itself to those who are righteous.... The knowledge is not universally helpful; it tells of the destruction of some and thus comforts only the apocalyptists."[15] Further work needs to be done in thinking through the different typologies of wisdom that are attested in varieties of texts; where different types of wisdom seem compatible and where they clash; and how these relate to the perceived worldview of the text.

Another feature of wisdom literature that has been noticed and deserves further exploration is that while revelation is not absent as a source for wisdom, the writers of wisdom literature draw much more heavily on traditional opinions. They aspire not to originality, but rather they are concerned with "adapting religious traditions for use in their

---

14. Cf. Sir 34:1–8. See Collins, "Wisdom, Apocalypticism, and Generic Compatibility," 172; Richard A. Horsley, "The Politics of Cultural Production in Second-Temple Judea" (paper presented at the Annual Meeting of the Society of Biblical Literature, Denver, 17 November 2001 and reprinted in this volume), 133–34; and Lester L. Grabbe, "Papers by D. Harrington and B. Wright: A Reply" (paper presented at the Annual Meeting of the Society of Biblical Literature, New Orleans, 23 November 1996), 2.

15. Jon L. Berquist, *Judaism in Persia's Shadow: A Social and Historical Approach* (Minneapolis: Augsburg Fortress, 1995), 187–88. See also Randal A. Argall, "Reflections on 1 Enoch and Sirach: A Comparative Literary and Conceptual Analysis of the Themes of Revelation, Creation and Judgment" *Society of Biblical Literature 1995 Seminar Papers* (SBLSP 34; Atlanta: Scholars Press, 1995), 350–51. Argall's essay is a synopsis of what can be found in much more detail in his book, *1 Enoch and Sirach: A Comparative Literary and Conceptual Analysis of the Themes of Revelation, Creation and Judgment* (SBLEJL 8; Atlanta: Scholars Press, 1995).

own time."[16] This, of course, is a feature that helps to differentiate wisdom from apocalyptic writings in which revelation plays the determinative role.

Identifying how the specific characteristics of a text are linked to a worldview holds promise for understanding the interrelationship of wisdom and apocalyptic, yet also cautions us away from sliding once more into the dichotomy of labeling a text as either apocalyptic or wisdom. Contributing to the tendency to dichotomize (and to label more texts as apocalyptic rather than wisdom) is our clarity about the constellation of elements that would indicate an apocalyptic worldview (even acknowledging several variations), whereas we are less certain about what it means to say that a text exhibits a wisdom worldview. So, for example, typical of an apocalyptic worldview is the important role that supernatural agents and the heavenly world play in human affairs, the expectation of eschatological judgment and reward or punishment beyond death, and the perception that something is fundamentally wrong with the world.[17] The wisdom worldview has been characterized by Crenshaw as beginning "with humans as the fundamental point of orientation. It asks what is good for men and women. And it believes that all essential answers can be learned in experience."[18] And as Collins also says:

> This worldview involves more than a point of orientation. It also involves a set of assumptions about the universe. It affirms a world where there is an organic connection between cause and effect; where human fulfillment, such as it is, is to be found in this life; and where wisdom can be attained from accumulated experience without recourse to special revelations.[19]

Two things limit the usefulness of this characterization of wisdom: (1) it works better as a characterization of the Hebrew wisdom texts, but does not characterize the Wisdom of Solomon or other texts from the Hellenistic and Roman periods[20] and (2) this worldview may not be distinctive to wisdom alone in ancient Israel.

---

16. Berquist, *Judaism in Persia's Shadow*, 165. Cf. Collins, "Wisdom, Apocalypticism, and Generic Compatibility," 169–70.
17. Collins, "Wisdom, Apocalypticism, and Generic Compatibility," 171.
18. Crenshaw, *Old Testament Wisdom*, 17–19.
19. Collins, "Wisdom, Apocalypticism, and Generic Compatibility," 169.
20. Cf. Collins, "Response to George Nickelsburg," 4–5 ("Even when Job and Qoheleth question this worldview or dissent from it, it still frames the discussion.").

These observations about the state of definitional issues, especially in the study of wisdom but also to some degree in apocalyptic, lead me back to George's thesis and his cautions about these scholarly categories: (1) that we tend to dichotomize wisdom and apocalyptic when studying a text, insisting that the categories are mutually exclusive or at least that one label should prevail; (2) that we assume "generic incompatibility" when the opposite is true; (3) that we believe too much in our definitions of these categories and forget that they are merely constructs, "windows" onto an "ancient landscape;" and (4) that we do not tend to give the categories enough flexibility to understand texts that come from different times, locations, and contexts. While I would agree completely with all of these observations, in the area of wisdom literature the reverse problem is at least as great. Before we can more fully understand the relationship between wisdom and apocalyptic, and where the boundaries between these categories are most permeable, we need to work text by text on the definitional issues of wisdom. And as we look at texts in which the boundaries between wisdom and apocalyptic are blurred (the texts in which there is generic compatibility), we need to ask about types of wisdom, context, worldview, tradition, and revelation as sources for wisdom and how the themes that are found in both wisdom and apocalyptic are shaped by the specific worldview of the text.[21]

I find George's designation *"texts that complicate the categories"* especially helpful for a few reasons: the texts in which both wisdom and apocalyptic features are clearly evident most strongly push us to work out the interrelationship of wisdom and apocalyptic with some precision; they force the issue of definitions, dichotomous labeling, and what it is that we seek to know through the use of these categories. From the period following the Maccabean revolt as the ideas in apocalyptic literature became more acceptable in Judaism (for example, resurrection, judgment, the impact of the heavenly world on the human lives, etc.), one finds many more texts that combine elements of wisdom and apocalyptic in ways that challenge our understanding—texts which in form are not apocalypses and yet do not fit clearly within the types of wisdom literature (e.g., Qumran rule codes, testaments).[22] It is also a designation that fits well with the challenges of early Christian texts (for example Q, James, and the *Epistle of Barnabas*). The Qumran corpus seems especially

---

21. A good example of this approach is Argall, "Reflections on *1 Enoch* and Sirach," 337–51, in which he examines shared themes, literary, and conceptual features of *1 Enoch* and Sirach and comes to the conclusion that it is their worldviews that set these two books apart.

22. Collins considers the form and content of testaments in "Wisdom, Apocalypticism, and Generic Compatibility," 178–79.

rich here, allowing us to look at this designation from many different angles: by noting the features of an apocalyptic worldview in texts that are not apocalypses and which are varied in form; by studying four of the five different types of wisdom (excluding mantic wisdom) which are reflected in these texts; and lastly, by comparing the range of ways that apocalyptic and wisdom are brought together in these texts. For example, 4QInstruction has many similarities to Sirach in form and content and yet also repeatedly calls upon the sage to gaze upon the "mystery that is to come." On the other hand, there are the Hodayot and the hymnic parts of 1QS that are clearly not wisdom texts and yet are loaded with all sorts of wisdom elements (especially revelatory and theological wisdom), and also exhibit an apocalyptic worldview.

Institutions and Social Settings

In the second part of his essay, George argues that in order to understand the interrelationship of wisdom and apocalypticism we need to try "to reconstruct the institutions, social settings, and functions that gave rise to this literature" in order "to avoid the elusive abstraction that sometimes attends the history of ideas."[23] In particular, we need to work at understanding the producers of these texts and their real-life social worlds to the extent that we are able, even though this is not an interest of the texts themselves. He has risked framing an early hypothesis about "Developments in Israelite Wisdom Circles," following a first assessment of figures and functions in early Jewish texts.[24] His observation that as we look at the interrelationship of wisdom and apocalyptic literatures, "we shall *not* discover that Ben Sira and the authors of *1 Enoch* and Daniel were really clones of one another.... Nonetheless, they appear to be different species of the same genus...."[25] challenges us to notice their close proximity in terms of geography, education, functions, and class even as we recognize how strikingly different are their worldviews and the different scribes and scribal allegiances represented by these texts.[26]

---

23. Nickelsburg, "Wisdom and Apocalypticism," 30.
24. Ibid., 34–35. This hypothesis, as George acknowledged, is risky. In my view it raises the complexities involved in moving from literary texts and figures to institutions and social settings. Similarly, I do not find the terminology, "wisdom circles," to be helpful—it is too general and too poorly defined.
25. Ibid., 35.
26. Ibid., 34–36. In fact, his call for setting up tables or grids to plot "text, titles or self-designations, functions, and settings" would be useful for bringing precision to our descriptions of the scribes who produced these writings.

The issue of specifying the social locations of the producers of these texts, the scribes, has been the focus of much scholarship over the past dozen years and has also been a central focus of the SBL Wisdom and Apocalypticism Group. On the one hand, what has emerged are more detailed, but broad hypotheses about who these various scribes were and their background in society. For example, Jon Berquist provides rather full hypotheses about the social locations of the producers of wisdom literature and apocalyptic literature in the postexilic period. His observations about the scribes who produced wisdom literature include: they were among the most literate segments of Jerusalem society; although they may well have been active within the temple they sought other truths to be found outside of the temple system; they were trained in foreign languages and their education had an international character to it, which would allow them to oversee the bureaucratic affairs involving other nations and provinces; they worked for the government, the temple, local merchants and other employers; they contributed to the social maintenance of society's power institutions; they presented the opinions of society's chief authorities as immutable; while their social functions included educating the young, they served the powers that be in a daily way through their scribal activity.[27] Berquist sees the scribes who produced apocalyptic literature as deriving from the same social location as the scribes who produced wisdom, "the knowledge experts of Jerusalem, who operate within the middle management of the imperial-colonial bureaucracies."[28] But unlike the scribes who produced wisdom, those who produced apocalyptic literature felt they were in a position of relative deprivation when compared to their superiors, and they were frustrated by their lack of power to change the system.[29] Aware that they could not change the systems in which they worked, these groups of scribes undertook different responses: in wisdom literature the scribes teach people how to succeed within society and the current institutions, whereas in apocalyptic literature the scribes "create a rhetorical power that legitimates their own dissatisfaction by claiming God's displeasure at the system led by their superiors. Destruction of the system seems inevitable,"[30] though it will happen through God's intervention and not by human hands. These very full hypotheses provide

---

27. Berquist, *Judaism in Persia's Shadow*, 161–72. On the issue of a wisdom school or wisdom schools, see also p. 162, and Fox, *Proverbs*, 7–8, who summarizes the scholarship on this subject.
28. Berquist, *Judaism in Persia's Shadow*, 187.
29. Ibid., 184–87.
30. Ibid.

helpful reconstructions against which to test out the evidence of individual texts. They may, however, mislead people into thinking that we know more about these scribes than we possibly can, and they also lump together wisdom scribes and apocalyptic scribes by too simplistically attributing to them one sort of stance in relationship to the systems within which they live and work.

On the other hand, another approach has been to try to discern the specific social world of the scribes on a text-by-text basis, asking a variety of social world questions such as: Where are they located socially? For whom would these scribes have worked? With whom would they have associated? What was their relationship to the people in power? What do they advocate for/against in society? What sort of authority do they seem to have? What was authoritative for them? Does the polemic in the text give hints of possible rivalries between scribal groups?[31] Richard Horsley represents a growing trend in this text-by-text scholarship in his conclusion that we learn a great deal about the producers of these texts through an examination of their attitudes toward the current imperial regime(s), and their attitudes toward the temple, the priesthood, and the ruling aristocracy in Judea.[32] Further, according to Horsley's analysis, their choice among differing types of wisdom depended precisely on these things (thus, traditional proverbial wisdom is found in texts which are basically pro-status quo whereas mantic wisdom and higher wisdom through revelation tend to be the wisdoms of choice for those who are opposed to the status quo or those who are part of a resistance movement).[33] While quite helpful for its detailed text-by-text analysis and for its attention to the

---

31. So, for example, Benjamin G. Wright III concludes (in "Putting the Puzzle Together: Some Suggestions Concerning the Social Location of the Wisdom of Ben Sira," reprinted in this volume, 111–12), after looking at Sirach, *1 Enoch* and *Aramaic Levi*, that despite many common interests, they held "competing notions of scribal wisdom and priestly legitimacy. Their concerns and claims show that in the late third to early second century B.C.E., besides having to confront and to deal with outsiders and foreign cultural influences, different Jewish groups who had varying assessments of the Jerusalem priesthood and Temple were actively engaged in an inner-Jewish struggle for power."

32. Horsley, "Politics of Cultural Production."

33. This simplified overview does not begin to do justice to Horsley's rich analysis. For more on *1 Enoch*, see Horsley, "The Politics of Cultural Production," 137–41; Patrick A. Tiller, "Israel at the Mercy of Demonic Powers: An Enochic Interpretation of Post-Exilic Imperialism" (reprinted in this volume); and Argall, "Reflections on *1 Enoch* and Sirach," 350–51. For more on Sirach, see Horsley, "The Politics of Cultural Production," 133–37; and Benjamin G. Wright III, "'Put the Nations in Fear of You:' Ben Sira and the Problem of Foreign Rule" in *Society of Biblical Literature 1999 Seminar Papers* (SBLSP 38; Atlanta: Scholars Press, 1999), 77–93. For more on Daniel, see Horsley, "The Politics of Cultural Production," 141–44.

social indicators in different texts, one wonders whether this sort of approach will also lead us to new ways of dichotomizing.

Conclusion

Eight years down the road are we any wiser for George Nickelsburg's essay, "Wisdom and Apocalypticism in Early Judaism"? Certainly many of the same stumbling blocks remain in trying to understand the interrelationship of wisdom and apocalypticism in early Judaism, and although we have been wary of the dichotomizing tendencies of the past, much in current research has led to different (but still somewhat dichotomizing) ways of defining the divide between the various types of wisdom and the differing perspectives of the scribes who produced it. Yet his essay has proved tremendously generative in any number of ways. His comment about scholarly reification and abstraction of wisdom and apocalyptic[34] has prompted an approach that sets the terms aside and works more deductively and descriptively out of the texts. His concern that we try to reconstruct the social and cultural realities around the production of the texts[35] has challenged us to search in the details of each individual text for what we might learn about the producers of these texts, their commitments and relationship to their social world. He has reminded us that our definitions of the genre apocalypse and related terminology only take us so far—that there is great diversity and there really are not any pure genres out there.[36] His designation "texts that complicate the categories"[37] is especially helpful in recognizing that the boundaries between wisdom and apocalyptic are very permeable and not sharply drawn in reference to Jewish literature in the Greco-Roman period. Although George cautiously included only the Wisdom of Solomon and the Qumran Scrolls under this heading in his essay, I suspect that eight years later he would include many more texts under this designation. Perhaps the best way to bring this response to an end is to remind us of George's challenge to think holistically about these texts, because "the similarities in texts that *we have decided* belong to different categories are not really all that strange after all, because in the wholeness of life in antiquity they were tied together in ways that we have yet to understand."[38]

---

34. Nickelsburg, "Wisdom and Apocalypticism," 19.
35. Ibid., 34–35.
36. Ibid., 34–37.
37. Ibid., 28.
38. Ibid., 37.

RESPONSE TO SARAH TANZER

George W. E. Nickelsburg

After eight years of study on the topic of "Wisdom and Apocalypticism," Sarah Tanzer's response to my paper and her reflections on these years of study suggest that we still find ourselves on terrain that we have not clearly mapped and that we do not understand very well. We have worked through many texts, tried to place them in their generative contexts, and asked many good questions about texts and contexts. Yet the answers continue to elude us. She notes that while we know quite a bit about apocalypticism, having at hand as a partial control an analysis of the genre of apocalypse, we are still in the dark about the category that is generally called "wisdom."

I will comment briefly on the larger picture, suggesting three overarching commonalities between "wisdom" and apocalypticism, and within them, some points of difference. I will also conclude with three questions that will be relevant for the next stage of investigation.

1. The "mysterious ingredient" in "wisdom" to which James L. Crenshaw refers in his study of "Old Testament Wisdom" is the purposeful, "systematic," and sometimes obsessive quest to understand how things are or should be and why.[1] Crenshaw hints at this in the chapter headings of his 1998 edition (italics, mine): "The *Pursuit* of Knowledge," "The *Search* for Divine Presence," "The *Chasing* after Meaning," "The *Quest* for Survival," "The Widening *Hunt*." One seeks to understand one's world, how to live aright in it, and how it relates to God's greater designs and purposes. The notion of searching and seeking is important. One does not simply know these things; one must think about them, ask about them, and observe nature and human conduct to (try to) find some answers. If we tie this to the question of social location, we arrive at the one description of the sage that has been preserved from ancient Israel. The verbs speak for themselves.

---

1. James L. Crenshaw, *Old Testament Wisdom: An Introduction* (Atlanta: John Knox, 1981), 17.

> On the other hand he who *devotes* himself
> to the *study* of the law of the Most high
> will *seek out* the wisdom of all the ancients,
> and will *be concerned* with prophecies;
> he will *preserve* the discourse of notable men
> and *penetrate* the subtleties of parables;
> he will *seek out* the hidden meanings of proverbs
> and be at home with the obscurities of parables. (Sir 38:1–3 RSV)

As Ben Sira notes, this is a full-time profession and not an avocation (38:24). One must have the leisure to think that is not available to those whose trades and occupations demand their full-time attention. The sage or scribe, however, must direct his attention to a consideration of how things are or should be. It would be worth considering to what degree the "wisdom" literature, broadly construed, is permeated with language about seeing, thinking, and considering.[2] The activity that I have in mind is typical of literature like the Wisdom of Ben Sira, as the passage above indicates. It also pertains to a work like *1 Enoch,* where one is exhorted to "observe" the heavens and the earth, and to understand what one sees, and where the seer is taken to see the hidden places of the universe and to peer into the obscure future. However, to confuse the categories further, the process also pertains to the activity of those who study the Torah. Striking here, as in Sir. 39:1 and 3, is the use of the verb *darash* or *biqqēsh.*[3] To study the Torah is to search after a meaning that is not immediately apparent and that may be completely elusive, and this may involve great effort (*Jub.* 23:17; 1QS 6:6; 8:14–15). Thus, though we may distinguish between "sapiential" texts and halakhic exegesis, as I have, they have in common the persistent search for the right knowledge and understanding of God's will.

2. This pursuit of understanding focuses on the issue of what is right and what is wrong and on the consequences that follow from this. On a mundane, albeit very practical level, it may involve boorish conduct at a banquet that leads to social ostracizing or foolish companionship with the powerful that puts one in their debt. More seriously, proverbial wisdom lays out, often in poetic parallelism, the consequences of obeying or disregarding the will of God. Halakhic exegesis asks what God's will is. Apocalyptic wisdom takes on the big issues of whether divine justice is,

---

2. Here I am indebted to a graduate seminar paper on *2 Baruch* written some years ago by Frances Flannery at the University of Iowa.

3. Rodney A. Werline, *Penitential Prayer in Second Temple Judaism: The Development of a Religious Institution* (SBLEJL 13; Atlanta: Scholars Press, 1998), 111–13.

in fact, present in the (history of) the phenomenal world. But as Wis 1–5 indicates, this issue is not limited to the writings that we call apocalypses. Indeed, these big issues of "theodicy" leap across categories and types of apocalyptic and other sapiential thought. Qoheleth and Job are concerned with the issue. And like Job, the authors of 2 Baruch and especially 4 Ezra wrestle with the issue, Ezra to the point of obsession.

3. Finally, there is the issue of how one knows or where one goes for the knowledge that leads to understanding. One may reflect on the results of practical experience. "There is someone who ... and this happens to him/her." One may appeal to nature—often with the admonition to "observe." The admonition may occur in an apocalypse (1 En. 2:1–5:4; 101:1) and in other nonapocalyptic "sapiential" contexts. Thus, Matt 7:26–30 and Luke 12:24–31, as they draw on their Q source, appeal to the example of the birds and the flowers. The appeal to observe the heavens and the earth appears also in 2 Macc 7:28 in a mother's exhortation that her son act rightly by dying for the Torah. Common to all these texts is not only the appeal to "observe" nature, but also the purpose of such observation—to act rightly or to see that others have acted wrongly. For Ben Sira, the scribe looks for enlightenment in the tradition, which for him includes the Torah, the prophets, and the writings and traditions of the wise. Here the Enochic authors part company with him. Although, in fact, they draw on Scripture at many points, they do not acknowledge the fact. Instead they claim to have received a special revelation, through dreams, visions, and heavenly journeys. They assert that this is an ancient revelation (to Enoch), but, in fact, it is new revelation. Scripture is not sufficient. The author of chapters 24–26 draws on the imagery of Isa 65–66, but he anchors the authority of his information not in the prophetic word about the new Jerusalem, but in a visionary journey in which Enoch himself actually saw these future realities. For the author of the Animal Vision, the history of the world—including the sins of Israel, the enlightenment of the chosen, and the judgment that will set things right—was seen in Enoch's dream vision. This striking difference in epistemology may well be tied to the apocalypticist's world view, as Sarah Tanzer suggests. Because the Enochic authors experience their world as an alienating environment, they appeal to special revelation that will resonate with their audience and thus guarantee the veracity of their claims that the end is at hand and that God's judgment will right the injustices that they now perceive.

Three questions follow from this: (1) Are the three rubrics proposed in these theses shared by all the texts generally thought to be "sapiential" or "apocalyptic," and/or can the rubrics be refined to fit the evidence better? (2) If so, do the rubrics help to distinguish this group of texts from the macro-contents of other types of texts? If not, of what sort are the exceptions?[4] (3) Do the rubrics provide a tool for dividing the texts in the group into sub-groups?

As modern scholars, we get caught in traps of our own making, when we attempt to lock certain clusters of motifs and emphases into exclusive categories like "wisdom" and "apocalyticism." We shall do better to study the texts broadly and comparatively, in order to *see* what we find where—especially when we do not expect to find it there—and to *observe* what patterns emerge from this comparative endeavor.

---

4. See, e.g., my comments on revelation in Ben Sira: George W. E. Nickelsburg, "The Nature and Function of Revelation in *1 Enoch, Jubilees,* and Some Qumran Documents," in *Pseudepigraphic Perspectives: The Apocrypha and Pseudepigrapha in Light of the Dead Sea Scrolls: Proceedings of the International Symposium of the Orion Center for the Study of the Dead Sea Scrolls and Associated Literature, 12–14 January, 1997* (ed. E. G. Chazon et al.; STDJ 31; Leiden: Brill, 1999), 118.

PART 2:
WISDOM AND APOCALYPTICISM IN EARLY JUDAISM

WISDOM, APOCALYPTICISM, AND THE PEDAGOGICAL ETHOS OF 4QINSTRUCTION*

Matthew J. Goff

INTRODUCTION

In recent years the sapiential and apocalyptic traditions and the ways in which they intersect have been prominent topics of scholarly debate.[1] At this point it is well established that the two traditions are by no means mutually exclusive. This is evident, for example, in *1 En.* 42, in which Lady Wisdom appears.[2] Biblical and deuterocanonical sapiential texts contain some material that is more in keeping with apocalypticism than traditional wisdom. Eliphaz's first response to Job is based on a description of a vision (Job 4:12–21). Ecclesiastes 3 presents a deterministic understanding of the natural order and in that sense can be compared to the apocalypses.[3] But Ecclesiastes shows minimal interest in eschatology,

---

* This essay is a revised version of a paper delivered at the Annual Meeting of the Society of Biblical Literature in Toronto, Ontario, 24 November 2002.

1. For a good summary of the relevant issues, see John J. Collins, "Wisdom, Apocalypticism and Generic Compatibility," in idem, *Seers, Sibyls and Sages in Hellenistic Roman Judaism* (JSJSup 54; Leiden: Brill, 1997), 385–404, and, in the same volume, "Wisdom, Apocalypticism and the Dead Sea Scrolls," 369–83. See also H.-P. Müller, "Mantische Weisheit und Apokalyptik," in *Congress Volume: Uppsala, 1971* (VTSup 22; Leiden: Brill, 1972), 268–93; John G. Gammie, "Spatial and Ethical Dualism in Jewish Wisdom and Apocalyptic Literature," *JBL* 93 (1974): 356–85; Michael E. Stone, "Lists of Revealed Things in the Apocalyptic Literature," in *Magnalia Dei: The Mighty Acts of God: Essays on the Bible and Archaeology in Memory of G. Ernest Wright* (ed. F. M. Cross et al.; Garden City, N.Y.: Doubleday, 1976), 414–51; James C. VanderKam, "The Prophetic-Sapiential Origins of Apocalyptic Thought," in idem, *From Revelation to Canon: Studies in Hebrew Bible and Second Temple Literature* (JSJSup 62; Leiden: Brill, 2000), 241–54; Jonathan Z. Smith, "Wisdom and Apocalyptic," in idem, *Map Is Not Territory* (Chicago: University of Chicago Press, 1993), 67–87; Andreas Bedenbender, *Der Gott der Welt tritt auf den Sinai: Entstehung, Entwicklung und Funktionsweise der frühjüdischen Apokalyptik* (ANTZ 8; Berlin: Institut Kirche und Judentum, 2000), 62–87, 264–65.

2. George W. E. Nickelsburg, *Ancient Judaism and Christian Origins: Diversity, Continuity, and Transformation* (Minneapolis: Fortress, 2003), 103–4.

3. Ecclesiastes 3 is an important text for von Rad's claim that apocalypticism develops out of the wisdom tradition, a view that has encouraged debate but, as is well known,

whereas the determinism of apocalyptic literature often supports a claim that the final judgment has already been revealed (e.g., Dan 11:40–12:3). Wisdom of Solomon 5 has a judgment scene that is reminiscent of accounts of judgment in apocalyptic literature, and there is similar material in Ben Sira.[4]

The Dead Sea Scrolls have increased significantly the evidence available for the study of wisdom vis-à-vis apocalypticism. The sapiential texts from Qumran were among the last of the Dead Sea Scrolls to be published.[5] Their contribution to the assessment of Jewish wisdom in the Second Temple period has begun to be examined in earnest only recently.[6] 4QInstruction, the longest Qumran wisdom text, demonstrates that a sapiential text from this period can combine elements from both apocalypticism and traditional wisdom.[7]

---

cannot stand as originally formulated. See Gerhard von Rad, *Wisdom in Israel* (trans. J. D. Martin; Philadelphia: Westminster, 1972), 263; idem, *Old Testament Theology* (trans. D. M. G. Stalker; 2 vols.; New York: Harper & Row, 1962–1965), 2:306–8.

4. Shannon Burkes, "Wisdom and Apocalypticism in the Wisdom of Solomon," *HTR* 95 (2002): 21–44. Regarding Ben Sira, see, e.g., 5:1–8; 23:16–21. See further Randal A. Argall, *1 Enoch and Sirach: A Comparative Literary and Conceptual Analysis of the Themes of Revelation, Creation and Judgment* (SBLEJL 8; Atlanta: Scholars Press, 1995), 211–47.

5. Torleif Elgvin et al., *Qumran Cave 4. XV: Sapiential Texts, Part 1* (DJD 20; Oxford: Clarendon, 1997); John Strugnell and Daniel J. Harrington, *Qumran Cave 4. XXIV: Sapiential Texts, Part 2. 4QInstruction (Musar le Mēvin): 4Q415ff. With a Re-edition of 1Q26* (DJD 34; Oxford: Clarendon, 1999). See also Donald W. Parry and Emanuel Tov, *Calendrical and Sapiential Texts* (DSSR 4; Leiden: Brill, 2004).

6. The scholarship on Qumran wisdom texts includes Charlotte Hempel et al., eds., *The Wisdom Texts from Qumran and the Development of Sapiential Thought* (BETL 159; Leuven: Leuven University Press/Peeters, 2002); John Kampen, "The Diverse Aspects of Wisdom at Qumran," in *The Dead Sea Scrolls after Fifty Years: A Comprehensive Assessment* (ed. P. W. Flint and J. C. VanderKam; 2 vols.; Leiden: Brill, 1998), 1:211–43; John J. Collins, "Wisdom Reconsidered in Light of the Scrolls," *DSD* 4 (1997): 265–81; Daniel J. Harrington, *Wisdom Texts from Qumran* (London: Routledge, 1996).

7. Matthew J. Goff, *The Worldly and Heavenly Wisdom of 4QInstruction* (STDJ 50; Leiden: Brill, 2003); Eibert J. C. Tigchelaar, *To Increase Learning for the Understanding Ones: Reading and Reconstructing the Fragmentary Early Jewish Sapiential Text 4QInstruction* (STDJ 44; Leiden: Brill, 2001); Torleif Elgvin, "An Analysis of 4QInstruction" (Ph.D. diss., Hebrew University of Jerusalem, 1997); Armin Lange, *Weisheit und Prädestination: Weisheitliche Urordnung und Prädestination in den Textfunden von Qumran* (STDJ 18; Leiden: Brill, 1995).

Elgvin has argued that 4QInstruction is composed of an older layer of practical advice in the tradition of Proverbs that was later expanded with apocalyptic material. See, e.g., his "Wisdom and Apocalypticism in the Early Second Century B.C.E.—The Evidence of 4QInstruction," in *The Dead Sea Scrolls Fifty Years after Their Discovery: Proceedings of the Jerusalem Congress, July 20–25, 1997* (ed. L. H. Schiffman et al.; Jerusalem: Israel Exploration Society/Shrine of the Book, Israel Museum, 2000), 226–47. The influences from the wisdom and apocalyptic traditions on 4QInstruction are too intermingled to separate them into different strata. For elaboration of this view, see Goff, *Worldly and Heavenly Wisdom*, 13–17.

4QInstruction (1Q26, 4Q415–18, 423) is devoted to the moral and intellectual training of its addressee, or, as the text calls him, *mebin* (מבין; "understanding one").[8] In this paper I will argue that 4QInstruction combines the eudaemonistic and educational mindset of traditional wisdom with an apocalyptic worldview.[9] To show this I will discuss not only the kinds of knowledge the *mebin* can learn but also the role of revealed wisdom, in the form of the *raz nihyeh* (רז נהיה), in his education. I will also consider why the *raz nihyeh* is presented as an important source of wisdom.

Pedagogy and Knowledge in 4QInstruction

In terms of genre, 4QInstruction is a wisdom text.[10] The document includes a substantial number of admonitions regarding ordinary aspects of life, as in traditional wisdom. For example, 4Q416 2 ii 6–7 contains a vetitive urging that the addressee avoid indebtedness, a prominent theme in 4QInstruction, Proverbs, and many other wisdom writings.[11] 4QInstruction is driven by a pedagogical ethos. This is clear from texts such as 4Q418 81 17: "Be very intelligent, and from all your teachers increase learning (מיד כול משכילכה הוסף לקח)." In a similar vein, 4Q416 2 iii 14–15 reads: "Have understanding in all the ways of truth, and all the roots of iniquity perceive." 4QInstruction presumes some sort of instructional setting and strives to instill a love for learning in the *mebin*.

John J. Collins has emphasized that one common thread throughout wisdom literature is "its use as instructional material."[12] The stress on education in 4QInstruction is characteristic of the sapiential tradition. 4QInstruction is in continuity with Proverbs in that both have an explicit pedagogical purpose (Prov 1:1–7). There is also an emphasis on learning

---

8. Eibert J. C. Tigchelaar, "The Addressees of 4QInstruction," in *Sapiential, Liturgical and Poetical Texts from Qumran: Proceedings of the Third Meeting of the International Organization for Qumran Studies, Oslo 1998* (ed. D. Falk et al.; STDJ 35; Leiden: Brill, 2000), 62–75.

9. Kasper Bro Larsen, "Visdom og apokalyptik i Musar leMevin (1Q/4QInstruction)" [Wisdom and Apocalyptic in Musar leMevin (1Q/4QInstruction)], *DTT* 65 (2002): 1–14.

10. Strugnell and Harrington, DJD 34, 28–33.

11. Compare, e.g., 4Q418 88 3, "Take care for yourself lest you go surety," with Prov 17:18, "It is senseless to give a pledge, to become surety for a neighbor." See also 4Q416 2 ii 17–18; 4Q416 2 iii 15–16; 4Q417 2 i 17–20; Prov 6:1–5; 17:5; 19:1; 28:27; 29:7; Ahiqar 105, 137. For more on this issue, note Catherine M. Murphy, *Wealth in the Dead Sea Scrolls and the Qumran Community* (STDJ 40; Leiden: Brill, 2002), 163–209; J. David Pleins, *The Social Visions of the Hebrew Bible: A Theological Introduction* (Louisville: Westminster John Knox, 2001), 452–513.

12. Collins, "Wisdom Reconsidered," 281.

in the apocalyptic tradition.[13] According to *1 En.* 82 and 105, for example, Enoch is enjoined to teach the knowledge that he has received through revelation. The visions of Daniel have an instructional intent (11:33). Analogously, Baruch is depicted as giving teachings to Israel (e.g., *2 Bar.* 44–45; 76:5). The sapiential and apocalyptic traditions differ in terms of pedagogy in that the former provides practical advice regarding specific areas of ordinary life more consistently than the latter.[14] Apocalyptic literature often encourages its intended audience to be righteous, as in, for example, the Epistle of Enoch (e.g., *1 En.* 94:1). In a broad sense, this goal is compatible with ethical instruction in the wisdom tradition. However, the posture toward ethics in the apocalypses is almost always geared toward the teleological goals of achieving rewards and avoiding punishment after death, whereas this is never the case in traditional wisdom.[15] Wisdom texts that provide an eschatological backdrop for their admonitions, such as the Wisdom of Solomon and 4QInstruction, can be understood as examples of influence from the apocalyptic tradition on late sapiential texts.[16]

The addressee of 4QInstruction can learn many different kinds of knowledge drawn from both the sapiential and apocalyptic traditions. Some accord with traditional wisdom while others reflect an apocalyptic worldview. The *mebin* learns, for example, to practice moderation with food (4Q416 2 ii 18–20) and filial piety (4Q416 2 iii 15–19). These tropes are commonplace in the sapiential tradition. He is also given instruction regarding his elect status. He is told, for example, that he is among the lot

---

13. For more on education in the Second Temple period, see David M. Carr, *Writing on the Tablet of the Heart* (Oxford: Oxford University Press, 2005); James L. Crenshaw, *Education in Ancient Israel* (ABRL; New York: Doubleday, 1998).

14. Apocalypses do contain advice on specific practical topics that is reminiscent of the wisdom tradition, but such material is by no means prominent in this corpus. For example, *1 En.* 91:4 includes an admonition encouraging the addressee to avoid "hypocrites." Instruction regarding negative types of people who should be avoided is commonplace in the wisdom tradition (e.g., Prov 29:27; 4Q424 1 10). See also *4 Ezra* 14:13: "Now therefore, set your house in order and reprove your people; comfort the lowly among them and instruct those that are wise." Such material is too general to claim with confidence that it reflects influence from the wisdom tradition, but this possibility cannot be discounted outright.

15. Alan F. Segal, *Life after Death: A History of the Afterlife in Western Religions* (New York: Doubleday, 2004).

16. John J. Collins, "The Eschatologizing of Wisdom in the Dead Sea Scrolls," in *Sapiential Perspectives: Wisdom Literature in Light of the Dead Sea Scrolls. Proceedings of the Sixth International Symposium of the Orion Center, 20–22 May 2001* (ed. J. J. Collins et al.; STDJ 51; Leiden: Brill, 2004), 49–65; Torleif Elgvin, "Early Essene Eschatology: Judgment and Salvation according to Sapiential Work A," in *Current Research and Technological Development on the Dead Sea Scrolls: Conference on the Texts from the Judean Desert, Jerusalem, 30 April 1995* (ed. D. W. Parry and S. D. Ricks; STDJ 20; Leiden: Brill, 1996), 126–65.

of the angels (4Q418 81 4–5). The *mebin* can also learn about the nature of the final judgment (4Q416 1; 4Q418 69 ii).

The Acquisition of Wisdom in 4QInstruction — The רז נהיה

How does the *mebin* obtain wisdom? The most important source of wisdom for the addressee is the *raz nihyeh* (רז נהיה). This enigmatic phrase occurs over twenty times in 4QInstruction but elsewhere only three times, in the Book of Mysteries and the Community Rule (1Q27 1 i 3–4 [2x] [par 4Q300 3 4]; 1QS 11:3–4).[17] The phrase combines the word *raz*, a Persian loan-word that means "mystery," with the Niphal participle of the verb "to be."[18] There has been much debate on how to translate this phrase.[19] I prefer the translation "the mystery that is to be" over options that more strongly emphasize the future sense of the phrase such as the "mystery to come." The *raz nihyeh* refers to revealed knowledge that pertains to the entire scope of history. The meaning of the expression is not limited to the eschatological future.[20] This is suggested by 4Q417 1 i 3–4, which reads: "Gaze [upon the mystery that is to be and the deeds of old, from what has been to what exists through what] [will be] ... [for]ever ([והבט֯] ברז נהיה ומעשי קדם למה נהיה ומה נהיה במה] ... [יהיה])" (cf. 4Q418 43 2–3). Elgvin has suggested that this passage attests a three-fold division of time.[21] This claim is supported by 4Q418 123 ii 3–4, which associates a tripartite division of time with the mystery that is to be: "Everything that exists in it, from what has been to what will be in it (כול הנהיה בה למה היה ומה יהיה בו) ... His period

---

17. 4Q415 6 4; 4Q416 2 i 5 (par 4Q417 2 i 10–11); 4Q416 2 iii 9, 14, 18, 21 (par 4Q418 9 8, 15; 4Q418 10 1, 3); 4Q417 1 i 3, 6, 8, 18, 21 (par 4Q418 43 2, 4, 6, 14, 16); 4Q417 1 ii 3; 4Q418 77 2, 4; 4Q418 123 ii 4; 4Q418 172 1; 4Q418 184 2; and 4Q423 4 1, 4 (par 1Q26 1 1, 4). The phrase has been plausibly reconstructed in 4Q415 24 1; 4Q416 17 3; 4Q418 179 3; 4Q418 190 2–3; 4Q418 201 1; 4Q418c 2; 4Q423 3 2; 4Q423 5 2; and 4Q423 7 7. The mystery that is to be is often accompanied by the preposition ב. See also Strugnell and Harrington, DJD 34, 28–29; Tigchelaar, *To Increase Learning*, 205.

18. Elliot R. Wolfson, "Seven Mysteries of Knowledge: Qumran E/Sotericism Recovered," in *The Idea of Biblical Interpretation: Essays in Honor of James L. Kugel* (ed. H. Najman and J. H. Newman; JSJSup 83; Leiden: Brill, 2004), 177–213.

19. For an overview, see Goff, *Worldly and Heavenly Wisdom*, 30–42. Daniel J. Harrington has claimed that the רז נהיה refers to a separate educational text that 4QInstruction encourages the *mebin* to study. See his *Wisdom Texts*, 49; idem, "The Raz Nihyeh in a Qumran Wisdom Text (1Q26, 4Q415–418, 423)," *RevQ* 17 (1996): 549–53. The teachings connected to this phrase are never presented as citations from a physical document.

20. Murphy, *Wealth in the Dead Sea Scrolls*, 207.

21. Elgvin, "Analysis of 4QInstruction," 259.

which God revealed to the ear of the understanding ones through the mystery that is to be."

The mystery that is to be is a focal point of instruction. This is clear, for example, from 4Q417 2 i 10–11: "[Gaze upon the mystery] that is to be, and grasp the birth-times of salvation and know who is inheriting glory and who ini[qu]ity." In this instance this mystery makes eschatological knowledge available to the *mebin*. In 4Q417 1 i 6–8 the mystery that is to be is associated with the knowledge of good and evil. The *raz nihyeh* is also connected to mundane aspects of the addressee's life. For example, knowing the mystery that is to be is to encourage the *mebin* to practice filial piety (4Q416 2 iii 18–19). Studying this mystery will also help him have success at raising crops. This is evident from 4Q423 3 2, even though it is fragmentary: "... [through the mystery] that is to be. So you will walk, and al[l your] c[rops will multiply]" (cf. 1Q26 2 2; 4Q418 103 ii).[22] Another fragmentary passage associates the *raz nihyeh* with instruction on marriage (4Q416 2 iii 20–21).

The mystery that is to be is able to provide different kinds of knowledge because it refers to a divine plan that orchestrates the flow of events. Like the Treatise on the Two Spirits (1QS 3:13–4:26), 4QInstruction has a deterministic mindset.[23] 4Q417 1 i 10–12 reads: "He has expounded for their un[der]standing every d[ee]d so that one may walk in [the inclination] of their understanding ... in proper understanding were made [known the secr]ets of his plan, along with his walking [perfe]ctly [in all] his [de]eds." Lines 18–19 of this fragment affirm that one who studies the mystery that is to be will understand how the divine plan of the natural order unfolds: "And you, understanding son, gaze into the mystery that is to be and know [the path]s of all life. The way that one conducts himself he appoints over [his] deed[s]."[24] The disclosure of this mystery is to encourage the addressee to be moral and upright. This explains why the *raz nihyeh* is connected to specific realms of daily life such as filial piety and marriage. The point of 4Q416 2 iii 18–19 is not that God has revealed that parents should be respected. Rather, understanding the divine plan that orchestrates events has ethical implications. By living in an upright manner the addressee acts in

---

22. Strugnell and Harrington, DJD 34, 513–14; Tigchelaar, *To Increase Learning*, 146.

23. Torleif Elgvin, "The Mystery to Come: Early Essene Theology of Revelation," in *Qumran between the Old and New Testaments* (ed. F. H. Cryer and T. L. Thompson; JSOTSup 290; Sheffield: Sheffield Academic Press, 1998), 135; Lange, *Weisheit und Prädestination*, 60.

24. Strugnell and Harrington, DJD 34, 155. Also note 4Q418 77 2: "the mystery that is to be, and grasp the nature of humankind."

accordance with God's deterministic order. In this sense the revelation of the mystery that is to be fosters worldly wisdom.[25]

The Epistemology of 4QInstruction

Because of its reliance on revelation, the epistemology of 4QInstruction is much more in keeping with apocalypticism than biblical wisdom. In Proverbs wisdom is often presented as a capacity of the human intellect to discern the nature of the world and act accordingly.[26] By contrast, Daniel and *1 Enoch* claim to reveal wisdom from heavenly sources. In Daniel God is hailed as a "revealer of mysteries (גלא רזיא)" (2:29). In Proverbs one who divulges secrets is condemned as a gossip. For example, Prov 20:19 states: "A gossip reveals secrets (גולה־סוד); therefore do not associate with a babbler."[27] The term *raz* signifies a fundamental difference between biblical wisdom and the apocalyptic tradition.[28]

Neither Daniel nor *1 Enoch* attest the phrase *raz nihyeh*. But the term *raz* signifies revealed knowledge in both compositions. In the Hebrew Bible the term רז is found only in Daniel, in which it is used nine times (2:18, 19, 27–29, 30, 47 [2x]; 4:6). In most of these occurrences the word denotes knowledge that God gives Daniel. For example, Dan 2:28 exclaims that "there is a God in heaven who reveals mysteries (גלא רזין), and he has disclosed to King Nebuchadnezzar what will happen at the end of days." The word *raz* also refers to revealed knowledge in the Aramaic manuscripts of *1 Enoch*. For example, in chapter 106 Enoch transmits divine knowledge regarding the eschatological judgment to his father Lamech. Enoch claims that he received this information through revelation: "For I know the mysteries of (רזי) the holy ones, for that Lord showed (them) to me and made (them) known to me, and I read (them)

---

25. For another interpretation, see Florentino García Martínez, "Wisdom at Qumran: Worldly or Heavenly?" in *Wisdom and Apocalypticism in the Dead Sea Scrolls and in the Biblical Tradition* (ed. F. García Martínez; BETL 168; Leuven: Leuven University Press/Peeters, 2003), 1–15.

26. James L. Crenshaw, *Old Testament Wisdom: An Introduction* (rev. ed.; Louisville: Westminster John Knox, 1998 [orig. 1981]), 10.

27. Prov 11:13: "A gossip goes about telling secrets, but one who is trustworthy in spirit keeps a confidence"; 25:9: "Argue your case with your neighbor directly, and do not disclose another's secret."

28. For surveys of mystery language in the Second Temple period, see Markus Bockmuehl, *Revelation and Mystery in Ancient Judaism and Pauline Christianity* (Grand Rapids: Eerdmans, 1990); Raymond E. Brown, *The Semitic Background of the Term "Mystery" in the New Testament* (FBBS 21; Philadelphia: Fortress, 1968); B. Rigaux, "Révélation des Mystères et Perfection à Qumran et dans le Nouveau Testament," *NTS* 4 (1958): 237–62. See also E. Vogt, "'Mysteria' in textibus Qumran," *Bib* 37 (1956): 247–57.

in the tablets of heaven" (106:19; 4QEnᶜ 5 ii 26–27; cf. 93:2).²⁹ The term "mystery" is associated with revealed truths in many passages of *1 Enoch* that are not available in Aramaic.³⁰ While many of 4QInstruction's teachings are devoted to the worldly and practical success of its addressee in a manner reminiscent of Proverbs, the epistemology of the composition reflects an apocalyptic worldview.

The Study of Revealed Wisdom

One key difference between 4QInstruction's *raz nihyeh* and the *razim* of Daniel and *1 Enoch* merits further examination. In these apocalypses the revelation of visions and the bestowal of divine knowledge are narrated to the reader. In a sense, one can look over the shoulders of Daniel and Enoch as they receive revelations. The best example of this in the Enochic corpus is the Book of the Watchers. In the case of 4QInstruction the situation is somewhat different. The *raz nihyeh* has already been given to the addressee. For example, 4Q418 123 ii 4 discusses "His period which God revealed to the ear of the understanding ones through the mystery that is to be." Similarly, the Astronomical Book and the Epistle of Enoch recount revelation given to Enoch at an earlier point (*1 En.* 72:1; 103:1; cf. 81:2; 93:2). 4QInstruction differs from this Enochic material, and *1 Enoch* in general, in that the Qumran wisdom text contains no accounts of visions, otherworldly journeys, or angels transmitting divine knowledge. The document exhibits virtually no interest in the media of revelation. The author reminds the addressee that the mystery that is to be has been revealed to him already without describing this disclosure.

If Daniel and *1 Enoch* emphasize the disclosure and transmission of revelation, 4QInstruction underscores its contemplation. The mystery that is to be is combined often with what John Strugnell has called imperatives "of intellection," verbs that exhort the *mebin* to study and contemplate the mystery that is to be.³¹ He is told to "gaze" (נבט)

---

29. Michael Knibb, *The Ethiopic Book of Enoch* (2 vols.; Oxford: Clarendon, 1978), 2:248. See also George W. E. Nickelsburg, *1 Enoch: A Commentary on the Book of 1 Enoch Chapters 1–36; 81–108* (Hermeneia; Minneapolis: Fortress, 2001), 549. Also note that 4QEnᵃ 1 iv 5 (cf. *1 En.* 8:3) states that the Watchers reveal "secrets (רזין) to their wives."

30. See, for example, *1 En.* 16:3: "You were in heaven but (its) secrets had not yet been revealed to you and a worthless mystery you knew. This you made known to the women in the hardness of your hearts, and through this mystery the women and the men cause evil to increase on earth"; 41:3: "And there my eyes saw the secrets of the flashes of lightning of the thunder ... and the secrets of the clouds and of the dew"; 52:2: "There [in the west] my eyes saw the secrets of heaven, everything that will occur on earth."

31. Strugnell and Harrington, DJD 34, 29.

upon,"³² "examine" (דרש), "meditate" (הגה) upon, and "grasp" (לקח) this mystery.³³ 4Q417 1 i 6–8 illustrates the crucial role of the study of the *raz nihyeh* in the education of the addressee: "[Day and night meditate upon the mystery that is] to be. Inquire constantly. Then you will know truth and iniquity, wisdom and [foll]y you will [recognize] ... Then you will distinguish between g[ood] and [evil according to] [their] works." Knowledge is acquired in 4QInstruction not merely through the bestowal of the *raz nihyeh* itself but from continued reflection upon it once it has been revealed. Wisdom is a two-step process—revelation then contemplation. One could say that the *raz nihyeh* gives the addressee the key but he has to open the door himself.

The acquisition of wisdom through the study of revealed knowledge reflects a combination of ideas from the sapiential and apocalyptic traditions. 4QInstruction's repeated stress on study seems to reflect the pedagogical ethos of the sapiential tradition. The book of Proverbs teaches the importance of study and reflection. It begins by explaining that its contents are "For learning about wisdom and instruction, for understanding words of insight ... to teach shrewdness to the simple, knowledge and prudence to the young—Let the wise also hear and gain in learning, and the discerning acquire skill" (1:2–5). The value of study is also emphasized in Ben Sira (e.g., 6:32–37). The sapiential tradition places pedagogy in high regard, and 4QInstruction is similar to traditional wisdom in that sense. As mentioned at the outset of this essay, the acquisition of knowledge is an important theme in apocalyptic literature as well. The emphasis in 4QInstruction on the worldly success of the addressee, regarding specific areas of ordinary life such as the management of finances, suggests the pedagogy of the document draws on the sapiential tradition. The role of revelation in obtaining knowledge is a trope alien to the traditional wisdom of Proverbs but consistent with the apocalyptic tradition. This is also the case with regard to the teaching of 4QInstruction on topics such as the final judgment and the elect status of the addressee (4Q416 1; 4Q418 81).³⁴ The stress 4QInstruction places upon the study of the mystery that is to be, along with the types of knowledge

---

32. 4Q416 2 i 5 (par 4Q417 2 i 10); 4Q417 1 i 3, 18 (par 4Q418 43 2, 14). See also 4Q418 123 ii 5 and 1QS 11:19.

33. 4Q416 2 iii 9 (par 4Q418 9 8), 4Q418 43 4 (par 4Q417 1 i 6), and 4Q418 77 4. See Elgvin, "The Mystery to Come," 133.

34. These two major themes of 4QInstruction are never explicitly connected to the mystery that is to be. Since this mystery is associated with the entire scope of history, it is implied that all topics of instruction in the document are available through the *raz nihyeh*.

the document makes available, produces a form of education that combines elements from the sapiential and apocalyptic traditions.

Creation and the *Raz Nihyeh*

Why is the *raz nihyeh* such a potent source of knowledge for the addressee? The main reason is the relationship between creation and the mystery that is to be.[35] 4QInstruction presents creation itself as a mystery, or *raz*. When the *mebin* is told to study the *raz nihyeh* in order to learn the knowledge of good and evil in 4Q417 1 i 6–8, 4QInstruction explains this by affirming that "the God of Knowledge is a foundation of truth and by means of the mystery that is to be he has laid out its foundation and its works (וברז נהיה פרש את אושה ומעשיה)..." (lines 8–9).[36] The text then reads: "[with all wisd]om and all [clever]ness he has fashioned it (לכל חכ[מה ולכל] ער[מה יצרה])" (line 9).[37] The association between the *raz nihyeh* and the moment of creation cautions against understanding this expression in an exclusively future sense. The mystery that is to be relates to both the beginning and end of history. This mystery was the means by which God endowed the world with an overarching framework.[38] This explains why the *raz nihyeh* is the vehicle through which wisdom is obtained. In 4Q417 1 i 6–8 the knowledge of good and evil does not merely denote the intelligence required to make ethical decisions. This knowledge represents the acquisition of wisdom about the broader divine framework in which the human realm should be understood. This is also the case with the Treatise on the Two Spirits: "He knows the result of their deeds for all times [everlas]ting and has given them as a legacy to the sons of man so that they know good [and evil] (לדעת טוב [ורע])" (1QS 4:25–26). According to 4QInstruction, one can use the mystery that is to be to understand the natural order in a more comprehensive way because God used it to create the world. The claim that the divine act of creation is a revealed "mystery" implies that creation bears the stamp of a transcendent deity who cannot be fully understood without revelation. The term *raz* signifies not only the disclosure of revelation but also the heavenly knowledge that is revealed.

---

35. Matthew J. Goff, "The Mystery of Creation in 4QInstruction," *DSD* 10 (2003): 163–86.
36. Strugnell and Harrington, DJD 34, 151; Tigchelaar, *To Increase Learning*, 52.
37. For discussion of the reconstruction of this text, see Goff, "Mystery of Creation," 171.
38. Note 4Q417 1 i 12–13: "Seek these things continually and understand [al]l their outcomes. Then you will know the glory of his m[ight wi]th the mysteries of his wonder, and the mighty acts of his deeds" (cf. 4Q418 219 2).

Conclusion

The mystery that is to be is the main source of wisdom for the addressee of 4QInstruction. The knowledge that it offers relates to practical and mundane aspects of his life and more speculative topics such as the moment of creation and the final judgment. The *raz nihyeh* is able to provide such knowledge because it is associated with a deterministic divine plan that is revealed to the addressee. One is able to understand the world by means of the mystery that is to be in part because God created the world by means of this mystery. Knowing the *raz nihyeh* allows the addressee to appreciate the utter scope of God's dominion. The revelation of the mystery that is to be is intended to produce a sense of reverence and humility in the addressee. The mystery that is to be is designed not only to supply knowledge but also to guide behavior. The conduct of the *mebin* is to be characterized not only by righteousness but also by study. In 4QInstruction revelation does not provide wisdom outright. It is the result of constant reflection upon revealed knowledge. By endorsing the study of revealed wisdom, 4QInstruction merges the pedagogical ethos of the sapiential tradition with an appeal to revelation that is characteristic of an apocalyptic worldview.

THE *PSALMS OF SOLOMON*
AND THE IDEOLOGY OF RULE*

Rodney A. Werline

INTRODUCTION

The need for a critical examination of the *Psalms of Solomon* in our ongoing investigation of wisdom and apocalyptic literature is illustrated by recent historical Jesus studies' reliance on the old synthetic scholarly construction of apocalypticism, in which scholars examined apocalyptic texts and formulated lists of motifs and characteristics. Then, when any text contained one of these features in the list, the interpreter labeled the text "apocalyptic." For example, John Dominic Crossan uncritically perpetuates that unhistorical synthetic view in setting Jesus against the "apocalyptic" view of the kingdom for which he quotes *Pss. Sol.* 17 at length along with the *Testament of Moses,* the Parables of *1 Enoch,* and Dan 7.[1] Even some specialists on the *Psalms of Solomon* take *Pss. Sol.* 17 as an example of "apocalyptic messianism."[2]

The discussion that follows will examine some basic problems in interpreting the *Psalms of Solomon* through an investigation of its ideology of rule. Using the information gleaned from the examination of the texts, I shall make suggestions about the authors' most probable social location and situation. Finally, I shall reexamine the problem of the genre and the worldview of the *Psalms of Solomon*. Does this text fit the

---

* While I was writing this paper I benefited from several conversations with Richard Horsley. He also graciously read the manuscript and gave valuable suggestions. I am grateful to him for his help. Of course, I am responsible for any shortcomings that this essay might contain. This essay first appeared in Society of Biblical Literature 2000 Seminar Papers. Only slight revisions have been made.

1. John D. Crossan, *The Historical Jesus: The Life of a Mediterranean Peasant* (San Francisco: Harper, 1992), 107, 284–86; idem, *Jesus: A Revolutionary Biography* (New York: HarperCollins, 1994), 40, 56.

2. Robert B. Wright, "Psalms of Solomon," *OTP*, 2:642. I follow Wright's translation throughout this essay. For the Greek text, see Alfred Rahlfs, ed., *Septuaginta, id est Vetus Testamentum iuxta* LXX *interpretes* (vol. 2; Stuttgart: Deutsche Bibelstiftung, 1935).

category of apocalyptic literature either in form or worldview? Although, as I shall argue, the *Psalms of Solomon* cannot be understood as apocalyptic literature, comparisons between this text and apocalyptic texts should contribute to this Group's primary interest—a clearer understanding of what constitutes apocalypticism.

Interest in the ideology of rule directs attention primarily to *Pss. Sol.* 1, 2, 8, and 17, all of which struggle to come to grips with Roman conquest and rule over Judea. The final form of *Pss. Sol.* 17, of course, must come from the Herodian period, since certain events described in this psalm happened only when Herod took control of Palestine.[3] The individual psalms (*Pss. Sol.* 3, 4, 6, 9, 10, 12, 13, 14, 15, 16) could contribute to understanding the *Psalms of Solomon's* ideology of rule.[4] These psalms provide glimpses into the authors' struggles in the midst of shifting power in Jerusalem. Further, these other psalms' descriptions of the ideal pious scribe prove invaluable for interpreting the image of the anointed one in *Pss. Sol.* 17.

Historical Background and Allusions

Psalms of Solomon 1, 2, 8, and 17 contain rather obvious references to the historical events connected with Pompey's arrival in Jerusalem in 63 B.C.E.[5] His appearance in Jerusalem came as a result of a civil war between Hyrcanus II and Aristobulus II. The rival Hasmoneans and their supporters appeared before Pompey when he interceded in their dispute. A third group of Jews, who wanted neither of these men to rule, petitioned Pompey to restore the old priestly theocracy. When Aristobulus suspiciously left Pompey's company after the general had told the parties to wait for his decision, Pompey followed him to Jerusalem. Hyrcanus's supporters opened the gates of the city to Pompey and his armies, while

---

3. Kenneth Atkinson ("On the Herodian Origin of Militant Davidic Messianism at Qumran: New Light from *Psalm of Solomon 17*," *JBL* 118 [1999]: 435–60) argues for this date of *Pss. Sol.* 17. Marinus de Jonge ("The Expectation of the Future in the Psalms of Solomon," in idem, *Jewish Eschatology, Early Christian Christology, and the Testaments of the Twelve Patriarchs* [NovTSup 63; Leiden: Brill, 1991], 14) also believes that the *Psalms* may have been updated and redacted, but he is not confident that one could now isolate and date the various layers of the text. Cf. André Caquot, "Les Hasmonéens, Les Romains et Hérode," in *Hellenica et Judaica: Hommage à Valentine Nikiprowetsky* (ed. A. Caquot et al.; Leuven: Peeters, 1984), 213–18.

4. George W. E. Nickelsburg, *Jewish Literature between the Bible and the Mishnah* (Philadelphia: Fortress, 1981), 209–12.

5. For Josephus's account, see *Ant.* 14.3–4; *J. W.* 1.6–7. For a lengthy discussion of issues related to the historical and social setting, see Atkinson, *I Cried to the Lord: A Study of the Psalms of Solomon's Historical Background and Social Setting* (JSJSup 84; Leiden: Brill, 2004).

Aristobulus and his followers barricaded themselves in the temple. Pompey eventually took the temple, although with significant bloodshed. According to Josephus, the soldiers slaughtered the priests who were in the process of sacrificing. Entering the holy of holies itself, Pompey reportedly looked around and exited without destroying, looting, or vandalizing the sanctuary. Judea became a Roman province with Hyrcanus installed as high priest, but without the status of kingship. Aristobulus and his family were taken as prisoners to Rome.

Several passages in the *Psalms of Solomon* reflect the circumstances associated with Pompey's siege and capture of Jerusalem. *Psalms of Solomon* 2:1–2 speaks of Pompey's use of a battering ram and his entrance into the sanctuary (cf. *Ant.* 14.4; *J.W.* 1.7). *Psalms of Solomon* 8:16 refers to the meeting between Pompey and the Jewish parties; verses 16b–17 depict Hyrcanus's supporters opening the gates of the city to the general; and verses 18–22 describe the slaughter in Jerusalem and the taking of prisoners. *Psalms of Solomon* 17 refers to Pompey's triumph (v. 7), the killing that took place in Jerusalem upon his entrance into the temple area (v. 11), and the exile of Aristobulus and his family (v. 12). *Psalms of Solomon* 2 also mentions Pompey's death in Egypt in 48 B.C.E. during the civil war in Rome, for the passage pictures his corpse floating ignobly on the waves (v. 27).

At least one psalm, number 17, shows signs of later redaction as some features originate from the period of Herod's reign.[6] The end of the Hasmonean dynasty as described in this psalm—"He hunted down their descendants and did not let even one of them go" (v. 9b)—comes at the hand of Herod, who systematically removed every Hasmonean threat to his kingship. The statement, "So he did in Jerusalem all the things that gentiles do for their gods in their cities" (v. 14), also fits Herod's reign more than Pompey's brief stay in Jerusalem. *Psalms of Solomon* 17:18b–19a connects the "lawless one's" advance on the city with a famine: "For the heavens withheld rain from falling on the earth. Springs were stopped, (from) the perennial (springs) far underground (to) those in the high mountains." A famine occurred when Herod besieged Jerusalem, not when Pompey invaded.[7] Therefore, sometime after Herod's rise to power, the "lawless" foreigner or "alien" who attacked the Jews no longer referred to Pompey but to the Idumean.

---

6. See also Atkinson, "On the Herodian Origin," 440–44.
7. Atkinson, "On the Herodian Origin," 443 n. 21; Josephus, *J.W.* 1.17–18; *Ant.* 14.16.

Deuteronomic Critique of Rule in the *Psalms of Solomon*

The *Psalms of Solomon* extensively quotes or alludes to biblical materials. For its understanding and explanation of the events that led to the end of Judean autonomy and beginning of Roman rule, the text employs Deuteronomic ideology.[8] According to Deuteronomic thought, disastrous events result from the people's and/or the rulers' sins. In the case of the city falling to Rome in 63 B.C.E., blame lies especially with the Jerusalem rulers and foremost with the Hasmoneans.

The collection begins with a slight twist on Deuteronomic ideology. In Psalm 1, which was perhaps composed at a later date as an introduction to the entire corpus as well as to *Pss. Sol.* 2, Zion expresses surprise at Rome's assault. She had previously perceived herself as prosperous, which according to Deuteronomic ideology is the reward for righteousness (vv. 1–3).[9] However, verses 4–8 explain that the foreign invasion resulted from Hasmonean policies and activities. First, the author seems to criticize the Hasmoneans' military campaigns of expansion (v. 4).[10] For example, John Hyrcanus I immediately had seized the opportunity upon the death of Antiochus VII to subdue some neighboring territories.[11] Second, alluding to Isa 14:13, the psalmist charges the Hasmoneans with attempting to exalt themselves like pagan kings: "They exalt themselves to the stars."[12] According to *Pss. Sol.* 2, such Hasmonean actions profaned the temple (v. 8). While Zion may not have been able to see the sins of her children because they committed them in secret (v. 7), God saw them and brought punishment as Deuteronomic ideology demands. In fact, according to such cause and effect ideology, the presence of punishment confirms that sin has been committed; the two are inextricably linked.

Psalms of Solomon 2 also employs this same sin-punishment ideology. Making clear allusions to historical events, the author attributes the catastrophe to Judean sins (vv. 7–8). His charge that the people sinned by not "listening" (v. 8b) may reflect the frequent Deuteronomic exhortation to "listen to" or "obey" (שמע) all God commands the people. This interpretation is quite probable, if, as most scholars think, the *Psalms of Solomon* has a Hebrew *Vorlage*.

---

8. See Nickelsburg, *Jewish Literature*, 204.

9. Wright, "Psalms of Solomon," 651 n. 1.

10. Cf., e.g., Bar 1:1–3:8, which opposes Judas's siege of the Akra and continued aggression against Antiochus V, and 1QpHab. Daniel, as is well known, also does not place hope in Hasmonean policy (Dan 11:34).

11. See Emil Schürer, *History of the Jewish People in the Age of Jesus Christ (175 B.C.–A.D. 135)* (ed. G. Vermes et al.; 3 vols.; Edinburgh: T&T Clark, 1973), 1:206–10.

12. Wright, "Psalms of Solomon," 651.

The author of *Pss. Sol.* 2 also responds to the historical crisis with a confession of God's righteousness: "I shall prove you right, for your judgments are right, O God" (v. 15). Von Rad labeled this kind of declaration a "Gerichtsdoxologie."[13] During the Second Temple period, such confessions become a standard, formulaic feature in penitential prayers, which Deuteronomic ideology also markedly influenced. Like *Pss. Sol.* 1, the author of *Pss. Sol.* 2 believes that the disaster in Jerusalem reveals that sin filled the city, even though her beauty masked her deeds. God saw through the appearances and brought judgment (v. 18).

Psalms of Solomon 8, like *Pss. Sol.* 1, depicts Zion as initially expressing surprise that such tragedy has visited Jerusalem (vv. 1–6). Then, like *Pss. Sol.* 1 and 2, the author of *Pss. Sol.* 8 interprets the disaster Deuteronomically. The punishment comes as a result of the leadership, especially the Hasmoneans, whose sins the author catalogues by using stock polemical rhetoric (vv. 9–13). The rulers are guilty of incest (v. 9b), adultery (v. 10b), robbing the temple (v. 11), and uncleanness that defiles the sacrifices, especially not following proper laws about sex after menstruation (v. 12). *Psalms of Solomon* 2:11–14 indicts the Judean rulers for similar behavior. These accusations resemble the content of CD 5:6–8:

> And they also defiled the temple, for they did not keep apart in accordance with the law, but, instead lay with her who sees the blood of her menstrual flow. And each man takes as a wife the daughter of his brother and the daughter of his sister.[14]

Such polemical language actually does not reveal much about the disagreements between those responsible for the *Psalms of Solomon* and the Hasmoneans. Instead, it mostly identifies the Hasmoneans as the enemy and connotes the authors' opinion that their rule is illegitimate.[15] Finally, *Pss. Sol.* 8 also includes two proclamations of God's righteousness for bringing punishment (vv. 7, 23–24).

---

13. See Rodney A. Werline, *Penitential Prayer in Early Judaism: The Development of a Religious Institution* (SBLEJL 13; Atlanta: Scholars Press, 1998), 52.

14. The translation is from Florentino García Martínez and Eibert J. C. Tigchelaar, *The Dead Sea Scrolls Study Edition* (2 vols.; Leiden: Brill, 1997), 1:557.

15. For a discussion of polemical language, see Luke. T. Johnson, "The New Testament's Anti-Jewish Slander and the Conventions of Ancient Polemic," *JBL* 108 (1989): 419–41. Johnson shows that ancient polemical language must be understood as connotative rather than denotative. Authors and speakers drew on stock polemical language to speak about their opponents. Thus, such language does not provide a factual description of the opponents. Rather, the language indicates to the reader or hearer that those are the people to be disliked.

With a few variations, these same Deuteronomic features appear in *Pss. Sol.* 17, a passage about a messianic king. In this psalm, however, the author makes the remarkable claim that the Hasmoneans came to power in the first place because of Judean sin (v. 5). Typically in Deuteronomic thought, God punishes the nation by sending a pagan king and his army against the people. Indeed, Pompey and later Herod perform this task in the *Psalms of Solomon*. The author of *Pss. Sol.* 17, however, places the Hasmoneans in this role. By assigning them this function, the *Psalms of Solomon* highlights the illegitimacy of their rule and erodes their power. Further, in order to denounce the way in which the Hasmoneans came to power, the author charges them with usurping the kingship by force. He alludes to the Davidic covenant in 2 Sam 7, which promises kingship to the Davidic line: "Those to whom you did not (make the) promise, they took it by force" (v. 5b).[16] Beginning with Aristobulus I (104–103 B.C.E.) and continuing until the arrival of Pompey, Hasmonean rulers assumed the title "king."[17] For the author of *Pss. Sol.* 17, this claim to kingship "despoiled the throne of David" (v. 6). Like pagan kings whom God sends to punish the people, including Pompey (see below), the Hasmoneans' arrogance brings their end, for God rewards them for their sin (vv. 6–10).

Thus, Deuteronomic ideology in the *Psalms of Solomon* produces several layers of critique. First, and explicitly, it subverts rule by the Hasmoneans. They did not rise to power on their own merit or on the merit of the Jews, but because of the people's sin. They were punishment from God. Clearly the authors disagree with the Hasmonean policies of expansion and their adoption of royal titles. All these errors pollute the temple. Their fall to Rome proves the illegitimacy of their rule and is the way in which God punishes them. Second, the *Psalms of Solomon* also employs Deuteronomic ideology in objection to the establishment of Roman power in Palestine. Pompey does not take Jerusalem by his own power, but by an act of God's wrath against the Jerusalem rulers. Pompey is God's unwitting puppet in the affairs of Palestine and in the history of God's people.

---

16. I alter Wright's translation, in which he seems to think that the author believed that the Hasmoneans took something away from those associated with the psalmist. If the reference to God's "promise" is the Davidic covenant, the Hasmoneans took the kingship.

17. Schürer, *History*, 1:216–17.

Pompey as a "Dragon" and God as "Savior"

The notion that Pompey, a pagan, is the instrument of God's wrath draws on a recurring motif in biblical and Second Temple literature. For example, in Isaiah God calls the king of Assyria "the rod of my anger" (Isa 10:5) and sends him against Jerusalem. The king of Assyria, however, becomes arrogant and boastful, and he refuses to acknowledge that he served as God's "ax" (10:10–19). Therefore, even though God sends the foreign king against Israel because of its sins, God punishes him. Similar concepts appear in reference to the king of Babylon in Isa 14, the king of Tyre in Ezek 28, Pharaoh in Ezek 31–32, and Antiochus IV in Dan 11:40–45.[18]

Like these other foreign powers, some of which assaulted Jerusalem, Pompey fails to recognize that God has given the city into his hand. Instead, he is boastful and arrogant about his accomplishments. He celebrates by taking Aristobulus II, his family, and other Jews to Rome for his triumphal procession. These exploits and attitude invite the authors of the *Psalms of Solomon* to recall the motif of God punishing the foreign power. Thus, the *Psalms of Solomon* celebrates the news of Pompey's death in Egypt after the battle of Pharsalus in 48 B.C.E. Indeed, the author of *Pss. Sol.* 2 gloats that God responded to his intercessory prayer by bringing Pompey's death:

> And I did not wait long until God showed me his insolence pierced
>   on the mountains of Egypt,
>   more despised than the smallest thing on earth and sea.
> His body was carried about on the waves in much shame,
>   and there was no one to bury him, for he (God) had despised
>   him with contempt (2:26–27).

Other biblical motifs occur in the discussion of Pompey's end in *Pss. Sol.* 2. The author explains: "He did not consider that he was a man.... He said, 'I shall be lord of land and sea'" (vv. 28–29). Despite his claims, the text labels him a "dragon" (v. 25) who did not understand that God is king (vv. 29b–30). The designation of Pompey as a "dragon" also has biblical precedents. The image, which biblical authors originally adopted from Canaanite and other ancient Near Eastern mythologies, depicts the forces of chaos that challenge God and threaten the order of the universe. Biblical authors eventually used this image to speak of ancient Near Eastern rulers. The authors saw them as defiant against God like chaos

---

18. De Jonge, "Future in the Psalms of Solomon," 8.

monsters because they harassed God's people and because of the chaos that they caused in the region. Pharaoh is called a dragon in Ezek 29:3, as is Nebuchadnezzar in Jer 51:34.[19] Daniel 7 depicts ancient Near Eastern empires as beasts that rise from the sea, which cause havoc in the world and threaten God's people.

With these biblical motifs and images, the *Psalms of Solomon* interprets Pompey as another oppressive and imperial chaos dragon that God humbles and dishonors like all preceding monsters. Since Pompey is representative of Roman power in the region, the author of *Pss. Sol.* 2 is also critiquing Roman rule. God is king over the earth, and by implication God's kingdom stretches over land and sea. Roman rule in Palestine, and indeed the world, continues only because God permits it, or because Rome is in rebellion against God. The authors believe that God will someday bring an end to this rebellion.

In discussions of Roman rule, the *Psalms of Solomon* consistently affirms God's role as "savior" (σωτήρ; e.g., 2:32; 8:33; 17:1, 3, 34, 46). Certainly this is traditional biblical language.[20] In the context of Greco-Roman ideology, however, where generals and emperors are quick to make such proclamations about themselves, the appellation takes on new significance. Greeks recognized good rulers as "saviors" because of their abilities to conquer those forces that threatened the order of the state.[21] These rulers restored and protected civilization.[22] Thus, the Thessalonians honored Philip of Macedon as "savior" (σωτήρ), as well as "friend" (φίλος) and "benefactor" (εὐεργέτης).[23] Several of the Ptolemies and Seleucids adopted the title σωτήρ for themselves, bestowed it upon deceased relatives, or were acclaimed such by their citizens.[24] Greek citizens could also call Roman generals "saviors."[25] As a marble inscription in Mytilene attests, Pompey himself received the titles

---

19. Wright, "Psalms of Solomon," 653 n. a².
20. See, e.g., Ps 106:21; Isa 43:3, 11; 45:15, 21; 49:26; 60:16.
21. For the definitive presentation on this subject, see Simon R. F. Price, "Rituals and Power," in *Paul and the Empire: Religion and Power in Roman Imperial Society* (ed. R. A. Horsley; Harrisburg, Pa.: Trinity Press International, 1997), 47–71. For a convenient summary, see John L. White, *The Apostle of God: Paul and the Promise of Abraham* (Peabody, Mass.: Hendrickson, 1999), 99.
22. Price, "Rituals and Power." White also notes that this role of the ruler has a religious parallel among the Greeks. "[T]he major gods came to be associated with the power of civilization over chaos" (99).
23. W. Foerster, "σωτήρ," *TDNT* 7:1007–8.
24. Ibid., 1008–9.
25. Ibid., 1008.

of "benefactor," "savior," and "restorer" when he granted freedom to the city.[26]

Although Pompey settled the civil unrest caused by the dispute between Hyrcanus II and Aristobulus II, the Jews did not recognize or acknowledge Pompey as "savior." Josephus, in fact, remembers this event as the moment that the Jews lost their freedom and came under Roman rule (*Ant.* 14.4). The *Psalms of Solomon*, of course, refuses to recognize Pompey as "savior," even if his arrival brought the end of illegitimate Hasmonean rule. For the *Psalms of Solomon*, the title "savior" belongs only to God. With this language, then, the *Psalms of Solomon* challenges the Greco-Roman ideology of rule. Pompey is not ruler of "land and sea" (cf. 2:26, 29).[27] He is simply a "dragon" whom God, the true σωτήρ, defeats and dishonors.

The Messiah of Psalms of Solomon 17

Until the final quarter of the last century, *Pss. Sol.* 17 stood as the *locus classicus* for understanding Jewish messianic expectation (sometimes inappropriately characterized as "apocalyptic"). The basic assumption was that in the time of Jesus the Jews hoped for a Davidic king who would overthrow Roman rule and establish a new political state. Not only does this position inadequately represent the variety in Jewish hopes for the future, it also fails to represent the peculiar features of the *Psalms of Solomon*, for, as I have argued, one must view these psalms as a response to particular crises. Further, the description of a messianic king in this text must be read within the social, historical, and ideological context of the author and those who shared his beliefs. The author constructed his image of an anointed king so that it addressed the most pertinent problems his group faced. Concerns about the group's social circumstances appear in the text. Infusing the text with his own ideology, the author portrays a messiah who will also apparently be the benefactor and patron to the "pious"; this messiah sees the world from the author's perspective.

The first indication in *Pss. Sol.* 17 that something has gone wrong for the author's group arises in verse 5: "Because of our sins, sinners rose up against us, they set upon us and drove us out." According to scholarly consensus, the sinners are the Hasmoneans.[28] These "sinners" apparently

---

26. Ibid..
27. See also 1 Macc 8:23, which uses similar language to speak of the extent of Roman rule.
28. For an exception to this position, see Johannes Tromp ("The Sinners and the Lawless in Psalm of Solomon 17," *NovT* 35 [1993]: 344–61), who holds that the sinners are Romans.

persecuted the "pious," a label that designates the author and his associates. The problem reaches such proportions that the pious must flee into the wilderness (v. 17) as the "lawless ones" are chasing them (v. 18). Furthermore, every stratum of society is failing to function properly: "No one among them in Jerusalem acted (with) mercy or truth" (v. 15b); "For there was no one among them who practiced righteousness or justice" (v. 19); "The king was a criminal and the judge disobedient, (and) all the people sinners" (v. 20). For the author, his civilization is in chaos, and he and his associates are disenfranchised.

Elsewhere in the *Psalms of Solomon* comparable tensions exist between the pious and sinners.[29] Although it is impossible to conclude that all these references to opponents are Hasmoneans, the authors of the *Psalms of Solomon* certainly felt socially, if not on occasion physically, threatened. They seem vulnerable to religious/political leaders more powerful than they. Most likely the shifts in power within Palestine from one party to another in the late Hasmonean and the beginning of the Roman era, including Herodian rule, made life difficult for the authors of the *Psalms of Solomon*. Several passages suggest that some had lost social power and had been pushed to the margins. For example, *Pss. Sol.* 4:9–13, 20–22 implies that some people associated with the author may have lost property and suffered financially in other ways at the hands of powerful people: "[F]or they deceitfully empty many people's houses and greedily scatter (them)... for they defraud innocent people by pretense." Similarly, it is probably not a coincidence that Psalm 5 contains a prayer that describes God as "the shelter of the poor," a righteous judge, and a strong man whose house cannot be plundered (vv. 1–4). In this psalm, the author also understands himself as a member of a persecuted group (v. 5).

Despite the difficulty of the situation and the chaos in his society, the author of *Pss. Sol.* 17 continues to profess that "God is king" (vv. 1, 34, 46) and "savior" (σωτήρ; v. 3). The human rulers who claim to have power actually have none, and their future destruction is certain. God will restore order by raising up a messianic king. Unlike the Hasmonean rulers, the anointed one can legitimately assume the throne because he is a son of David (v. 21). As God's vice-regent on earth, he will shatter unrighteous rulers and purge Israel of the Gentiles who are trampling it down (vv. 22–27, 41, 51). The language of the text is militant—"To smash the arrogance of sinners like a potter's jar" (v. 23)[30]—even though it is

---

29. E.g., 2:6, 12, 16, 25; 4:21, 24; 12:1, 4; 14:4; 15:6.

30. Atkinson ("On the Herodian Origin," 444–45) and John J. Collins (*The Scepter and the Star: The Messiahs of the Dead Sea Scrolls and Other Literature* [New York: Doubleday, 1995], 54–55). Atkinson demonstrates that similar ideas appear in five Qumran scrolls from the

reminiscent of Pss 2:9, 104:7, and Isa 11:2–4. The messiah's deeds, therefore, bring the removal of the Romans and all Jewish leaders who assist them in their rule.

After the anointed one removes all the wicked from the land, he begins the restoration and reestablishment of a just, civil society as the *Psalms of Solomon* envisions it. He gathers a "holy people" to him and leads them in righteousness (v. 26). Throughout the *Psalms of Solomon*, the text refers to the members of the community as the "pious" (ὅσιος), the "righteous" (δίκαιος), and the "holy ones" (ἅγιος).[31] These designations have special meaning for the author of *Pss. Sol.* 17, and he probably would have used the terms "pious," "righteous," and "holy ones" only for himself, his fellow scribes, and any Jews who had a similar theology. While the author of *Pss. Sol.* 17 probably did not think that the benefits of the messiah's rule were for him and those associated with him alone to the exclusion of the rest of Israel, his language reflects his concern about his own social situation in the present and future eras. Undoubtedly, because he and his associates are pious, they will benefit from the messiah's arrival and rule. Thus, under the rule of the messiah, they will have a better status than they had under the Hasmoneans and the Romans.

A cornerstone of the new society that the messiah inaugurates is the establishment of justice: "And he will establish justice for the tribes of the people that have been made holy by the Lord their God" (v. 26b).[32] As Richard Horsley argues, the verb κρίνειν does not mean "to judge" in the typical English sense of making judicial decisions.[33] Rather, the term has the connotation of the Hebrew word שפט, which expresses the idea of "deliverance" or "establishing justice." According to Horsley, the "terms have connotations of deliverance, grace, and salvation, and that God's judging or justice 'regulates the social relationships of the people' and asserts the rights of the oppressed against the oppressors."[34] In the Hebrew Bible, the spirit of God comes upon individuals so that they bring deliverance and liberation from oppressors. This model appears in

---

Herodian period: 4Q161; 4Q285; 4Q246; 4Q252; 4Q174. See also Atkinson, *I Cried to the Lord*, 151–75.

31. For "pious," see, e.g., 2:36; 3:8; 4:1, 6; 8:23; 9:3; 10:6; 17:16. For "righteous," see, e.g., 2:34; 3:3, 4, 5; 4:8. For "holy ones," see 17:32, 43.

32. Here I have departed from Wright's translation of the phrase: "he will judge the tribes."

33. Richard A. Horsley, *Jesus and the Spiral of Violence: Popular Jewish Resistance in Roman Palestine* (San Francisco: Harper & Row, 1987), 203–6; idem, *Whoever Hears You Hears Me: Prophets, Performance, and Tradition in Q* (Harrisburg, Pa.: Trinity Press International, 1999), 69, 106–7.

34. Horsley, *Jesus and the Spiral of Violence*, 203–4.

Isa 11, where the spirit of the Lord rests upon the Davidic ruler and also gives him the spirit of "wisdom," "understanding," "counsel," "might," "knowledge," and "the fear of the Lord" (Isa 11:2). These special attributes then empower him to establish justice, that is, to deliver and to vindicate the "poor" (vv. 3b–4). With the "word of his mouth" and "the breath of his lips" he "kills the wicked" (v. 4b). The author of *Pss. Sol.* 17 relies upon this very text, Isa 11:2–4, for his description of the messiah and his activities in verses 29 and 37. Hence, whereas the judges during the Hasmonean and Roman rules were "disobedient," which resulted in an unjust society in which the righteous were oppressed, the messiah will bring and maintain a just world. In *Pss. Sol.* 4 God effects a similar kind of judgment against the wicked (e.g., 4:24). In order to preserve justice, the author of *Pss. Sol.* 17 says that the messiah "disciplines" (παιδεῦσαι) the nation (17:42).[35]

While the author of *Pss. Sol.* 17 relies on biblical images and language to depict the messiah's peaceful rule, he is also clearly attempting to make sharp distinctions between the messiah and the Hasmoneans and Romans. Unlike them, the messiah does not place his confidence in military might and heavy taxation (v. 33). Instead, he resembles the king in Zech 9:9–10 who comes to Jerusalem riding humbly on an ass and bringing peace, cutting off the chariot, the war horse, and the battle bow (cf. *Pss. Sol.* 17:33a). The restrictions placed on the king in Deut 17:14–17 also prevented him from amassing horses and silver.[36] The messiah places his hope in God (*Pss. Sol.* 17:39), and thus he is like the pious, who "hope" in God their "savior" (17:3). He is also "strong in the fear of God" (v. 40). Although biblical literature often states that the righteous fear God, this is also a favorite image for the authors of the *Psalms of Solomon*.[37] Therefore, this messianic king will not display the arrogance of Pompey and the Hasmoneans (cf. 17:6, 13, 23, 41). He understands that God is king, and he glorifies and honors God (17:30). In fact, there will be no arrogance in the society that the messiah establishes, and, as a result, no one will be oppressed. If anyone has lost property, the messiah will restore it, for he redistributes the land according to tribal inheritance (v. 28). Again, while this is good biblical tradition, it is also in line with the deeds of a great benefactor. Surely, the end of oppression and the security of one's property comprise part of the deepest hope of the author and his community who both live at the margins of their world.

---

35. Other psalms depict God as disciplining the righteous (see, e.g., 3:4; 7:3, 9; 10:2; 13:7, 8; 16:11).
36. De Jonge, "The Future in the Psalms of Solomon," 12.
37. E.g., 2:33; 3:12; 4:23; 5:18; 12:4; 13:12; 15:13.

After the messiah has purged the land of arrogant, oppressive Gentile overlords and has established a just society, *Pss. Sol.* 17 depicts Gentiles returning to Jerusalem in order to praise the glory of the messiah, Jerusalem, and God (vv. 30–31, 34; cf. Isa 66:18–19). As they come from the ends of the earth to the city, they bring the dispersed Jews with them, an image based upon Isa 66:20.

Thus, the author of *Pss. Sol.* 17 has chosen his words with care and intention, for the language used to speak of the messiah comprises the same words that other texts in the *Psalms of Solomon* employ to describe the ideal pious person. Such language has acquired special meaning in the *Psalms of Solomon*, and it carries the author's particular ideology. As a result, the messiah lives up to the author's ideals, and, indeed, he resembles the psalm's scribal author. His rule is legitimate. With all this in mind, the meaning of verse 43 becomes apparent: "His (i.e., the anointed king's) words will be as the words of the holy ones among the sanctified peoples."[38] The author's messiah is a king and a benefactor to the "pious" and to those Jews who share the author's ideas.

Social Location

This textual analysis of *Pss. Sol.* 17 now allows for suggestions about the social location and identity of the *Psalms of Solomon's* authors. In the late nineteenth century, Julius Wellhausen proposed that Pharisaic circles produced the *Psalms of Solomon*.[39] His position dominated scholarship for a large part of the twentieth century. Late in the last century, however, possible new identities for the group emerged as some suggested that the text originated from a group of Essenes.[40] Other interpreters noted similarities between the *Psalms of Solomon* and the Qumran scrolls.[41]

However, each of these suggestions seems either to go beyond the evidence or to appear incompatible with certain features of the text. The literature from the era in which the *Psalms of Solomon* emerged actually

---

38. Although I have preserved Wright's translation "holy ones," I do not accept his identification of the "holy ones" as angels. I maintain that the designation refers to pious humans, probably the author's scribal circle.

39. For an extended listing of those who accept this thesis, see Kenneth Atkinson, "On the Herodian Origin," 437 n. 4. For a review of the *Psalms of Solomon* in modern research, see Joseph L. Trafton, "The *Psalms of Solomon* in Recent Research," *JSP* 12 (1994): 3–19.

40. E.g., André Dupont-Sommer, *The Essene Writings from Qumran* (New York: Meridian, 1962), 296; Robert R. Hann, "The Community of the Pious: The Social Setting of the *Psalms of Solomon*," *SR* 17 (1988): 169–89.

41. Atkinson, *I Cried to the Lord*; Otto Eissfeldt, *The Old Testament: An Introduction* (New York: Harper & Row, 1965), 610–13.

provides little information about Pharisaic doctrines, and the presentation of the Pharisaic ideas in literature from the common era does not significantly resemble those of the *Psalms of Solomon*. Consequently, the idea that the authors of the *Psalms of Solomon* were Pharisees is unacceptable. Similarly, Robert Hann's proposal that the text is the product of second-generation disenfranchised Essene priests suffers in part from one significant feature of *Pss. Sol.* 17.[42] The author looks for a restored Davidic kingship, not a restored priesthood; Davidic kingship will be the instrument for restoring a just society. The author's main concern is about Hasmonean, and then Roman, oppressive rule, not about priests.

More recent proposals that the *Psalms of Solomon* originates from a group of scribal retainers offers a more suggestive proposal about the authors' social location and explanation of the problems that they had to confront.[43] As scribes they, of course, would have possessed the ability to write and could have acquired the rather thorough knowledge of biblical traditions demonstrated in the text. Their comments about loss of power imply that they at one time lived nearer the center of power, probably in Jerusalem. They may have functioned as scribal retainers sometime during Hasmonean rule, though their exact relationship to the central power remains obscure. However, in the constant shift of power in Jewish Palestine, these scribes became disaffected; they lost their station and power. The text does not reveal the precise political shifts that caused this change in status.

In an earlier era, Ben Sira, himself a scribe, recognized that one had to be cautious when relating to the powerful (Sir 13:9).[44] That retainers could fall in and out of favor during this period is further confirmed by the stories of the Pharisees during the reigns of Alexander Jannaeus and Salome Alexandra. Any hope that the scribes who wrote the *Psalms of Solomon* might have had about recovering their position when Rome arrived, if indeed they held such notions, was not realized. In the early Roman and Herodian periods, their status did not improve. For these reasons, these scribes anticipated the arrival of the Davidic messiah. In that future era, this scribal group would no longer live on the margins. Life under the Davidic messiah, as these scribes imagine it, would mean that they would be nearer the center of power and that the injustices that they suffered at the hands of the rulers of this world would cease.

---

42. Hann, "Community of the Pious," 176.
43. Horsley, *Jesus and the Spiral of Violence*, 203–6; *Whoever Hears You Hears Me*, 69, 106–7.
44. See R. A. Horsley, "Social Relations and Social Conflict in the Epistle of Enoch," in *For a Later Generation: The Transformation of Tradition in Israel, Early Judaism, and Early Christianity* (ed. R. A. Argall et al.; Harrisburg, Pa.: Trinity Press International, 2000), 100–115.

The Psalms of Solomon and Apocalypticism: Comparisons, Contrasts, and Questions

Literary Form

Although earlier generations of scholars included the *Psalms of Solomon* in their broad synthetic category of apocalyptic literature, in regard to genre, this classification is untenable. The *Psalms of Solomon* does not demonstrate the features of Judean apocalypses according to the consensus definition in *Semeia* 14.[45] The text does not assume the form of a narrative that contains a revelation from an "otherworldly being" about events in a transcendent world that influences the terrestrial order. As Nickelsburg states, "There is here no concept of two corresponding levels of reality: the heavenly and the earthly, the mythical and the historical."[46] The reference to Pompey as a "dragon" clearly exemplifies the difference between the *Psalms of Solomon* and the apocalyptic text of Daniel. In the *Psalms of Solomon*, the term "dragon" functions as a simple metaphor. Certainly, the word carries the rich meanings and symbolism of this image in the Hebrew Bible traditions and other ancient Near Eastern mythologies. However, this is quite different from the way that the author of the apocalypse in Dan 7 uses the dragon imagery. In that chapter, the dragon is a character in a grand vision that the author casts into a narrative that portrays human history and the events that will lead to the eschaton. When the Ancient of Days appears, the dragon will be destroyed, and the righteous will be delivered. This kind of fantastic imagery is simply not a feature of the *Psalms of Solomon*.

The proper literary category for the *Psalms of Solomon* is a collection of psalms. The parallels, both in language and form, between the text and the biblical psalms are numerous. The psalms upon which I have focused, *Pss. Sol.* 1, 2, 8, and 17, exhibit the characteristics of biblical psalms, especially the so-called Zion hymns, wisdom psalms, psalms about the sinful history of the nation, psalms of deliverance, and laments.[47] The writing of psalms is widely attested in Second Temple Jewish literature, and the editing of the biblical psalms might still have been in process when the *Psalms of Solomon* was written. Hence, the activity of writing, editing, and

---

45. John J. Collins, "Introduction: Towards the Morphology of a Genre," *Semeia* 14 (1979): 9.

46. Nickelsburg, *Jewish Literature*, 209.

47. For more on form, see Claus Westermann, *Praise and Lament in the Psalms* (trans. K. R. Crim and R. N. Soulen; Atlanta: John Knox, 1981).

compiling psalms continued to be significant during this period, a phenomenon that continues to receive little attention in modern scholarship.

IDEOLOGY

I have already established that the *Psalms of Solomon* especially relies on Deuteronomic ideology to critique Hasmonean and Roman rule. Ostensibly, the Deuteronomic worldview represented in the *Psalms of Solomon* seems to be in complete opposition to what is generally regarded as the apocalyptic worldview. Deuteronomic thought is anchored in the covenant and its requirements. Israel's behavior determines whether blessings or curses visit the people. Thus, according to this line of thought, problems arise because the people have sinned. Repentance serves as the way to remove the punishment and regain divine favor. On the other hand, modern interpreters typically hold that apocalypticism reflects a kind of determinism. Problems that come upon the Jews are the result of demonic forces in the world that often assume the form of oppressive empires. Because demonic forces pose a threat that humans cannot overpower, God defeats the powers and brings deliverance for the righteous. While waiting for God's final victory, the proper responses of the righteous are hope and faithfulness. For example, the apocalyptic visions in Dan 7–12 reflect these features. In chapter 7, Daniel can only watch as the four beasts arise from the sea. The end of the final kingdom, which climaxes with a reference to Antiochus IV, comes by divine intervention—the arrival of the Ancient of Days. Daniel 10–12 contains a lengthy historical apocalypse and interpretation. Once again, the apocalypse indicates that historical events, including the beginning and end of empires and the rise and fall of rulers, are predetermined. Only at the completion of this scenario does Michael arrive and deliver the people and the end come.

Daniel 9, however, presents a curious combination. The text contains a penitential prayer that is marked by Deuteronomic ideology. At the same time, the prayer occurs within the context of Daniel receiving the proper interpretation of Jeremiah's seventy years. As is well known, the seventy years become seventy weeks of years, an apocalyptic timetable. In this text, then, Deuteronomic covenantal cause-and-effect and apocalyptic determinism stand together, the author apparently oblivious to the contradictions between the two worldviews. However, the problem with Dan 9 may not reside so much in Daniel as it does in the rigid scholarly reifications of the category "apocalyptic" that assume what must be in an apocalypse.

Likewise, one might think that the *Pss. Sol.* 17 reflects a degree of historical determinism in the author's ideology. Is this a reason why Wright characterized the messianism as apocalyptic?[48] The author of *Pss. Sol.* 17 believes that God will raise up the messianic king according to "the time known to you, O God" (v. 21). This may not be a sufficient basis for finding determinism in the text, and it is certainly not enough evidence to conclude that the text displays "apocalyptic messianism."

Dissident Scribes

While the *Psalms of Solomon* is not an apocalypse, it reflects a social situation similar to some apocalyptic texts. Like the scribes of the *Psalms of Solomon*, the *maskilim* in Daniel were also probably a group of dissident scribes.[49] In Daniel, the nation as a whole is suffering under a foreign ruler. Further, some of the *maskilim* most likely died for their faith (Dan 11:33). At the end of time, when Michael delivers the people and the resurrection occurs, the *maskilim* are vindicated and receive special treatment: "They will shine like the stars" (v. 3). Thus, the authors of Daniel imagined an end to the historical crisis in which the problems that they faced found a resolution especially suited for them. Further, as Horsley has recently argued, dissident scribes may be responsible for the Epistle of Enoch (*1 En.* 92–104).[50] This text seems to claim that wealthy rulers are oppressing the righteous, perhaps through deceitful business contracts, corrupt courts, and powerful connections to imperial rulers. Under the weight of such suffering, the author encourages the righteous by reminding them that God will punish the powerful, oppressive rulers. The Epistle of Enoch "imagines, somewhat vaguely, a future societal life without sin, without oppression by the wealthy and powerful."[51] The *Psalms of Solomon* displays similar features. Like the *maskilim* and the scribes of the Epistle of Enoch, the scribes in the *Psalms of Solomon* envisioned a future in which they regained their positions of influence. They would again enjoy a prominent status when the messiah arrived. Thus, we find texts from scribes with similar social locations, yet they write in very different ways.

Conclusions

The *Psalms of Solomon* proves a useful text for examining several issues in the ongoing investigations into apocalyptic literature. First, the

---

48. Wright, "Psalms of Solomon," 662, 667 n. p.
49. For a description of the *maskilim*, see Werline, *Penitential Prayer*, 72–74, 85–86.
50. Horsley, "Social Relations," 115.
51. Ibid.

text clearly does not fit into the literary category apocalypse, contrary to the vague characterizations of earlier scholars. The imprecision and misunderstanding resulted in part from the method of studying apocalyptic literature whereby scholars formulated lists of motifs and characteristics that occurred in apocalypses. These lists, then, were applied to other texts, and when anything on the list appeared in a text, the interpreter called the text apocalyptic. D. S. Russell's work provides an example of this approach, and he includes the *Psalms of Solomon* in his list of apocalyptic texts.[52] As the final section of my essay shows, the *Psalms of Solomon* shares a few motifs with some apocalypses from about the same era. However, there is a difference between sharing a motif and completely adopting apocalyptic ideology. But how does one distinguish between these two possibilities?

Second, studies in apocalypses have tended to reify the category and to make broad sweeping statements about such literature. For example, as I noted above, it is generally assumed that apocalyptic ideology is deterministic and that one would not expect to find Deuteronomic thought in an apocalypse. Examples from apocalypses demonstrate that this assumption is false, however; apocalypses can be ideologically inconsistent. On the other hand, when a text like the *Psalms of Solomon* exhibits perhaps a hint of determinism, one must not rush to label its ideology as apocalyptic.

Third, social location and conflict do not determine genre. Scholars have often claimed that every apocalypse arises from an oppressed group, even though we know that this is not always the case. For example, the Astronomical Book of *1 Enoch* was, by all indications, not born in suffering. Further, those who are oppressed do not always write in the form of an apocalypse. The *Psalms of Solomon* testifies to this. The social situation of the authors of this text somewhat resembles the social setting of the *maskilim* in Daniel and the scribes of the Epistle of Enoch. The genres of the respective literary products, however, are quite different.

Fourth, scholars have expressed general discomfort in speaking about apocalyptic "groups" and "conventicles," and for good reasons. I agree with Horsley that more investigation needs to be done into the possibility that some protest literature was written by dissident scribes. In this way, we can move away from thinking that every text has a community. Further, the possibility that such texts are the product of scribes might answer the question of why our categories of wisdom and apocalypticism seem to be breaking down. A characteristic of scribes is that

---

52. D. S. Russell, *The Method and Message of Jewish Apocalyptic: 200 BC–AD 100* (Philadelphia: Westminster, 1964), 57–58, 104–39, 233.

they are educated. If so, it seems quite possible that they were familiar with and could draw on a variety of themes, motifs, and forms from many texts. They obviously did not rigidly work within, or feel confined to, modern scholarly devised literary categories, including the category "apocalyptic." These categories as scholars have applied them simply do not accord with what one finds in a text like the *Psalms of Solomon*. The categories prove to be more scholarly invention than the actual manner in which ancient Jewish authors operated.

PUTTING THE PUZZLE TOGETHER: SOME SUGGESTIONS CONCERNING THE SOCIAL LOCATION OF THE WISDOM OF BEN SIRA

Benjamin G. Wright III

INTRODUCTION

A significant part of the agenda of the Wisdom and Apocalypticism in Early Judaism and Early Christianity Group during the course of its work has included the exploration of the social locations of texts traditionally labeled "wisdom" or "apocalyptic." The phrase "social location" can mean several different things, among them the attempt to identify the person, people, groups, or communities (if they were gathered into such coherent social bodies) responsible for a text or to find the place in the social landscape where a text most likely originated. This paper takes the first tack.

In the course of the 1995 Steering Committee planning meeting for the 1996 sessions for what was then the Wisdom and Apocalypticism in Early Judaism and Early Christianity Consultation (it only later became a Group in the SBL), Richard Horsley made the remark that after the discussions of Sirach in the previous year's meetings someone needed to "send up some trial balloons" concerning the social location of this work. I wrote this paper to take up that challenge. For several years prior to that meeting, I had been thinking about how to read the clues in Ben Sira's book that I thought might indicate how he fit into the social fabric of the Judaism of pre-Maccabean Palestine.[1] The sources for this period are few, and those that do exist frustrate the exegete since the evidence they provide is, for the most part, tantalizingly indirect and often expressed in ambiguous and/or mythic language. In this paper, which was the first of several that I ended up writing on issues related to this topic, I suggest

---

1. I presented some preliminary thoughts on these issues in a paper entitled "Seeking the Sublime: Aspects of Inner Jewish Polemic in the Wisdom of Ben Sira," presented at the Annual Meeting of the Society of Biblical Literature, Washington, D.C., 20 November 1993.

that, among other things, Jesus ben Sira was aware of and intended some elements of his book to address criticisms of the Jerusalem priesthood and temple by other groups of Jews (priests/scribes?) critical of those institutions.[2] These other Jewish groups were cognizant of people like Ben Sira, who were connected with the Jerusalem priests and who supported them. Three works that are roughly contemporary with Sirach express these kinds of criticisms: (1) the Book of the Watchers (*1 En.* 6–36), (2) the Astronomical Book (*1 En.* 72–82)—two of the oldest portions of *1 Enoch*—and (3) the *Aramaic Levi Document*.[3] An additional factor in this scenario is that these factions might possibly have been in some sort of dialogue with each other.

The most difficult hurdle to get over in such an enterprise is to reconstruct a social situation, in which various individuals or groups may be in conflict, from texts that may only allude to those conflicts and never explicitly indicate who the intended targets of the polemic are or with

---

2. This initial "trial balloon" paper sparked my interest in a range of issues related to the relationship between *1 Enoch, Aramaic Levi,* and Sirach, which I explored in subsequent publications. See "Fear the Lord and Honor the Priest: Ben Sira as Defender of the Jerusalem Priesthood," in *The Book of Ben Sira in Modern Research* (ed. P. C. Beentjes; BZAW 255; Berlin: de Gruyter, 1997), 189–222; "Sirach and 1 Enoch: Some Further Considerations," in *The Origins of Enochic Judaism: Proceedings of the First Enoch Seminar* (ed. G. Boccaccini; Turin: Zamorani, 2002), 179–87; "Wisdom, Instruction and Social Location in Ben Sira and *1 Enoch,*" in *Things Revealed: Studies in Early Jewish and Christian Literature in Honor of Michael E. Stone* (ed. E. G. Chazon et al.; JSJSup 89; Leiden: Brill, 2004), 105–21; "Ben Sira and the Book of the Watchers on the Legitimate Priesthood," in *Intertextual Studies on Ben Sira and Tobit* (ed. J. Corley and V. Skemp; CBQMS 38; Washington, D.C.: Catholic Biblical Association of America, 2005), 241–54; "1 *Enoch* and Ben Sira: Wisdom and Apocalyptic in Relationship," to appear in *The Early Enoch Tradition* (ed. G. Boccaccini and G. W. E. Nickelsburg; Leiden: Brill).

3. The Book of the Watchers and the Astronomical Book probably date to at least the third century B.C.E. J. T. Milik, *The Book of Enoch* (Oxford: Clarendon, 1976), dates the Qumran manuscripts of these sections to the second century B.C.E. Since they are surely not the autographs, the composition of the books must be earlier. On the dating of the Enochic corpus, see George W. E. Nickelsburg, *Jewish Literature between the Bible and the Mishnah* (Philadelphia: Fortress, 1981), 46–55, 150–51. For the Book of the Watchers, see now George W. E. Nickelsburg, *1 Enoch: A Commentary on the Book of 1 Enoch Chapters 1–36; 81–108* (Hermeneia; Minneapolis: Fortress, 2001). On a third-century B.C.E. date for *Aramaic Levi*, see Michael E. Stone, "Enoch, Aramaic Levi and Sectarian Origins," *JSJ* 19 (1988): 159 n. 2; Robert A. Kugler, *From Patriarch to Priest: The Levi-Priestly Tradition from Aramaic Levi to Testament of Levi* (SBLEJL 9; Atlanta: Scholars Press, 1996), 222–24. Sirach is usually dated somewhere around 180 B.C.E. See Patrick W. Skehan and Alexander A. Di Lella, *The Wisdom of Ben Sira* (AB 38; New York: Doubleday, 1987), 8–10. On the relationship between the *Aramaic Levi Document* and the Greek *Testament of Levi*, see H. W. Hollander and M. de Jonge, *The Testaments of the Twelve Patriarchs: A Commentary* (SVTP 8; Leiden: Brill, 1985), as well as Kugler's discussion and the literature cited in *From Patriarch to Priest*.

whom they may be in disagreement.⁴ It is precisely these kinds of confrontations that constitute the "trial balloon" aspect of this paper. While Ben Sira and the communities represented by *Aramaic Levi* and the Enochic works may be contemporary and even deal with the same themes, can we then move from those "observations" to creating a social world in which these people know of each other and attack or respond to each other? Randal Argall, reading Sirach and *1 Enoch* against one another, has shown that they treat identical themes—revelation, creation, judgment—and articulate them similarly.⁵ How does one, or even can one, move from literary theme to social reality?

What I propose to do is a bit different from what Richard Horsley and Patrick Tiller did in their 1992 SBL paper, "Ben Sira and the Sociology of the Second Temple."⁶ Horsley and Tiller employ the insights of Gerhard Lenski in an attempt to sketch the contours of Judean society at the time of Ben Sira and to understand where he fits in the network of the social structure and the system of social relations revealed in his book.⁷ In addition, they compare briefly the picture of a "stable and quiet" Judean society, as Ben Sira paints it, with that of *1 Enoch*, whose social world reveals "intense social conflict."⁸ Their study provides important background for the analysis that I want to make, and their conclusions hint that they think Sirach and *1 Enoch* betray the kinds of social interactions that I want to consider.

Indeed, several recent studies have suggested some relation between Sirach and *1 Enoch*. George Nickelsburg, commenting on Sirach's and the

---

4. In this paper I speak of groups or even communities behind the Enochic works or *Aramaic Levi*. I make this claim cautiously. While certainly some ancient works might be the product of individual motivation outside the framework of a larger group or community and its concerns, these texts indicate that more than some isolated individual is at work. For instance, in both cases, the patriarch of the work speaks to "sons" who are to take the patriarch's advice or to inherit a written version of the patriarch's wisdom/revelation. Devices such as this suggest that some group has preserved the teachings of the patriarch through a chain of transmission. See my article, "From Generation to Generation: The Sage as Father in Early Jewish Literature," to appear in *Biblical Traditions in Transmission: Essays in Honour of Michael Knibb* (ed. C. Hempel and J. Lieu; Leiden: Brill).

5. Randal A. Argall, 1 Enoch *and* Sirach: *A Comparative Literary and Conceptual Analysis of the Themes of Revelation, Creation and Judgment* (SBLEJL 8; Atlanta: Scholars Press, 1995).

6. Presented originally to the Sociology of the Second Temple Group, San Francisco, 1992, and subsequently published as Richard A. Horsley and Patrick Tiller, "Ben Sira and the Sociology of the Second Temple," in *Second Temple Studies III: Studies in Politics, Class and Material Culture* (ed. P. R. Davies and J. M. Halligan; JSOTSup 340; Sheffield: Sheffield Academic Press, 2002), 99–103.

7. Gerhard Lenski, *Power and Privilege* (New York: McGraw-Hill, 1966).

8. Horsley and Tiller, "Ben Sira and the Sociology of the Second Temple," 103.

Epistle of Enoch's relative treatments of the rich and poor, has speculated as to whether "the poor of Ben Sira's time" could have produced the Epistle.[9] In two brief, but suggestive remarks, Saul Olyan links the polemics of the *Testament of Levi* and *1 Enoch* with Sirach. Olyan thinks that both the *Testament of Levi* and *1 Enoch* advance the claims of the Levites to the priesthood against the pretensions of the Aaronids/Zadokites.[10] He contrasts these claims with Ben Sira's "refusal to recognize the existence of the Levites as a group," and he further comments that "we may have evidence here [in *1 En.* 89:73] of a contemporary Levitic theology opposed to Ben Sira's pan-Aaronid exclusivism."[11]

The two most detailed treatments of Sirach and *1 Enoch* are by Randal Argall (noted above) and by Gabriele Boccaccini in his book *Middle Judaism*.[12] Argall's study is primarily concerned with the literary themes and forms that Sirach and *1 Enoch* have in common. At the conclusion of the book he ventures several tentative conclusions about a social connection between the works.[13] After summarizing the differences between *1 Enoch* and Sirach, he comments, "Such differences are the stuff of conflict.... it is enough to make the case that each tradition views the other among its rivals."[14]

Boccaccini also looks at the literary similarities and differences among several themes contained in Sirach and *1 Enoch*, but he takes the next step of claiming that these literary aspects reveal that Ben Sira is aware of apocalyptic theologies and that he is writing against them. Boccaccini's literary analysis provides hints that he thinks might indicate

---

9. George W. E. Nickelsburg, "Social Aspects of Palestinian Jewish Apocalypticism," in *Apocalypticism in the Mediterranean World and the Near East* (ed. D. Hellholm; 2nd ed.; Tübingen: Mohr Siebeck, 1989), 651. See also, Nickelsburg, *Jewish Literature*, 149.

10. Saul Olyan, "Ben Sira's Relationship to the Priesthood," *HTR* 80 (1987): 279–80.

11. Ibid., 280.

12. Gabriele Boccaccini, *Middle Judaism: Jewish Thought 300 B.C.E to 200 C.E.* (Minneapolis: Fortress, 1991).

13. Argall's assessment of the dates of the different portions of *1 Enoch* relies on that of Nickelsburg. He wants to use those portions of *1 Enoch* that are contemporary with Sirach, as I do here. Primarily for reasons of space, I have limited this paper to the Book of the Watchers and the Astronomical Book, while Argall has included in his study the Epistle of Enoch (*1 En.* 92–105). I include the Epistle in "Wisdom, Instruction and Social Location." On the Epistle, see also George W. E. Nickelsburg, "Revealed Wisdom as a Criterion for Inclusion and Exclusion: From Jewish Sectarianism to Early Christianity," in *"To See Ourselves as Others See Us": Christians, Jews, "Others" in Late Antiquity* (ed. J. Neusner and E. S. Frerichs; Scholars Press Studies in the Humanities; Chico, Calif.: Scholars Press, 1985), 74–77. Victor Tcherikover originally suggested a possible connection between Sirach and the Epistle of Enoch in *Hellenistic Civilization and the Jews* (New York: Atheneum, 1982), 151. See also Nickelsburg, "Social Aspects," 651.

14. Argall, 1 Enoch *and Sirach*, 250.

direct social confrontations between Ben Sira and these apocalyptic groups. Commenting on the theme of covenant in Sirach, he writes,

> Ben Sira is intent on reaffirming the centrality of the covenant and the retributive principle, overcoming the aporias and doubts of Job and Qohelet. At the same time he *directly* confronts the suggestions of the apocalyptic movement. The calm and systematic style of this wisdom book should not lead us to lose sight of the terms of a bitter debate, addressing such precise referents and urgent questioning.[15]

I will sketch out several literary and conceptual themes that I think show that Ben Sira and the communities represented by 1 *Enoch* and *Aramaic Levi* knew and responded to each other's criticisms. Combined with the scholarly insights into the possible social locations of these works, I think enough clues are at hand to argue that the communities behind these works are, in significant ways, engaged in ongoing confrontation with each other over what are considered foundational issues for Jews in the period before the Maccabean Revolt.

Problems of the Calendar

"It is difficult to overstress the importance of the calendar." So Michael Stone concludes about the character of third century B.C.E. Judaism.[16] And calendrical concerns are certainly in evidence in the documents at issue here. More important to stress, however, is that in some places the question of which calendar is the correct one arises in contexts that could be interpreted as polemical. Several different calendrical systems appear in these texts, and the issue at stake is which system—one of the possible solar ones or a lunar (or, luni-solar) one—ought to prevail and what that means for how the Jewish festivals and observances get set. The Qumran community, as is well known, used a solar calendar, but that calendar's origins come earlier than the founding of the group.[17]

Aramaic Levi, the Book of the Watchers, and the Astronomical Book all display the use of a solar calendar. Because *Aramaic Levi* is so fragmentary, it is difficult to ascertain exactly how the solar calendar functioned in the document, but probably the work utilizes a calendar like the one at Qumran. Such a conclusion depends on the reports of

---

15. Boccaccini, *Middle Judaism*, 80, emphasis added.
16. Stone, "Enoch, Aramaic Levi," 166.
17. On the Qumran calendar, see Shamaryahu Talmon, "The Calendar Reckoning of the Sect from the Judean Desert," *ScrHier* 4 (1958): 162–99.

Levi's children given in *Aramaic Levi* 65–72.[18] Michael Stone and Jonas Greenfield argue that several characteristics of the dates for the births of Levi's children are consistent with a Qumran-like solar calendar. These include: (1) the numbering of months rather than naming them; (2) the births of three of the children exactly three months apart putting them on the same date and day of the week; (3) two cases, for which dates are provided, where the birth falls on a Wednesday, an important day of the week in the Qumran calendar; and (4) Kohath's birth on the morning of the first day of the first month, morning being the time that the day began at Qumran.[19]

The Book of the Watchers also preserves clues that an important part of the Enochic visionary traditions was the revelation of the workings of the astronomical bodies. Even though the solar calendar is not mentioned per se in the Book of the Watchers, the work depends on such a calendar. Chapters 33–36 appear to be a summary account intended to end the work, and 33:2–4 in particular constitute a condensed version of the Astronomical Book. As in the Astronomical Book, the angel Uriel shows Enoch the "gates of the heavens" and how the stars that come out of them determine the calendar.[20] Chapters 34–36 also speak of the gates of heaven, although the astronomical scheme in these chapters differs somewhat from that of the Astronomical Book.[21]

The Astronomical Book contains the most extensive and detailed treatment of a 364-day solar calendar.[22] The angel Uriel shows Enoch the intricacies of the movements of the sun, moon, and stars in and out of the gates of heaven. This revelation establishes the solar year as the fundamental basis for the reckoning of seasons and festivals. In two places in the Astronomical Book as we now have it, 75:2 and 82:4–7 (which is an apparent intrusion into the astronomical material), and in one apparent addition to the book, 80:2–8, there are polemical passages directed at

---

18. On the Greek *Testament of Levi* and the Aramaic portions of *Aramaic Levi*, see Michael E. Stone and Jonas C. Greenfield, "Remarks on the Aramaic Testament of Levi from the Geniza," *RB* 86 (1979): 214–15; Kugler, *From Patriarch to Priest*, 23–59. Although it was not yet available to me, almost certainly the newly published edition of *Aramaic Levi* will be the most up-to-date discussion. See Jonas C. Greenfield, Michael E. Stone, and Ester Eshel, *The Aramaic Levi Document* (SVTP 19; Leiden: Brill, 2004).

19. Stone and Greenfield, "Remarks," 224.

20. Argall, *1 Enoch and Sirach*, 52. See the notes to these chapters in Matthew Black, *The Book of Enoch or 1 Enoch: A New English Edition* (SVTP 7; Leiden: Brill, 1985), 180–81.

21. Argall, *1 Enoch and Sirach*, 52.

22. The Aramaic fragments of the Astronomical Book found at Qumran show that the version used by the Qumranites was more extensive than that preserved in the Ethiopic *1 Enoch*. See Milik, *Book of Enoch*; Black, *Book of Enoch*. The solar year constitutes a central feature of both forms of the book.

those who do not use the Enochic calendar.[23] *First Enoch* 75:2 and 82:4–7 contain an attack on those who do not reckon the four epagomenal days in the calendar, which bring it to 364 days. Otto Neugebauer notes that 75:2 "could refer to the lunar calendar of the Jews (which has no intercalary days)," although it must be noted that the argument just as easily could be directed at those who use a solar calendar that does not reckon those four days.[24] *First Enoch* 80:2–8 inveighs against "sinners" whose "years shall become shorter, and their seeds shall be late in their lands and fields." These people are presumably those who do not use the Enochic solar calendar, but a different solar, a lunar, or a luni-solar one that rapidly gets out of sync with the solar year. The book of *Jubilees* and the people at Qumran later utilize this 364-day calendar in decidedly polemical contexts. Nickelsburg's comment on these materials is apt at this junction, "Behind all this [the problems concerning calendar evidenced in these works] appears to have been a bitter calendrical dispute with the Jewish religious establishment."[25]

Ben Sira's comments about the heavenly bodies reveal a position on the calendar directly in contrast to that of *Aramaic Levi* and the Enochic works. Sirach 43:2–8, the major section in which Ben Sira speaks of the sun and moon, is part of a larger section on the works of creation, and his comments on these two heavenly bodies can, and I think should, be read as a polemic against a solar calendar. The sun is of interest to Ben Sira primarily because it is hot. Six of the eight cola devoted to this celestial body describe its fiery nature. It "parches the earth and no one can endure its blazing heat" (43:3). The sun is much hotter than a furnace, and it "breathes out fiery vapors" (43:4). Nowhere does Ben Sira attribute to it any calendrical function. By contrast, his section on the moon focuses almost exclusively on the role it plays in setting the calendar. The moon, Ben Sira says, governs the changing seasons (עתות), the festivals (מועדים), and the pilgrimages (חגים). As its name implies, the moon gives the month its name, and it serves as an "army beacon" (כלי צבא).

Remarkably, Ben Sira not only denies the sun the role it plays in the solar calendar but does so in contrast to the function explicitly attributed

---

23. On this "intrusion of nonastronomical material," see Black, *Book of Enoch*, 252, 411; Nickelsburg, *Jewish Literature*, 48.

24. Black, *Book of Enoch*, 402. James VanderKam notes, however, that the polemic about the four epagomenal days does not necessarily oppose use of a lunar calendar. He argues that the Astronomical Book presents a 364-day calendar apparently without any active opposition to the calendar that regulated the cult in Jerusalem. See "The 364-Day Calendar in the Enochic Literature," *Society of Biblical Literature 1983 Seminar Papers* (SBLSP 22; Chico, Calif.: Scholars Press, 1983), 164.

25. Nickelsburg, *Jewish Literature*, 48.

to it in the Priestly creation account in Genesis.²⁶ Genesis 1:14–15 ascribes a cooperative role to the sun and moon when it comes to calendars. "God said, 'Let there be lights in the vault of the heavens to separate the day from the night, and let them serve as signs both for festivals and for seasons and for years.'"²⁷ Such a contravention of the P narrative, which Ben Sira certainly knows, can best be understood as his attempt not to make even an apparent concession to the calendrical stance taken by Jews, like those who produced and used *Aramaic Levi*, the Book of the Watchers, and the Astronomical Book, who claim the priority and foundational character of a solar calendar.

The Secrets of God and Creation

Ben Sira's opposition to any reliance on the sun for calendrical reckonings seems to represent one particular instance of more general suspicions that he has about the entire enterprise of moving beyond the law and inquiring into those subjects that are inscrutable: the secrets of the created order and the future. Several passages in his book could be brought to bear here, but the *locus classicus* is Sir 3:21–24.

> 3:21 Things too marvelous for you, do not investigate,
> And things too evil for you, do not research.
> 3:22 On what is authorized, give attention,
> But you have no business with secret things.
> 3:23 And into what is beyond you, do not meddle,
> For that which is too great has been shown to you.
> 3:24 For many are the thoughts of the sons of men,
> Evil and erring imaginations.²⁸

---

26. See Olyan, "Ben Sira's Relationship," for the affinities that Sirach has with the Priestly source of the Pentateuch regarding the role and place of the priests.

27. Alexander Rofé, "The Onset of Sects in Postexilic Judaism: Neglected Evidence from the Septuagint, Trito-Isaiah, Ben Sira and Malachi," in *The Social World of Formative Christianity and Judaism* (ed. J. Neusner et al.; Philadelphia: Fortress, 1988), 43–44, also notes this problem.

28. I have used the translation of Argall, *1 Enoch and Sirach*, 74, who argues for adopting the reading of MS C from the Geniza for 3:21b against Skehan and Di Lella, *Wisdom of Ben Sira*, 158, who use MS A. To judge from the Greek translation, the situation is more complicated than simply following one manuscript or the other. I would follow MS A for the verbs, since elsewhere in Sirach ἐκετάζω (Gk. colon b) only translates Hebrew חקר (11:7, 13:11), but I prefer the adjectives used in MS C, where Greek χαλεπώτερα seems to reflect a *Vorlage* more like MS C's רעים. Thus, 3:21 might be translated "What is too marvelous for you, do not seek, and what is too harsh/difficult/evil for you do not investigate." The Hebrew of Sirach (except for MS F) can be most conveniently found in The Historical Dictionary of the Hebrew

Some scholars have read these verses as a polemic against Jewish participation in Greek philosophical inquiry and discussion. Patrick Skehan and Alexander Di Lella summarize it this way, "Ben Sira cautions his readers about the futility of Greek learning, its goals and techniques, and also reminds them of what the Lord has bestowed on them.... Hence it is better for the enlightened Jew to follow the certainties and true wisdom of the law revealed to Moses than to strive after the often contradictory musings and uncertain opinions of the Greek thinkers."[29] While it is true that Ben Sira wants his readers to adhere closely to the precepts of Moses, perhaps even in the face of what he might consider foreign encroachment, this passage makes better sense when read against the backdrop of the mysteries revealed to Enoch and Levi, especially cosmological speculation and eschatological realities, and together with others that seem to address similar kinds of inner-Jewish concerns.

Ben Sira makes clear in this section that he does not want his students engaged in certain kinds of inquiry. Only God can reveal those things that are "too marvelous," "too difficult/evil," or that are "hidden." Investigation of these esoteric matters is not only unwise, but, even more, it is forbidden.[30] The passage is conspicuously characterized, however, by its vagueness as to the subject of the inquiry. What kinds of things are "too marvelous" or "hidden"?

The dangerous content of the questioning might be indicated by two Hebrew terms. The first, the adjective פלאות (3:21, the Gk. is probably ἰσχυρότερα), may refer to delving into the "works of God," particularly the secrets of God's creation. In the two other places where פלאות is used in Sirach, the first, 11:4, modifies "the works of God" (מעשי יהוה) and refers to the way that human fortunes can unexpectedly change. The second occurrence, 43:24, comprises part of an extended poem on the wonders of creation (42:15–43:33), where פלאות describes "the works of God," but here God's "works" are the incredible creatures/monsters that live in the sea. Elsewhere in this poem Ben Sira uses the related Hebrew word נפלאות to indicate the unfathomable wonders of God's creation. At the beginning of the poem (42:15) he exclaims, "I shall recall the works of

---

Language, *The Book of Ben Sira: Text, Concordance and an Analysis of the Vocabulary* [Hebrew] (Jerusalem: Academy of the Hebrew Language and Shrine of the Book, 1973), and Pancratius C. Beentjes, *The Book of Ben Sira in Hebrew* (VTSup 68; Leiden: Brill, 1997). For MS F from the Geniza, see Alexander A. Di Lella, "The Newly Discovered Sixth Manuscript of Ben Sira from the Cairo Geniza," *Bib* 69 (1988): 226–38.

29. Skehan and Di Lella, *Wisdom of Ben Sira*, 160–61. See also Martin Hengel, *Judaism and Hellenism* (Philadelphia: Fortress, 1974), 139–40.

30. On this passage, see Argall, *1 Enoch and Sirach*, 74–76, 250.

God (מעשי אל) ... through the word of the Lord are his works (מעשיו)." These works are filled with God's glory (v. 16), and even the "holy ones of God" cannot recount "the marvels/wonders of God (נפלאות יהוה)." At the end of the poem, Ben Sira extols God for his power and inscrutable nature. Returning to God's works in 43:32–33, he says, "Many more things than these are marvelous (נפלא?) and powerful. Only a few of his works I have seen. It is the Lord who has made all things and to those who fear him he gives wisdom."[31]

In one passage for which no Hebrew is extant, Ben Sira makes God's position as creator reinforce the role of God as judge. In 18:4–7, he again claims that God's creation, and hence God, cannot be fathomed. No one can describe "God's works" or measure his power. One cannot penetrate the "wonders of the Lord (καὶ οὐκ ἔστιν ἐξιχνιάσαι τὰ θαυμάσια τοῦ κυρίου)." This is the same sentiment found in the poem on creation in chapters 42 and 43.

The second important term is the noun נסתרות (3:22, Gk. κρύπτα), which probably refers to what the future holds. The term occurs elsewhere in Sirach in the initial section of the poem on creation in chapter 42. Ben Sira claims that God knows the depths of the human heart and that he "discloses both the past and the future and he reveals the deep secret things (נסתרות)" (42:19). The verbs in this verse, מחוה and מגלה, refer to revealing, and נסתרות occurs in parallel with "the past and future." The word, then, in the context of this poem on God's works, probably connotes both revelation and creation. The universe comprises not only the created order (visible and invisible), but also the things that God ordains. The past and future, the created order, these are all things that God has "made." Thus, while the "secret things" in this poem could refer to hidden aspects of creation, they almost certainly refer as well to matters of past and future. The poem culminates in the claim that the creator gives wisdom (revelation of the future and the secrets of creation?) to those who fear him (43:33). Further on in 48:25, the same term is used of Isaiah, who "foretold what should be till the end of time, hidden things (נסתרות) that were yet to be fulfilled." In this passage, Ben Sira intends the term to mean matters pertaining to the eschatological future. The most likely content of the נסתרות into which 3:22 prohibits investigation is events of the future, perhaps the eschaton. One can only speculate at

---

31. Skehan and Di Lella follow the Greek here because of the fragmentary nature of MS B, which only has the first word and part of the last word fully legible. On the basis of the traces on the manuscript, the Hebrew Language Academy edition of the Hebrew reconstructs the verse, רוב [מ]אלה נפ[ל]א וחק[ק. I have translated on the basis of this reconstruction.

this juncture as to whether Ben Sira's ambivalent attitude toward revelation of the future reflects his awareness of eschatological speculation of the kind found in *1 Enoch* and *Aramaic Levi*.

It is no accident, in my estimation, that the secrets of creation and revelation of the future are precisely two of the more conspicuous subjects treated in the Astronomical Book, the Book of the Watchers, and *Aramaic Levi*. During Enoch's visions of the Astronomical Book and the Book of the Watchers, he learns the inner workings of the created order. In his ascent to heaven in *1 En.* 14, Enoch encounters God in the heavenly temple, who reveals the impending judgment of the Watchers. Several scholars have understood this revelation as *1 Enoch*'s condemnation of the Jerusalem priesthood, a group for whom Ben Sira has great sympathy.[32]

Although there is some dispute about how the fragments of the Qumran manuscripts of *Aramaic Levi* should be divided and how they should be ordered, 4Q213b 3–4 apparently deals with the story of Dinah.[33] According to the order determined by Stone and Greenfield in DJD 22, the fragment should follow a report in Greek (MS Athos, Koutloumous 39) about Levi receiving visions, but it is not clear if these fragments are part of the contents of Levi's revelations. The text of the fragment does not correspond with anything in the Greek *Testament of Levi*, but similar material appears in *Jub.* 30, where it is part of the author's concerns about Jewish endogamy. In fact, 4Q213b 3–4 5 looks very similar to *Jub.* 30:7.[34] Given the subject matter and the similarity to *Jubilees*, one might reasonably suggest that the *Aramaic Levi* fragment also deals with more than a simple historical report of the Dinah story, but that it also concerns matters of endogamy generally, and in *Aramaic Levi* priestly endogamy in particular.

Later, in *Aramaic Levi* 82–106 Levi's speech to his children predicts that his descendants in later generations will not follow his instruction. In the beginning of the section, Levi admonishes his children both to learn and to teach wisdom (as well as "reading, writing, and instruction"). In

---

32. See below on the priesthood. On this interpretation of the Book of the Watchers, see George W. E. Nickelsburg, "Enoch, Levi and Peter: Recipients of Revelation in Upper Galilee," *JBL* 100 (1981): 575–600; David Suter, "The Priesthood and Apocalyptic" (paper presented at the Annual Meeting of the Society of Biblical Literature, San Francisco, 21 December 1981; my thanks to the author for making his paper available to me); and idem, "Fallen Angel, Fallen Priest: The Problem of Family Purity in 1 Enoch 6–16," *HUCA* 50 (1979): 115–35.

33. Kugler's analysis in *From Patriarch to Priest* differs from that of Michael E. Stone and Jonas C. Greenfield in DJD 22.

34. Stone and Greenfield, DJD 22, 35.

102–106 Levi makes clear that his descendents will abandon that wisdom and will "walk in the darkness of Satan/perversity ... will become fools." They will turn to wickedness and evil (106). This prediction is not, however, given in the form of predictions received in a vision, but it reads more like a testament.

By contrast, although he understands himself to be a sage with prophet-like inspiration (see ch. 24), Ben Sira admits that he has seen only a small portion of God's works (43:32), and he does not claim to know what the future holds. It is not that God does not reveal these things; he plainly has (to Isaiah, for instance) and does, but the things that God has already given are plenty to contemplate, and these are the only things that are "authorized" (3:22). I read this admonition as Ben Sira's warning to his students to stay grounded, so to speak, to confine their study to the law of God where true wisdom is to be found and where God's authorized revelation is located (Sir 24). In sum, rather than Greek philosophical inquiry, this passage addresses unauthorized interest in things that God has withheld from general human understanding. Ben Sira worries about what he considers to be an unhealthy concern for matters too great to be understood and too difficult, perhaps even too dangerous, to investigate, the secrets of God's creation and the revelation of the future, subjects treated at length in *1 Enoch* and *Aramaic Levi*.[35]

Dream Visions and Ascents

In addition to the investigation of certain unauthorized subjects, the possible methods of receiving such "revelation" are also a target of Ben Sira's polemic. In 34:1–8, Ben Sira takes on dreams and visions.

34:1 Empty and false are the hopes of the senseless,
and fools are sent winging by dreams.
34:2 Like one grasping at shadows or chasing the wind
is whoever puts his trust in dreams.
34:3 What is seen in dreams is a reflection
that mirrors the vision of the onlooker.
34:4 Can the clean produce the unclean?
Can the liar ever speak the truth?
34:5 Divination, omens and dreams are unreal;
what you already expect, the mind depicts.

---

35. If Argall's translation of 3:23 is accepted, Ben Sira is even aware that these matters have "been shown" to some of his students or that rival wisdom teachers are promulgating them. See *1 Enoch and Sirach*, 76.

34:6 Unless it be a vision specially sent from the Most High,
fix not your heart on it.
34:7 For dreams have led many astray,
and those who base their hopes on them have perished.
34:8 Without deceit the law is fulfilled,
and well-rounded wisdom is the discourse of the faithful.[36]

This section cautions against relying on dreams and visions generally, but it tells little about the content of those dreams. Martin Hengel thinks that the passage is directed against mantic traditions or magical practices, and Skehan and Di Lella refer to the prohibition of divination and paying heed to omens as "pagan and untrustworthy."[37] Indeed, one could read the passage as a general admonition about the problems connected with dreams and dream interpretation, since dreams and their interpretations were of general interest throughout antiquity.[38] In light of the apprehensions that Ben Sira has about different calendars and unauthorized investigations into God's secrets, however, I think that a text like 34:1–8, which treats avenues of revelation that correspond to the ways in which *particular* communities legitimate their knowledge of these topics, probably constitutes Ben Sira's attempt to undercut such claims to divinely inspired knowledge.[39]

The mention of "divination" and "omens" almost certainly indicates Ben Sira's use of the Mosaic proscriptions against these practices, but they are not really the main focus of the passage. Clearly dreams are the real targets, since they are mentioned in verses 1, 2, 3, and 7.[40] Three times in 1 *En.* 13 and 14, Enoch says that his visions come in his sleep, and Ben Sira's remark in 34:1 that fools "are sent winging by dreams" may even be directed specifically at heavenly ascents in dreams, like Enoch's ascent to heaven and heavenly tour.[41] Although 4QLevi[a]ar is fragmentary, the text says that Levi lies down, and, after a lacuna in the text, he has a vision.

---

36. The Hebrew extant for this section in MS E only preserves portions of verse 1. I rely on the Greek for the remainder of the section.

37. Hengel, *Judaism and Hellenism*, 240; Skehan and Di Lella, *Wisdom of Ben Sira*, 409.

38. On dreams and dream interpretation generally, see Naphtali Lewis, *The Interpretation of Dreams and Portents* (Toronto: Hakkert, 1976); Patricia Cox Miller, *Dreams in Late Antiquity: Studies in the Imagination of a Culture* (Princeton: Princeton University Press, 1994).

39. Argall (1 Enoch *and Sirach*, 81) wants to read the passage this way as well. I arrived at the same conclusion independently.

40. Argall (ibid., 82) notes that by linking dreams with divination and omen reading, Ben Sira connects these practices with those of the nations found in Deut 18:10–11. He also wonders if the rhetorical question of 34:4 about purity indicates that the dreamers have separated themselves from the temple.

41 Ibid., 81.

It seems likely that some mention of sleep and/or a dream belongs here and thus, Levi's vision, like Enoch's, comes via a dream.[42] Ben Sira ridicules those who depend on dreams and visions, calling them "senseless" and "fools." He also recognizes the self-fulfilling nature of dreams; they are simply reflections of the one who is dreaming (vv. 3, 5).

Ben Sira paints himself into something of a corner here, however. Dreams and dream interpretations occur frequently in the Hebrew Bible. The exception he makes for dreams sent by the Most High (34:6) may refer to the biblical visions, but he nowhere says how one can decide between a divinely inspired dream and one that simply "mirrors the vision of the onlooker" (v. 3). The passage ends in verse 8 with the antithesis to "grasping at shadows," the fulfillment of the law. Here the law is placed in parallel with "well-rounded wisdom," which should be the discourse of the faithful. It is the law and its wisdom that should concern his students, not flights of fancy found in the dreams and visions of folks like Enoch and Levi.

Priests and Priesthood

The literary themes outlined above are suggestive by themselves, and they provide some evidence that Ben Sira was concerned with the kinds of problems and claims made in the Astronomical Book, the Book of the Watchers, and *Aramaic Levi*. Recent work on all these books has tried to find for each of them a location in the social world of ancient Judaism. In each case, the conclusions point to groups of priests and/or their scribal retainers, who are either supportive of or opposed to the priests who control the cult in Jerusalem. One finds criticism of the Jerusalem priesthood in a number of postexilic texts, such as Malachi, but the important and ultimately interesting thing about Sirach, the Book of the Watchers, *Aramaic Levi*, and perhaps the Astronomical Book, is that they are roughly contemporary works, they all treat various priestly concerns, and each may have originated in priestly or scribal groups.

Both Nickelsburg and David Suter have argued that the myth of the Watchers utilized in the Book of the Watchers reflects a criticism of the Jerusalem priesthood, and by extension the temple, over the issue of improper marriage relationships.[43] Nickelsburg concentrates on the cultic

---

42. On 4QLevi^aar, see Michael E. Stone and Jonas C. Greenfield, "The Prayer of Levi," *JBL* 112 (1993): 247–66; Stone and Greenfield, DJD 22.

43. Nickelsburg, "Enoch, Levi and Peter"; Suter "Fallen Angel, Fallen Priest." See also Martha Himmelfarb, *Ascent to Heaven in Jewish and Christian Apocalypses* (New York: Oxford University Press, 1993), 9–29.

language of *1 En.* 15:2–4, in which Enoch is to tell the Watchers that God has rejected their plea. In fact, God tells Enoch, the Watchers should be petitioning on behalf of human beings, not Enoch on their behalf (v. 2). Then comes their indictment, "Why have you [the Watchers] left the high heaven and the eternal holy one and lain with women and defiled yourselves with the daughters of men and taken to yourselves wives and acted like the children of earth ... yet you defiled yourselves with the blood of women" (v. 34). The fact that God lives in a heavenly temple attended by the angels, who are described as priests, has prompted the identification of the Watchers as priests who have fallen and defiled themselves with women and who have sinned in the eyes of the Enochic community by marrying illegitimately. Because of these actions, God has excluded them from the heavenly temple. Such antipriestly polemic clothed in myth is consistent with a number of other Second Temple texts that report similar problems and demonstrates that the priesthood is a longstanding and contentious issue in Second Temple Judaism. For instance, upon his arrival into Judea, Ezra finds that priests and Levites have married foreign women, a practice he wants halted, and later the *Damascus Document* evidences a similar polemic against the priesthood.[44] Nickelsburg subsequently concludes that "the easiest explanation [of the myth in *1 En.* 12–16] appears to be that the mythmaker has a grievance against the priesthood in his own time ... we have here in *1 Enoch* 12–16 an apocalyptic tradition emanating from circles in upper Galilee who view the Jerusalem priesthood as defiled and therefore under the irrevocable judgment of God."[45]

Suter argues that such criticism of the Jerusalem priesthood pervades all of *1 En.* 6–16. Chapters 6–11 have as a central part of the myth a concern that the fallen angels have become defiled by contact with women and blood, and that their offspring are *mamzerim*. *First Enoch* 12–16 evinces a continued interest in the same problem, but the sexual contact reflected in these chapters, according to Suter, "is defiling per se since it represents an illegitimate degree of relationship."[46] This concern suggests that the compiler of *1 Enoch* is worried about family purity, which in Second Temple Judaism is primarily a concern with priestly purity. Suter

---

44. Nickelsburg, "Enoch, Levi and Peter," 584–85; Suter "Fallen Angel, Fallen Priest," 124–28; Himmelfarb, *Ascent to Heaven*, 20–23. For a more recent treatment of the issue of marriage in Second Temple texts, see Martha Himmelfarb, "Levi, Phinehas, and the Problem of Intermarriage at the Time of the Maccabean Revolt," *Jewish Studies Quarerly* 6 (1999): 1–24.
45. Nickelsburg, "Enoch, Levi and Peter," 586.
46. Suter, "Fallen Angel, Fallen Priest," 118.

concludes, "There is a parallel between the separation that the myth seeks to draw between the angelic and human realms and the tendency toward endogamy in priestly marriages."[47] He further notes that other indicators in these chapters point to the priesthood as the problem for *1 En.* 6–16. The intercessory function ascribed to Enoch in *1 En.* 15 is a priestly function. The Watchers of *1 Enoch* who teach forbidden knowledge subvert the role of priest as teacher. The illegitimate marriages of the Watchers result in their expulsion from heaven just as priests who contract illegitimate marriages should be, in the mind of the Enochic author(s), prevented from serving in the temple.[48]

A concern with priestly purity could indicate that the Book of the Watchers emanated from priests who were convinced that the Jerusalem priests had transgressed purity rules and were defiled as a result. Other clues as well point to priests as the source of the criticisms expressed in *1 Enoch*. Stone argues that the "scientific" speculations found in the early parts of *1 Enoch* must have come from groups of "educated men and may possibly have been associated with the traditional intellectual groups, the wise and the priests." He further notes that the interest in calendar exhibited in the Book of the Watchers and the Astronomical Book is a traditional priestly matter.[49] In his SBL paper "The Priesthood and Apocalyptic," Suter takes an additional step. On the basis of the sociological analysis of Edward Shils, who studied the roles of intellectuals in society, and the connection made by Stone between apocalyptic and Jewish intellectual traditions, he argues that, since priests are major players in both the central institutional and the central cultural systems of ancient Judaism, and since the interests of these two systems are not identical, the concerns displayed in *1 Enoch* are not only *about* the priesthood but originate *within* priestly groups.[50]

The roles that Enoch, the protagonist of this mythic drama and likely representative of the community, plays, especially in the Book of the

---

47. Ibid., 122.
48. Ibid., 123–24. Suter also examines other Second Temple Jewish works, like the *Damascus Document*, that polemicize against the priesthood.
49. Michael E. Stone, "The Book of Enoch and Judaism in the Third Century B.C.E.," *CBQ* 40 (1978): 489. Olyan ("Ben Sira's Relationship," 280) suggests that the group behind *1 Enoch* was composed of "disenfranchised Levites," and "thus we have evidence here of a contemporary Levitic ideology opposed to Ben Sira's pan-Aaronid exclusivism."
50. See Suter "Apocalyptic and the Priesthood," 10–12, for the complete argument. He relies on two collections of Shils's scholarship, *The Intellectuals and the Powers and Other Essays* (Selected Papers of Edward Shils 1; Chicago: University of Chicago Press, 1972), and *Center and Periphery: Essays in Macrosociology* (Selected Papers of Edward Shils 2; Chicago: University of Chicago Press, 1975).

Watchers, also might give some indication of the group that produced the work. Enoch is called "scribe of righteousness" (15:1), and he performs scribal tasks in drawing up the petition of the Watchers. But, Enoch also plays the role of priest. He intercedes between God and the angels, thereby exercising the priestly prerogative of intercession with the deity. He has extraordinary access to the heavenly temple, a place that is the domain of priests.[51] As Suter notes regarding these two roles, "a scribal role need not preclude a priestly one, and may even point in that direction."[52] In addition, Enoch takes on prophetic characteristics, particularly as *1 Enoch* utilizes prophetic literary forms.[53]

A similar social situation is to be found in *Aramaic Levi*. Several elements suggest a priestly milieu for this work. Levi's position as the ancestor of the priests results in the glorification of the priesthood as an institution, even in a context in which the behavior of some priests is apparently condemned. Such approbation may constitute evidence of a priestly origin for the work. The centrality of the figure of Levi also points in the direction of priests. The polemic about proper marriage practices and the wickedness of some priests recalls that of *1 Enoch*. In sum, the central emphases of the work reflect priestly interests. Besides its calendrical interest, *Aramaic Levi* includes detailed sacrificial instructions (*Aramaic Levi* 13–60), and it emphasizes heavily the importance of the levitical line. Indeed, the levitical line is so central that in *Aramaic Levi* the "biblical verses referring to Judah, which came to be interpreted messianically, were transferred to Levi."[54] The *Testament of Levi*, for which *Aramaic Levi* most likely served as a source, attributes scribal characteristics to Levi the priest (8:17, 13:1–9, 14:4).[55] Stone makes this assessment of *Aramaic Levi*, "[T]he circles responsible for *Aramaic Levi* laid a very strong emphasis on the instructional function of the priesthood and this aspect of the priesthood attracted sapiential motifs."[56] These two roles

---

51. Himmelfarb, *Ascent to Heaven*, 23–25.

52. Suter, "Apocalyptic and the Priesthood," 9.

53. George W. E. Nickelsburg, "'Enoch' as Scientist, Sage and Prophet: Content, Function and Authorship in 1 Enoch" (paper presented to the Conference on Theology, Scientific Knowledge and Society in Antiquity, Center for Theological Inquiry, Princeton, 1993), 29. See also, Himmelfarb, *Ascent to Heaven*, 25. In addition, several authors note the relationship between Enoch's ascent in *1 En.* 14 and Ezekiel's vision of the chariot, which is a priestly text. On this relationship, see Suter, "Apocalyptic and the Priesthood"; Himmelfarb, *Ascent to Heaven*, 26–28.

54. Michael E. Stone, "Ideal Figures and Social Context: Priest and Sage in the Early Second Temple Age," in *Ancient Israelite Religion: Essays in Honor of Frank Moore Cross* (ed. P. D. Miller Jr. et al.; Philadelphia: Fortress, 1988), 580.

55. Himmelfarb, *Ascent to Heaven*, 30.

56. Stone, "Ideal Figures," 580.

subsumed under one figure, again are reminiscent of the roles attributed to Enoch.

From the first-person descriptions of what he does, together with the high praise accorded the sage/scribe, it is evident that Ben Sira himself belonged to that profession. Helge Stadelmann argues that he was, in fact, a priest, but without engaging those arguments in detail here, it is clear that he has a close relationship with and is very supportive of the priests who serve in the temple.[57] Olyan accepts Stadelmann's conclusions, and on the basis of passages such as 7:29–31 claims that "[i]t is not overstating the case to argue that Ben Sira all but equates the individual's relationship with God to the same individual's relationship to the priesthood."[58] In 7:29–31 Ben Sira adopts the language of the Shema and applies it to the layperson's relationship with God's priests: "*With all your heart*, fear God, and treat as holy his priests. *With all your might*, love your maker and do not forsake his servants. Fear God and honor the priest, and give their portion as you are commanded" (7:29–30). By intentionally using this language, Ben Sira lends heightened symbolic weight to the whole idea of the importance of the priesthood and its elevated station.[59]

Olyan goes even further and argues that the priestly ideology articulated by Ben Sira is consonant with the view of the P narrative of the Pentateuch in which Aaron and his descendants are the true priests.[60] Ben Sira is, like P, a proponent of a "pan-Aaronid" view of the priesthood through Phinehas with whom God made an eternal covenant. In many details, his description of Aaron is taken from the Pentateuch, but the "everlasting covenant" given to Aaron is given particular attention (45:7, 15, 25). Later in chapter 50, his praise of Simon II harks back to that of Aaron in chapter 45. The glorious description of Simon exiting the temple and blessing the people almost certainly stems from Ben Sira's personal experience, even though this poem was probably written after Simon's death.[61] Simon becomes the epitome of the high priest who fulfills the priestly covenant given to Aaron and Phinehas. Indeed the priests who accompany Simon in Ben Sira's description are called "sons of Aaron" (50:13, 16). By choosing this priestly theology over other possible approaches and by his general neglect of the Levites entirely, Olyan

---

57. Helge Stadelmann, *Ben Sira als Schriftgelehrter: Eine Untersuchung zum Berufsbild des vor-Makkabäischen Sofer unter Berücksichtigung seines Verhältnisses zu Priester- Propheten- und Weisheitslehrertum* (WUNT 2/6; Tübingen: Mohr Siebeck, 1981).
58. Olyan, "Ben Sira's Relationship," 263.
59. Ibid., 266.
60. Ibid., 267.
61. Skehan and Di Lella, *Wisdom of Ben Sira*, 9.

understands Ben Sira as rejecting the exclusivistic claims of the Zadokites to the high priesthood.[62]

The temple and its cult also find an important place in Sirach. Of course, one would expect such since that is where the priests whom Ben Sira supports serve.[63] God sends Wisdom to dwell in Jerusalem and in the temple in particular (24:10–12). Ben Sira notes specifically that Zerubbabel and Joshua "raised a temple, holy to the Lord, destined for everlasting glory" (49:12). Finally, 34:21–35:13 emphasize the importance of observing the cult properly. Ben Sira here stresses the relation between ethics and proper sacrifice, but not to the diminution of offering the proper sacrifice on the proper occasion.

The analysis of Horsley and Tiller suggests that Ben Sira's strong support of the Jerusalem priesthood (especially as represented in 7:29–31 and his praise of Simon II) and his first-person descriptions of the sage reflect his position in Jerusalemite society. They do not identify Ben Sira as a member of the priestly class, but as a "scribe-sage" who "clearly belonged to what Lenski called the retainer class."[64] They argue that such priestly retainers would have acted as intermediaries between the ruling class, primarily priests in ancient Judea, and the common folk. Clearly, according to Horsley and Tiller, some of the functions of the scribe-sage overlap with those of the priests. These functions, especially teaching the law (a responsibility of Aaron in 45:17, and hence of priests), would have been delegated to the scribe-sage by the priests. "In Ben Sira's Judea, the sages performed the functions that Lenski ascribes to 'the clergy' in societies of limited literacy: officials and diplomats as well as educators."[65]

The scribe-sage class to which Ben Sira belonged would naturally be dependent on the priestly ruling class for its own survival and social status. It would be both economically and politically vulnerable. Such a social position accounts well for Ben Sira's admonitions to his charges about their dealings with the ruling class. But scribes would also have a modicum of independence and retain a certain authority as the guardians of God's divine revelation and wisdom. Their role as teachers and interpreters of God's law might also bring them into conflict with their patrons. Horsley and Tiller argue that "[t]he sages had a clear sense of their own, independent of their patrons, of how the temple-state should operate in accordance with (their interpretation of) the covenantal laws.

---

62. Olyan, "Ben Sira's Relationship," 272, 275–76.
63. For a critical review of those who argue that Ben Sira is not really enamored of the temple cult per se, see Olyan, "Ben Sira's Relationship," 261–62.
64. Horsley and Tiller, "Ben Sira and the Sociology of the Second Temple," 99.
65. Ibid., 100.

Their high-priestly superiors, however, had regular dealings with the Hellenistic imperial officials and were susceptible to greater influence from the wider Hellenistic culture."[66] That independent interpretation of the law and divine wisdom seems to have resulted in the sages appropriating for themselves prophetic characteristics. This is true not only of Ben Sira (24:33; 39:1–11) but of Enoch as well.[67]

Competing Wisdoms and Confrontation

To take these pieces of evidence and to attempt to sketch out where and how Sirach, *1 Enoch,* and *Aramaic Levi* fit together is like trying to do a large jigsaw puzzle with only a few of the pieces. Despite the difficulty, I think that these pieces give some directions in which to work. In short, these works all demonstrate a common interest in calendar, dreams and visions, esoteric knowledge, and all apparently originate in scribal/priestly groups. The collocation of these themes, issues, and apparently similar social groups suggests to me that these texts represent competing groups/communities (and with Sirach and *1 Enoch* competing notions of wisdom) who know about each other, who do not really like each other, and who actively polemicize against each other although not necessarily directly. In what follows, I will set out in more detail what I think this picture looks like.

The fragmentary nature of *Aramaic Levi* necessitates more circumspection than is perhaps the case with *1 Enoch,* but it seems probable that the people who stand behind these works represent priests and scribes who are marginalized and even disenfranchised vis-à-vis the ruling priests in Jerusalem. They maintain that the temple service is defiled because of transgressions of family purity resulting from illegitimate marriages contracted by the Jerusalem priests. Part of their attack on those in power is expressed in *1 En.* 6–16 via the myth of the fallen Watchers and God's condemnation of them.[68] Although they, like Ben Sira, place great importance on understanding and wisdom, their wisdom and understanding are dependant on a different sort of authority, the ascent vision in which God reveals to the seer wisdom's true content. The ascent visions of Enoch and Levi provide the basis for their

---

66. Ibid., 102.

67. Ben Sira sees himself as having divine inspiration. See Horsley and Tiller, "Ben Sira and the Sociology of the Second Temple," 101; Stone, "Ideal Figures," 578. On Enoch as prophet, see Himmelfarb, *Ascent to Heaven,* 25; Nickelsburg, "Enoch, Levi and Peter."

68. I will not talk about the possible geographical location of such groups here. Nickelsburg ("Enoch, Levi and Peter") has suggested a Galilean provenance for them.

criticism of the Jerusalem priesthood, and God gives heavenly secrets, especially the workings of the calendar, directly to Enoch during his time in heaven. I am not arguing that these people do not depend on Torah at all; it is clear that they do.[69] But where their opposition to the Jerusalem priesthood and the concurrent service in the temple or their claims to certain kinds of "scientific" knowledge are concerned, they appeal to a higher authority, direct communication from God. And even though the Astronomical Book, for instance, does not appear to have originated as a polemical document, it seems to be employed polemically in its present context (75:2; 82:4–7). This wisdom is handed down as a sort of counter wisdom to that offered by other wisdom teachers, perhaps like Ben Sira, and, for a work like 1 *Enoch*, this counter wisdom has chronological precedence over the wisdom taught by someone like Ben Sira. Enoch received his revelation long before Moses did his. In the case of 1 *Enoch*, this revealed wisdom is apparently transmitted in written form that is legitimated by a prophetic inspiration. The "account" of Enoch's transmission of this knowledge to Methuselah makes this clear.

> And now, my son Methuselah, all these things I am recounting to you and writing down for you; and I have revealed to you everything, and given you writings of all these things. Keep, my son, Methuselah, the writings of your father's hand, that you may deliver them to the generations of eternity. Wisdom I have given to you and to your children, and to those who will be your children, that they may transmit it to their children, and to generations of generations forever, to whoever is endowed with wisdom; and they shall celebrate all the wise. Wisdom shall slumber, (but) in their mind those who have understanding shall not slumber, but they shall hearken with their ears that they may learn this wisdom, and it shall be better for those that partake of it than rich food. (82:1–3)[70]

Ben Sira, aware of the attacks mounted by these disgruntled priests and scribes, responds to their arguments. His rejection of the solar calendar, his warnings against seeking esoteric knowledge, and his strong defense of the priests who serve in the temple appear intended to counteract the criticisms of these other groups. Ben Sira is a scribe with strong priestly connections who imparts wisdom in *his* school (51:23). But the content of his wisdom is certainly different from that of his opponents. He includes in his book a number of extended poems on wisdom, the most well known being chapter 24. From the very beginning he sets up

---

69. See Nickelsburg, "'Enoch' as Scientist."
70. Translation taken from Black, *Book of Enoch.*

an equation that recurs several times: fear of the Lord is wisdom, and the one who desires wisdom fears the Lord and fulfills or obeys the law (1:26–27). For Ben Sira, true wisdom is to be found in Torah (24:23), and the one who fulfills the law finds wisdom (15:1).[71] But an additional, important idea accompanies the fulfilling of the law and hence the acquisition of wisdom, discipline (Hebrew usually מוסר, Greek, παιδεία). Wisdom is gained through disciplined study. This connection occurs often in Sirach, as for example, in 1:27 "the fear of the Lord is wisdom and discipline." According to 4:17, wisdom teaches "her children," but in the process she "will torment them with her discipline." The fool cannot continue with wisdom because he cannot bear her discipline (6:20–21). As a result, the many cannot acquire wisdom, but only those few who persevere in her training can (6:22). That training is the understanding of the law, the statutes and commandments given by God, which Ben Sira, as one who "will pour out teaching like prophecy" (24:33), understands and dispenses with divine inspiration. Ben Sira expects his students to be anchored thoroughly in the study of the law, the place where true wisdom can be found. His wisdom is to be understood in contrast with that taught by other wisdom teachers. Indeed, Argall's rendering of 3:23b ("for that which is too great for you was shown you"), if we accept it as a legitimate understanding of the text, could provide evidence that some of Ben Sira's students may have reported to him some of the competing wisdom of other teachers.[72]

In all of these works, however, the polemic is mostly indirect. That is, each of them seems to be directed to its own group rather than toward its opponents, and thus, the polemic functions as a way of providing inner group stability and cohesion. The wisdom that Enoch hands on to Methuselah is for those who have not "slumbered," presumably those who have inherited this Enochic revelation. *Aramaic Levi* is not so clear, but the emphasis on Levi as the primary actor could indicate that its intended audience was Levites or other priests disillusioned with the Jerusalem priests. Ben Sira apparently did not intend his teaching for those with whom he had difficulties and differences, but for his own students. This naturally raises the question that if these books were primarily intended for the in-group and not for the outside opponents,

---

71. The connection of law and Wisdom is thoroughgoing in Sirach, and the amount of scholarly literature on this subject is immense. For bibliography on these subjects, see Skehan and Di Lella, *Wisdom of Ben Sira*. For a view different from the usual identification of law and Wisdom in Sirach, see Boccaccini, *Middle Judaism*, 88–98.

72. Argall, 1 Enoch *and Sirach*, 75. His entire study is an extended argument for competing notions of wisdom in Sirach and *1 Enoch*.

then how would their antagonists know about their criticisms? At this point I can only speculate. It certainly is possible that, since these traditions were transmitted in writing, these people read each other's books. Priests (and their scribal retainers?), perhaps more than other Jews, would have need to go to Jerusalem, and these people may well have come into contact or conflict there. Criticism of the Jerusalem priests and/or the temple do not preclude going to the city. Almost certainly disciples could move from one teacher or "school" to another, and in their new situation, students might report the instruction given by their previous teachers.[73] In the face of a lack of substantial clues, the mechanisms of contact between these groups do remain obscure, however. Ben Sira, like his opponents, was trying to inculcate a certain set of cultural and religious values in his pupils/community. To do so he did not have to resort to direct literary confrontation, since that might have drawn unnecessary and, in his mind, unwarranted attention to such teachings. He possesses his own divinely inspired wisdom to pass on to subsequent generations. Those who grew up with warnings to pay no attention to fleeting and false dreams, or with admonitions against prying into the secrets of the universe, were less likely to do such things as adults. After all, Ben Sira was a diligent student of Israel's scriptures and what does Solomon's wisdom say but, "Train up a child in the way he should go, and when he is old he will not depart from it" (Prov 22:6).

Sirach, *1 Enoch, Aramaic Levi*—all three share much in common. In them we find competing notions of scribal wisdom and priestly legitimacy. Their concerns and claims show that in the late third to early second century B.C.E., besides having to confront and to deal with outsiders and foreign cultural influences, different Jewish groups who had varying assessments of the Jerusalem priesthood and temple were actively engaged in an inner-Jewish struggle for power.[74] The clues to the nature of that conflict are extant in works such as *1 Enoch, Aramaic Levi,* and Sirach. The people who composed and used these works had a great deal at stake in the outcome—power and social position and control. In this "trial balloon" of a paper, I have attempted to fill in some of the missing pieces of the puzzle and to suggest that the struggle was not one

---

73. If Josephus (*Life* 2) is to be believed, he spent quite a peripatetic youth moving from one sect to another. Presumably his personal involvement with different groups was one source of his knowledge of their thought. See also, Argall's translation and interpretation of Sir 3:23 (above, this section).

74. Of course, some of the conflict probably had its origins in different assessments of and participation in Hellenistic culture by different groups. This is, indeed, the most usual way of interpreting some of the issues I have treated above. See Horsley and Tiller, "Ben Sira and the Sociology of the Second Temple."

conducted in ignorance of the opposition, but that it was a confrontation engaged in by participants who knew about and were responding specifically to each other.

ISRAEL AT THE MERCY OF DEMONIC POWERS: AN ENOCHIC INTERPRETATION OF POSTEXILIC IMPERIALISM*

Patrick A. Tiller

INTRODUCTION

The second dream vision of book 4 of *1 Enoch* (the Animal Apocalypse) is an allegorical review of human history from Adam until the ideal future age.[1] The period from the Babylonian exile until the predicted end of the present age (apparently meant to arrive during the Maccabean revolt) is included in what we may call the allegory of the seventy shepherds. This section is an interpretation of the history of exilic and postexilic Judea (the author is not so interested in the rest of Israel) under various foreign dominions. In the process of interpreting history (including the author's present), the text promotes an ideology that competes with the dominant ideology of the temple-state and with that of the Seleucid Empire. The interpretation of the allegory is relatively straightforward because the writer has embedded in the text two sets of indicators of meaning. The first is the allegorical component. The second is the reuse of older textual (and oral, though these are harder to discover) traditions. We will first consider the external referent of the shepherds by investigating the internal workings of the allegory. We will then consider the antecedent traditions that seem to be incorporated within the story. Finally we will consider whether we can use these two sets of interpretive clues to understand the implied interpretation of Judean history. According to this Dream Vision, imperial rule over Judea

---

* This is a revised version of a paper that was presented at the 1999 meeting of the Society of Biblical Literature. It is published here in basically its original form in order to provide the reader the state of the discussion at that time. No attempt has been made to update it in the light of later discussions or publications.

1. On the characterization of the Animal Apocalypse as an allegory and the implications of that characterization for understanding it, see Patrick A. Tiller, *A Commentary on the Animal Apocalypse of* 1 *Enoch* (SBLEJL 4; Atlanta: Scholars Press, 1993), 21–28.

is nothing less than a replay of the descent of the Watchers with disastrous results for the whole earth.

THE ALLEGORY

The controlling allegory of the Animal Apocalypse is Israel as God's sheep. Before Jacob, the Sethite progenitors up to and including Isaac are symbolized as white cattle; the non-Sethites (particularly the Cainites) are symbolized as black cattle. The descent of the Watchers is represented by stars that fall to earth and cohabit with cows. The cows, in turn, give birth to elephants, camels, and asses (the giants). Seven beings "like white men" who represent the archangels carry out temporary judgment against the stars and the unnatural offspring of the stars and cows. After the flood in which most of the cattle are drowned, the surviving cattle again give birth to strange offspring. From one white bull comes a white sheep, which represents Jacob. From other cattle come various unclean, predatory, or scavenging animals and birds that threaten the sheep. These animals represent gentile contemporaries of Israel. The account contains an allegorical representation of the construction of the Jerusalem temple under Solomon and the subsequent abandonment of the temple, first by Israel and then by God. After the destruction of the first temple, the sheep-master (God) delivers the sheep (Israel) into the care of a series of seventy shepherds (angels) who are to tend the sheep and kill some of them (89:59-60). One may perhaps presume that this slaughter is not for food or sacrifice, but that it is a punishment for the sheep's abandonment of their house (Jerusalem) in 89:51. The sheep-master also appoints an auditor to count and record the actual number of sheep killed, because he knows that the shepherds will prove too zealous in their killing. This situation lasts until the final battle, which immediately precedes the final judgment, when the shepherds are punished for exceeding the sheep owner's command. The final age is marked by a transformation into white cattle of all who survive the judgment, a change that represents a restoration to adamic conditions.

The most important clue to the meaning and significance of the seventy shepherds is the internal function of the sign/symbol as indicated by its relationship to other signs within the allegory. In 1912, when R. H. Charles published his masterful commentary on *1 Enoch*, the identity of the shepherds was still "the most vexed question in Enoch."[2] Until

---

2. *The Book of Enoch or* 1 Enoch (2nd ed.; Oxford: Clarendon, 1912; repr., Mokelumne Hill, Calif.: Health Research, 1964), 200.

the beginning of this century, most attempts to explain the seventy shepherds assumed the identification of angels either with a series of seventy foreign or native kings or of seventy years.[3] By the time of Charles, however, there was a new consensus that the shepherds represent angels.[4] Charles's argument was based first on the fact that all other human figures in the allegory represent either angels or God. Second, these shepherds also correspond to the stars that fell to earth among the cattle earlier in the allegory because they are judged together in the final judgment. According to 90:24–25, the stars were the first to be judged, and they were put into a deep, fiery abyss. The shepherds were judged next and placed into the same abyss. The blinded sheep are the only other group to be judged, and they were placed in a separate abyss. Apparently there is one abyss for angels and one for humans. Since the shepherds and stars share a common judgment, they must both be angels. Third, the shepherds are associated with the angelic auditor who observed and recorded their deeds, since he is called "another" (89:61) one of them. That the auditor is an angel is clear from the fact that in 90:14, 17, and 22 he is said to be one of the seven white men of 87:2 who represent the seven archangels otherwise mentioned in 1 En. 20 and 81:5. If the angelic auditor can be called "another" of them, then they must also be angels.

The implications of these identifications go far beyond the simple determination of referents external to the allegory. They extend to the signification of the allegory itself. The close association of the stars and shepherds in the final judgment is an indication that both groups play a similar role in the allegory. Not only do the seventy shepherds and the "fallen" stars share a common judgment; they also face common foes in both the determination and the execution of that judgment. According to 88:1–3, three of seven individuals "like white men" (87:2) cast the stars into deep crevices in the earth to await judgment and send the elephants, camels, and asses into battle against each other. These events correspond quite transparently to the story as recorded in the Book of the Watchers (1 En. 1–36). In 1 En. 10:4–5 Raphael binds Asael and casts him into a

---

3. For a review of previous attempts at a solution, see Oscar Gebhardt, "Die 70 Hirten des Buches Henoch und ihre Deutungen mit besonderer Rücksicht auf die Barkochba-Hypothese," *Archiv für wissenschaftliche Erforschung des Alten Testaments* 2 (1872): 163–246. Gebhardt concluded that a solution was impossible without further textual evidence.

4. This was first suggested by J. Chr. K. von Hofmann, *Der Schriftbefwies: Ein theologischer Versuch* (2nd ed.; 2 vols.; Nördlingen: Beck, 1857–1860), 1:422. It was argued most carefully by Charles, *Book of Enoch*, 200, and François Martin, *Le livre d'Hénoch* (Documents pour l'étude de la Bible: Les Apocryphes de l'Ancien Testament; Paris: Letouzey et Ané, 1906), 217–18. See also Tiller, *Commentary*, 51–53.

rocky hole in the desert. In 10:9 God tells Gabriel to send the children of the Watchers into battle against each other. The judgment of the shepherds is closely modeled after that of the Watchers.

According to 90:22, one of the same seven white men was the auditor who was to count and record the number of sheep killed by the shepherds. Apparently God's economy is not completely different from that of the foreign empires with their official recorders and census takers. The function of this auditor was to guard against fraud. And, in fact, it was this auditor's report on the fraudulent (excessive) killing that instigated the sheep-master's violent intervention in 90:17. Again this series of events corresponds precisely to the account of the Book of the Watchers. According to *1 En.* 9, it was the archangels Michael, Sariel, Raphael, and Gabriel who noticed the violence brought about on earth by the giants and brought the Watchers' sins to God's attention. It was the angelic auditor who notified God of the excesses of the seventy shepherds and brought them bound to judgment before the sheep-master (90:22). Thus, the angelic auditor is explicitly identified as one of the archangels, and like the archangels of the Enochic tale of the Watchers (*1 En.* 9–10), it was his task to report to God on the misdeeds of errant angelic beings and then to bind them for judgment.

Thus the allegory of the seventy shepherds is designed with reference to the older myth of the Watchers. The larger allegory has within it the story of the descent and judgment of the Watchers who are allegorized as stars that fell from the sky and cohabited with cows. This, however, is not the end of the story. Like so much in apocalyptic literature, older myths become the key to understanding the present. The past is not only the past; it is also the model for understanding the present.

Interpretation of Antecedent Traditions

The Animal Apocalypse of *1 Enoch* clearly incorporates several earlier biblical and Enochic texts, though never by quotation and only rarely by the use of common words or phrases. As an allegory, it points to earlier texts by relating in allegorical form the events and situations described by these texts or by adapting the symbols of earlier texts. The allegorist has brought together a rich array of sacred Judean traditions to provide an allegorical retelling of Israel's history, which implicitly interprets the present condition of Judea as exile under the deficient care of delinquent angels. He combines the notions of seventy years (or periods) of exile, oppression by angelic beings, and divine punishment for sins to create a tapestry of traditions, woven together into a critique of the current Judean political establishment with its cooperation with foreign rulers.[5] Our task at this point is to define these traditions more precisely and to show how the writer of the Animal Apocalypse has interpreted these traditions and how they contribute to the development of the allegory.

Some of the traditions are too general to be traced to a particular text. The basic symbol of the Animal Apocalypse is that of shepherd/sheep. This is an ancient and common metaphor that is by no means limited to Israelite traditions. Paul Porter has conducted a careful investigation into the semantic domain of the animal metaphors of Dan 7–8, in the course of which he considers also the Animal Apocalypse.[6] He has shown that the metaphor of the shepherd is used not only in the Hebrew Bible but also throughout ancient Mesopotamia. It is used of the relationships between political and divine rulers and their subjects. As in the Animal Apocalypse, these rulers are sometimes criticized as wicked shepherds. Ezekiel 34 and Zech 11 provide excellent parallels and may even have influenced the shaping of the Enochic allegory. Ezekiel 34 contains a condemnation of the "shepherds of Israel" who failed to care for the sheep and a promise that God himself would gather the flock and personally "shepherd the flock with justice" (Ezek 34:16b). In Zech 11 the Lord declares that he will raise up a foolish shepherd who will eat the sheep instead of caring for the flock and then will be punished. In the Animal Apocalypse, as in Ezek 34, the shepherds are explicitly contrasted with the sheep-master. This provides a poignant reminder of the relationship that the Judeans' ancestors had once had with God, but which has been replaced by a destructive relationship with angelic substitutes. Plainly pseudo-Enoch sees his present time as one in which Judah is in some sense estranged from God as punishment for past failures. The real rulers of Judah, however, are not the local chieftains, priests, or elders (however one imagines the precise political organization of Judea at this time) or even the foreign representatives of the imperial court, but angelic beings whom God has commissioned to take his place in the care of his people. This assessment turns the imperial claims to divine descent on its head. Yes, there is something other-worldly behind the empire, but it is demonic, not divine.

---

5. The use of multiple traditions is also recognized by Carol Newsom ("Enoch 83–90: The Historical Résumé as Biblical Exegesis" [Unpublished seminar paper, Harvard University, 1975], 24–27). Although she understands the seventy shepherds primarily as "a systematic exegesis of Jeremiah 25" (25), she acknowledges that "the influence of Ez. 34 and Zech. 11 must not be discounted" (27), and she accepts the possibility of the multivalence of the number seven.

6. Paul A. Porter, *Metaphors and Monsters: A Literary-Critical Study of Daniel 7 and 8* (ConBOT 20; Uppsala: Gleerup, 1983).

Another of the more general traditions presupposed in the allegory is what David Bryan calls the "kosher mentality."[7] Using an anthropological approach, Bryan argues that the strict and consistent use of only non-kosher animals for all but the patriarchs before Jacob and Israel is a reflection of the idea of clean and unclean. The unclean animals evoke a sense of chaos, while the conflict between the unclean animals and the sheep evokes the perennial conflict between order and chaos. The whole history of Israel, then, is symbolically represented as an ongoing battle between the forces of chaos and the created order. Final restoration of all humans in the form of white cattle represents the final victory of order. The references during the period of the seventy shepherds to blind sheep in 89:74 and blind and deaf sheep in 90:7 bring the notion of anomaly even into the sheepfold. The author's present is one in which order is threatened by chaos. The problem, however, is not simply that life is chaotic. The real opponents are the angelic caretakers of Israel and the gentile nations that oppress the Judean people. The symbolism marks the foreign rulers as disordered, unnatural, and unclean-unfit for mixing with the Judean faithful. With this symbolic expression the allegory denies the claim that imperial rule is somehow benevolent; whatever benefactions it may bestow bring only disorder and chaos.

One somewhat more specific tradition that is presupposed in the allegory of the seventy shepherds is the interpretation of Jeremiah's predicted seventy years of exile, popularized by Daniel's seventy weeks of years (Dan 9:24–27).[8] Jeremiah 25 and the allegory of the shepherds share a common condemnation of Israel, a common punishment, a common time period, a common judgment upon the instruments of Israel's punishment (including the metaphorical sword in both cases), and significantly a common use of the shepherd symbol. Jeremiah is somewhat unique in the Hebrew Bible in that it uses "shepherd" to symbolize foreign rulers. The reinterpretation of Jeremiah's prophecy in the Animal Apocalypse is a clear sign of the rejection of the legitimacy of the contemporary temple-state. The seventy years of exile are not over. There is still a shepherd or two to go before the end.

---

7. David Bryan, *Cosmos, Chaos and the Kosher Mentality* (JSPSup 12; Sheffield: Sheffield Academic Press, 1995).

8. Carol Newsom ("Enoch 83–90," 24–27) and James VanderKam (*Enoch and the Growth of an Apocalyptic Tradition* [CBQMS 16; Washington, D.C.: Catholic Biblical Association of America, 1984], 165–67) derive most of the imagery from Jer 25 with a great deal of justification. The following discussion is heavily dependent upon their analyses. The richness of the traditions brought together here, however, seems to require a broader search. One of the traditions that scholars frequently appeal to in studies of this passage is the idea that each of the seventy nations of the world has an angel assigned to it. This seems unlikely. See Tiller, *Commentary*, 53.

What is by far the most important of Israel's sacred traditions for our text, however, is often overlooked in contemporary scholarship. That tradition is the specifically Enochic tradition of the Watchers. Over a century before the composition of the Animal Apocalypse, another Enochic sage composed the Book of the Watchers by bringing together two separate myths of divine or angelic descent. George Nickelsburg has already proposed that the Book of the Watchers was written near the end of the fourth century in response to the wars of the diadochi, "a time of bitter military conflict by a foreign power, and among foreign powers—conflict so fierce, incessant, and widespread as to lead our author to claim that the existence of the human race was threatened."[9]

In the Book of the Watchers, contemporary events are compared to the ancient myth of the Watchers. The reader understands that like the ancient giants, Alexander's heirs are consuming and destroying the earth. The Animal Apocalypse goes even further. The allegory of the shepherds declares that the current status of Judea under the domination of foreign powers is the direct result of disobedience to God. The ruin experienced by the faithful of Israel is being orchestrated by disobedient angels. The only proper response to such a situation is resistance. Those who cooperate are blind, apostate sheep. The foreign emperor falsely claims legitimacy on the grounds that the conqueror has the right to rule and that he can trace his ancestry to the gods. The true basis for his rule over Israel is that God has abandoned his people into the care of false shepherds. They are illegitimate rulers, whose place has been secured by disobedient angels. Fellow Judeans are called to spiritual vision and military resistance. Those who cooperate with such rule are cooperating with angelic rebellion against God as serious as the rebellion of the ancient Watchers whose sin brought about the flood. The story carefully identifies the shepherds with the stars in order to demonstrate that the ancient ante-diluvian events described in the Book of the Watchers correspond to the contemporary situation, and not only by analogy.

It is certainly possible to understand each of these adaptations of tradition in purely theological terms, but that is probably not the most satisfactory frame of reference. The one common thread that unifies all of the variegated elements of this allegorical tapestry is that each implies a critique of the current political regime. This critique is certainly aimed at the high priestly regimes of Jason and Menelaus. It would be a mistake, however, to assume that the critique is aimed solely at these "helleniz-

---

9. George W. E. Nickelsburg, "Apocalyptic and Myth in 1 Enoch 6–11," *JBL* 96 (1977): 391.

ing" high priests. The Animal Apocalypse itself is very clear about the scope of the critique. It goes back at least as far as the founding of the Second Temple, the sacrifices of which were "polluted" and "not pure" (89:73). If we follow the allegory, we are brought all the way back to the beginning of the exile when the seventy shepherds were first commissioned by the sheep owner.

Conclusions

In an Enochic book that plainly refers to the famous Enochic story of the fall of the Watchers, the intertextual clues lead one inexorably to understand the seventy shepherds in terms of a kind of *Urzeit-Endzeit* scheme. The horrors that were inflicted upon the earth by the Watchers and their giant offspring are now (at the time of composition) being experienced by the writer and his fellow Judeans. The writer acknowledges that God is rightfully punishing his people for past wrongs, but the rightful limits to that punishment have been violated. Like the shepherds of Ezek 34:8 or Zech 11, the foreign nations and the domestic political leaders have made fodder of the Judeans. Instead of feeding and caring for the flock, while killing a predetermined number, the angelic guardians have slaughtered the Judeans and allowed other nations to oppress them as well. Political rule has become a tool of supernatural oppression and exploitation.

It has become clear that the allegory is a political allegory. The story begins with cattle, which represent people differentiated only as Sethite and non-Sethite. It then moves to the birth of all kinds of animals, each of which represents a nation or ethnic group, and in the end returns to the transformation of all animals back into white cattle. This must be understood as the ultimate elimination of the separate identities of different nations. Even Israel does not survive as Israel, but it persists in the form of the original patriarchs of the Sethite line. There is no restored temple in the rebuilt Jerusalem. In this connection the use of Enoch as the hero begins to make sense. He represents the pious individual, not of Israel, but of generic humanity. The Animal Apocalypse is an extremely radical document. It criticizes not only enemy regimes, but even the propriety of any political, ethnically based regime. Granted, the history of Israel under Solomon was good, but it quickly degenerated when the people neglected God and his messengers.

In the light of these conclusions, we must reconsider how we understand the alignment of the Enochic writer in the context of Judean politics of the second century B.C.E. It is impossible to imagine that any of the claimants to power during the postexilic period could have won the loyalty of the allegorist. The usual view that this text supports Judas

Maccabeus and other rebels against Seleucid rule and against the Seleucid-appointed high priests is undoubtedly correct. The Maccabees are supported, however, not as national rulers, but as rebels. The text is not an antihellenizing document, supporting traditional high-priestly rule against political and religious change. The basis of all postexilic rule in Jerusalem has been cooperation with and subordination to the reigning foreign empire. Onias, no less than Tobias, could only rule with the approval of the Greek king. The Second Temple was understood to be impure, and its offerings were polluted.

In the books of Enoch, then, we have evidence of a group of pious sages who trace their existence back at least to the beginning of Seleucid rule.[10] They were as opposed to the so-called theocratic rule of Simon and Onias as to the so-called hellenizing rule of Jason, Menelaus, and the compromise high priest, Alcimus. Religious opposition did not begin with Jason, but at the latest with the transfer of power from Ptolemaic Egypt to Seleucid Syria. If one assumes that the Book of the Watchers was motivated by a similar sentiment, then the opposition began with the conquest of Alexander the Great or shortly thereafter. The simplistic view that the political scene of early second century Judea was characterized by competition between faithful Torah observance against innovative Hellenism is false. The books of Enoch display a third, more radical way.[11] The goal of history is an end of all political divisions. No longer will one people rule another. Rather the God of Israel will personally rule a unified people without the need for temple or king.

This study has further implications for how we interpret historical apocalypses. The historical review of the Animal Apocalypse has a real, interpretive function. It is not there simply to confirm the predictive powers of the claimed author, in this case, Enoch. At least for this apocalypse, the purpose of the historical review is to interpret history and to create a meaningful vision of reality. This reality includes the day-to-day realities of everyday experience, but it encompasses also the larger realities where God and the angels act and compete for power over this world.

---

10. The statement in *1 En.* 90:6, that "lambs were born from those white sheep, and they began to open their eyes and to see and to cry out to the sheep," seems to indicate that the writer identifies with the reform group symbolized by the lambs. See Tiller, *Commentary*, 102–16, 350–51.

11. See Randal A. Argall, *1 Enoch and Sirach: A Comparative Literary and Conceptual Analysis of the Themes of Revelation, Creation and Judgment* (SBLEJL 8; Atlanta: Scholars Press, 1995), 249–55, for speculation about one of the contexts in which Enochic opposition may have been expressed and nurtured.

THE POLITICS OF CULTURAL PRODUCTION IN SECOND TEMPLE JUDEA: HISTORICAL CONTEXT AND POLITICAL-RELIGIOUS RELATIONS OF THE SCRIBES WHO PRODUCED 1 ENOCH, SIRACH, AND DANIEL

Richard A. Horsley

Literature arises from and addresses historical circumstances. This common assumption in interpretation of modern literature is also valid for ancient literature. We interpreters of ancient Judean texts, however, have virtually no sources other than the extant texts to use to reconstruct their historical circumstances. And we have no training in how we might go about relating ancient Judean wisdom and apocalyptic literature to its historical social circumstances. The venturesome few who have inquired after who may have written apocalyptic literature such as Daniel and *1 Enoch* have spoken in terms of "movements," "groups," and "communities." Those concepts remain vague, with little or no indication of how they may have been comprised. Even vaguer is the "Judaism" to which they belonged. This modern construct tends to collapse the social structure, homogenize historically distinctive documents, and abstract a religion from the concrete dynamics of history. Those scholars who have investigated the occasion that evoked the writing of apocalyptic literature such as Daniel and *1 Enoch* often focus on a "crisis." This also is conceived in vague, often essentialist terms, such as the incursion of "Hellenism."[1]

An obvious step toward understanding who produced wisdom and apocalyptic literature and in what historical circumstances would be to investigate the structure and historical dynamics of Second Temple Judean society. Our analysis, however, can move beyond the abstract, synthetic "structural-functionalist" model of "advanced agrarian soci-

---

1. This study builds on previous examinations of the "social world" of wisdom and apocalyptic literature such as George Nickelsburg, "The Epistle of Enoch and the Qumran Literature," *JJS* 33 (1982): 333–48, and Philip R. Davies, "The Social World of Apocalyptic Writings," in *The World of Ancient Israel: Social, Anthropological, and Political Perspectives* (ed. R. E. Clements; Cambridge: Cambridge University Press, 1989), 251–71.

ety" derived from Gerhard Lenski that has been applied to monarchic Israel and late Second Temple Judea in recent decades, in at least two related respects.

First, Lenski's scheme, tends to obscure the basic division in ancient Near Eastern societies in an overly generalized scheme of horizontal stratification that attempts to accommodate evidence from feudal European and ancient Greek and Roman societies as well. In any preindustrial society where it takes ten people cultivating the soil to raise sufficient food to feed every noncultivator, there are basically two classes, the peasants who raise the crops and the rulers who take a percentage as tribute, taxes, or tithes. Moreover, if artisans, traders, and scribes cater to and are dependent on the ruling aristocracy, they do not constitute a "middle class." In ancient societies such as Second Temple Judea, moreover, there was no "structural differentiation" between religious and political-economic institutions. Rather than apply Lenski's complex model, therefore, we might do better to examine closely the considerable information provided by extant texts, particularly the book of Sirach. Once we recognize that literacy was limited basically to circles of scribes, the question of who produced (and used) sapiential and apocalyptic literature becomes a simple one, at least at a superficial level: the scribes. But that does not tell us much about wisdom and apocalyptic literature, since all texts were produced by scribes. Further analysis of Sirach, Daniel, and *1 Enoch* may help us understand the particular historical social circumstances, social interests, and effective social roles of those who produced these few extant examples of "sapiential" and "apocalyptic" literature in Second Temple Judea.

Second, the elaborate horizontal stratification in Lenski's model of agrarian societies may obscure the vertical divisions, the competing factions among the aristocracy. Such divisions obviously have implications for the military and scribal "retainers" who work for and are economically dependent upon the rulers. Just such vertical divisions among ruling aristocracies and their retainers, moreover, can result in historical conflicts and changes. The conflicts within the Jerusalem high-priestly aristocracy that led up to the Maccabean revolt and the split in the Hasmonean dynasty that continued after the initial Roman takeover of Judea offer two prime examples.

Just those examples, however, illustrate why we cannot consider Second Temple Judea in isolation. Judea was subject to a succession of empires. The imperial situation could decisively influence social-political dynamics in the temple-state. We can be more systematic in inquiring after the interaction between imperial relations and the struggle among factions for power in Judea itself. Even if some think that the basic structure was consistent through the Second Temple period, the Jerusalem high priesthood was contested, and its power waxed and waned in close connection with the imperial power relations.

Is it possible that the key to precisely who produced Sirach, Daniel, and the Enoch literature at certain historical junctures lies precisely in the relations between the imperial regime(s) and factions among the ruling aristocracy competing for power in Judea? Both Ben Sira's wisdom book and the Enochic and Danielic apocalyptic literature were produced by and for circles of scribes/sages. Which types of wisdom from the traditional scribal repertoire they utilized, however, may have depended on their respective stance toward the temple-state and its incumbents and toward the imperial regime. Although we are hampered by a paucity of documentary evidence for the Second-Temple period, we can nevertheless attempt to be specific in dealing with what we do have, with regard to document, place, social location, power relations, and social interests.

Ben Sira's Judea

Ben Sira's reflections on the role of the scribe/sage in relation to others (38:24–39:11) indicates that scribes/sages stand somewhere above the plowmen and artisans, on whose labor Jerusalem depends, yet subordinate and in service to the rulers.[2] Because he focuses on the city in which he himself surely lives (since he serves among rulers), he does not dwell long on the peasants "who handle the plow" and "drive oxen." He refers elsewhere to the "poor," "hungry," "needy," and "desperate," and he recites proverbial observations that "the poor are the feeding grounds for the rich" (13:19). He exhorts his fellow scribes to "stretch out your hand to the poor" with alms or loans and to rescue them from the worst predatory practices of the powerful (e.g., 29:1–20; 3:30–4:10). Peasants in such agrarian societies were almost always economically marginal, since their "surplus product" was expropriated by the rulers in the form of tithes and taxes and were thus vulnerable to falling into debt. Those who "rely on their hands," with whom Ben Sira is more directly acquainted, include artisans, smiths, and potters. The operations of the city depend on such folks, but they are of low status, basically serving the needs of the leisured who desire "signets of seals," patterned iron work, and glazed pottery (38:27–34).

---

2. The following depends on Richard Horsley and Patrick Tiller, "Ben Sira and the Sociology of the Second Temple," in *Second Temple Studies III: Studies in Politics, Class and Material Culture* (ed. P. R. Davies and J. M. Halligan; JSOTSup 340; Sheffield: Sheffield Academic Press, 2002), 74–107. My understanding of Sirach and *1 Enoch* is heavily indebted to Patrick Tiller.

Ben Sira deploys two juxtaposed sets of terms in reference to the ruling aristocracy of Judea. First, for rulers or officers of state he uses, interchangeably and apparently synonymously, several traditional Hebrew terms, especially *sr, mwšl,* and *šwpt*. They are usually used in construct (hence direct relationship) with "city," "people," and "assembly." Only *šwpt* is consistently translated in the Greek as κριτής. The other terms are rendered with a variety of overlapping Greek words: *sr* with μέγισταν, δυνάστες, and ἡγούμενος; and *mwšl* with ἡγούμενος, δυνάστες, κριτής, and κύριος. These terms are often used in parallel constructions, such that "chiefs of the people" and "rulers of the assembly" refer to the same figures and "the company of elders" and the "assembly of elders" refer to the same council of state (30:27 [33:19]; 39:4; 6:34; 7:14; 10:1–2, 3). These parallel and overlapping terms thus refer apparently to the ruling aristocracy, some of whom may have had particular responsibilities and many of whom probably had similar or overlapping functions.

Second, Ben Sira pictures the high priest in the temple surrounded by "a garland of brothers, . . . the sons of Aaron in their splendor holding out the Lord's offerings" (50:5–13). Since the (high) priests are the people's representatives to God, the people bring their offerings to the priests. Since the (high) priests are God's representatives to the people, established by everlasting covenant, so that they are given "authority and statutes and judgments" over the people, the latter are to "honor the priest" with their tithes and offerings as the way of "fearing the Lord" (7:29–31; 35:1–12; 45:20–22; 50:1–21). The "religious" relationships focused in the high priesthood in the Temple do not just legitimate but also constitute the political-economic structure of Judea. The people rendered up firstfruits, guilt offerings, choice shoulder cuts from animal sacrifices, and so forth to "honor the priest," because in the "everlasting covenant" by which the priesthood was bestowed upon Aaron, these had been allotted to him and his descendants as their heritage (7:29–31; 45:6–7, 15–16, 20–21).

These two sets of terms—rulers and officials on one hand and (high) priests on the other—refer not to separate "lay" and "priestly" aristocracies, but to one aristocracy that held political-economic-religious power. In actual practice it was not quite this simple, for not all of the wealthy and powerful families in Judea were priestly, as we shall see below. But for the most part, the "chiefs" and "rulers" and "judges" were apparently the "high-priestly" aristocracy among "the sons of Aaron." Some individual high priests, but by no means all, may have held particular offices (for instance, the "temple captain" known from the first century C.E.). The most prominent of Ben Sira's "chiefs," "rulers," and "judges," paralleled by "the sons of Aaron" around the high priest, therefore, appear to have constituted the γερουσία mentioned in both Antiochus

III's proclamation of restoration of the temple government in Jerusalem (Josephus, *Ant.* 12.142) and in the letter of the Hasmonean high priest Jonathan to Sparta a half-century later (1 Macc 12:6). Of course, the incumbents could change, as happened more than once in the generation immediately following Ben Sira and illustrated in the upstart Hasmonean high priesthood.

The principal role of the wise scribes, as Ben Sira mentions repeatedly, was to serve the "chiefs" and "rulers" (8:8). In his sustained discussion in 38:24–39:11, he takes pride in the scribes as advisers of ruling councils and members of courts who understand decisions and expound judgments, even as members of embassies to foreign lands (6:34, 7:14, 15:5, 21:17, 34:12). Since they do not "rely on their [own] hands" for sustenance, however, this means that they must be economically as well as politically dependent on patronage from the chiefs and rulers among whom they serve. This explains Ben Sira's admonition to bow low to the rulers and his extensive "professional" advice on deferential behavior and caution when dealing with the powerful (4:7; 8:1–2, 14; 13:9–11; 31:12–24).

Ben Sira and his scribal colleagues, however, have a clear sense of their own authority independent of the rulers among whom they serve. They view their own authority as grounded in "the wisdom of all the ancients" and their faithful "study of the law of the Most High" (38:34–39:1). They thus derive their authority, independent of the priestly aristocracy, from God and the revered cultural tradition (wisdom, prophecies, etc.). This suggests also that they had their own sense of how the temple-state should operate; that is, it should operate according to the sacred cultural tradition of which they were the professional guardians and interpreters. Despite their dependence on and vulnerability to their patrons among the ruling aristocracy, therefore, scribes such as Ben Sira could both criticize the aristocracy and take measures to mitigate its oppression of the poor (4:8–10; 13:3–4, 18–19; 29:8–9; 34:21–27).

Ben Sira's representation of Judean society thus reveals two major divisions that held potential for serious conflict, the peasants and the wealthy and powerful rulers:

> What peace is there between the rich and the poor?
> Wild asses in the wilderness are the prey of lions;
> Likewise the poor are feeding ground for the rich. (13:18–19)

The less ominous division lay between the rulers and the scribes/sages. As professional cultivators and guardians of Judean cultural tradition, the latter developed both a basis of their own authority independent of the rulers and criteria for the appropriate levels of exploitation of the peasantry and also codes for conducting the religious-economic relations of the temple-state. Therein lay considerable potential for serious conflict between rulers and their scribal retainers. Ben Sira's representation of Judean society and particularly of the rulers/high priesthood effectively obscures the way in which such potential for conflict might develop into actual conflict. Ben Sira treats Judea and the high priesthood as if it were an independent temple-state. In the grand hymn of praise of the ancestors at the end of the book, he grounds the authority of the high priesthood in the sacred tradition of Israel/Judea. We who have access to other literature, such as Ezra and Nehemiah and the books of the Maccabees, know better.

The Interaction of Local and Imperial Struggles for Power

Judea centered on the Second Temple was a creature of empire, initially of Persian imperial policy. The temple-state instituted in Jerusalem served several purposes simultaneously: a renewal of an indigenous people's service of their own deity, a local ruling class who owed their position to the imperial regime, and a financial administration for the imperial regime's revenues, the point of establishing an empire in the first place.[3] Besides restoring temples and their administrations throughout the empire, the Persian regime "promoted the codification and implementation of local traditional law as an instrument of the *pax Persica* throughout the empire."[4]

Far from the temple-state having been stabilized under a strong monarchical high priesthood (or a "diarchy" of high priest and local prince), there appears to have been a struggle for power in Yehud. Multiple conflicts emerged during the first generations of the restoration, as is evident in Haggai, Malachi, and Isaiah 56–66. By the mid-fifth century the various "big-men" in the region vying for influence included Jerusalem aristocrats aided by the Samaritan dynast Sanballat, a sheik in the Transjordan named Tobiah, who had ties of intermarriage and mutual interest with certain (priestly?) nobles in Yehud, and an Arab magnate named Geshem (Neh 2:9; 6; 13:28–30; etc.). As indicated in his memoir, the Per-

---

3. Jon Berquist, *Judaism in Persia's Shadow: A Social and Historical Approach* (Minneapolis: Fortress, 1995), 52–57, 63; Joachim Schaper, "The Jerusalem Temple as an Instrument of the Achaemenid Fiscal Administration," *VT* 45 (1995): 528–39.

4. Joseph Blenkinsopp, "The Mission of Udjahorresnet and Those of Ezra and Nehemiah," *JBL* 106 (1987): 409–21; idem, "Temple and Society in Achaemenid Judah," in *Second Temple Studies I: Persian Period* (ed. P. R. Davies; JSOTSup 117; Sheffield: Sheffield Academic Press, 1991), 24.

sian court sent Nehemiah as governor, escorted by mounted Persian troops, to reimpose order in Yehud and to regularize revenues for both the imperial regime and the Temple (Neh 5:4, 14; 10:26–29, 40).[5] Ezra's mission, also sponsored by the Persian imperial regime, aimed to consolidate the position of the previously exiled elite in Yehud. The people of the returned (*golah*) community were defined as the only true *Yehudim*, which either excluded the indigenous "people of the land" or subordinated them to the temple-state as lesser-status people.[6] Moreover, he promulgated only one form of Yehud's legal legacy, derived from the exiled and now restored Jerusalem ruling class as "the law of your God and the law of the king," effectively subordinating or excluding rival legal traditions and their proponents (Ezra 7:25–26). It is unlikely, however, that such subordination meant destruction. Rival factions, including priestly groups who were losing ground to the dominant elite, while leaving few traces of their interests and viewpoints, would likely have cultivated alternative Judean traditions.

Under the successor empires formed in the wake of Alexander's conquests, political affairs became even more complicated and contested in the Jerusalem temple-state. The principal complicating factor was the rivalry between the Ptolemaic empire in Egypt and the Seleucid empire to the east for control of Palestine. The Ptolemies prevailed in a series of wars throughout the third century before finally yielding control to the Seleucids right around 200 B.C.E. Thus, the dominant faction in Jerusalem and its rivals for power in Jerusalem and Judea alike had to deal regularly with competing imperial maneuvers and the potential for a sudden change in imperial overlord. And of course local power-brokers could seize any advantage as a factor in the imperial struggle for power.

Several sources suggest that the high priesthood had developed into a position of considerable prominence by the end of that period and the beginning of Ptolemaic rule. Hecataeus of Abdera, a Greek historian at the court of Ptolemy I, views Jerusalem as a temple-state headed by a revered high priest who has "authority over the people" (τοῦ πλήθους προστάσια) and who acts as "a messenger of God's commandments" and "announces what is ordained in assemblies" (in Diodorus Siculus, 40.3). Pseudo-Aristeas (96–98), an Alexandrian Jew probably writing in the second half of the second century B.C.E., offers a glowing description of the awesome appearance of the high priest in the

---

5. Norman Gottwald, *The Politics of Ancient Israel* (Louisville: Westminster John Knox, 2000), 110.

6. Blenkinsopp, "Temple and Society," 44–47; see also Richard A. Horsley, "Empire, Temple, and Community—But No Bourgeoisie," in Davies, *Second Temple Studies* I, 163–74.

midst of the other priests offering sacrifices in the temple. Pseudo-Hecataeus, a mid-second century B.C.E. source cited by Josephus (*C. Ap.* 1.187–189), mentions "Ezechias, a high priest of the Judeans, highly esteemed by his countrymen, intellectual, and an able speaker and unsurpassed as a man of business." This Ezechias, moreover, may be the same person as "Hezekiah the governor" inscribed on silver coins minted in Jerusalem dating to the late fourth century or early third century, which are also inscribed in paleo-Hebrew script (not Aramaic, as under the Persians). The combination of these sources suggests that Judea was indeed headed by a high priest under early Ptolemaic rule and that, if the high priest were also the "governor," he exercised considerable power in the temple-state of Jerusalem/Judea.[7] As evident in subsequent developments, however, other factions and power-brokers had not disappeared from the scene in Palestine and became significant factors in the struggles for power. The considerable prominence and power of the high priest in Judah, apparent at the outset of this period, changed under later Ptolemaic rule.

Since Tcherikover's critical reconstructions on the basis of the Zenon papyri and other sources, it has seemed clear that the hinterland of Palestine was dominated by a number of local figures who controlled certain limited territories and their populations.[8] Contrary to the policy in Egypt itself, the Ptolemaic regime entrusted military commands to certain local "big-men," such as "Tobias," apparently the descendent of Nehemiah's opponent east of the Jordan. Similarly, the Ptolemaic administrators farmed tax collection to some of these local power-holders.[9] This ad hoc administration of Syria-Palestine had far-reaching effects in the history of the Jerusalem temple-state, as it set up the struggle between and among the Tobiads and Oniads for control of Judah. Our source is the "Tobiah romance" that Josephus draws upon in his account (*Ant.* 12.157–236). Insofar as we place credence in this "romance" as a historical source, the following would be a compelling reconstruction.[10]

In the early third century, the high priests in Jerusalem held the tax contract from and/or paid the tribute to the Ptolemies. At one point the high priest Onias II stopped paying the sum of twenty talents a year, "on

---

7. Mark R. Kurtz, "The Social Construction of Judea in the Greek Period," *Society of Biblical Literature 1999 Seminar Papers* (2 vols.; SBLSP 38; Atlanta: Scholars Press, 1999), 1:58.

8. Victor Tcherikover, "Palestine under the Ptolemies," *Mizraim* 4/5 (1937): 9–90.

9. Roger Bagnall, *The Administration of the Ptolemaic Possessions outside Egypt* (Columbia Studies in the Classical Tradition 4; Leiden: Brill, 1976).

10. Dov Gera, *Judea and Mediterranean Politics, 219 to 161 B.C.E.* (Brill's Series in Jewish Studies 8; Leiden: Brill, 1998), see especially 36–57 in ch. 2, "The Tobiads: Fiction and History."

account of which [Onias] had received authority over the people (τοῦ λαοῦ προστασίαν) and obtained the high-priestly office (τῆς ἀρχιερατικῆς)" (*Ant.* 12.158–161). The Tobiad Joseph, who had married into the Oniad family, took the occasion to outbid Onias for the tax-contract, indeed maneuvered himself into the position of chief tax-collector for the entire province of Syria and Phoenicia (*Ant.* 12.184). It would fit the ad hoc Ptolemaic administration of tax revenues in Syria-Palestine to separate the role of tax-collector for an area from that of the ostensible local ruler, particularly if it involved a higher bid! It is possible, of course, that Joseph also took over the high priesthood, as implied in the Tobiad chronicle that reports that Onias was eager to give up the high priesthood (*Ant.* 12.163).

The deal that Joseph arranged with the Ptolemaic regime had serious and far-reaching implications for power relations within Judea, particularly insofar as the latter were closely interrelated with the shifting relations between the Ptolemaic regime and (ambitious, rival) local Palestinian power-holders. First (even if we do not find it credible that he took over the high priesthood from Onias II), in obtaining the tax-contract for Palestine, Joseph gained considerable power over affairs in Judea. Second, even if he retained the high priesthood, Onias's position was relatively weakened within Judea insofar as he no longer controlled the revenue for the imperial regime and was no longer the only or even the principal power-broker mediating between the imperial administration and the Jerusalem temple-state and people of Judea. Third, insofar as tax-farmers generally managed a considerable margin for themselves, Joseph like other magnates in Palestine under the Ptolemies, considerably enhanced his own wealth, which in turn led to a certain acculturation of local power-brokers who developed a taste for luxurious "Greek" lifestyles, and shifted to the use of the Greek language for administration and correspondence.[11] Fourth, insofar as the Tobiad family had long been maneuvering for power and position in Jerusalem, including intermarriage with the high-priestly family, Joseph could consolidate and build up an already existing network in the Jerusalem aristocracy.

It should thus not be surprising that as the imperial rivalry for control of Palestine came to a head toward the turn of the century, rival Oniad and Tobiad (and perhaps other) factions were struggling for power in Jerusalem and were prepared to seek advantages from the rival imperial regimes. Those rival factions, moreover, continued to

---

11. Seth Schwartz, "On the Autonomy of Judaea in the Fourth and Third Centuries B.C.E.," *JJS* 45 (1994): 165–66.

struggle for power under the Seleucids. At the very beginning of Seleucid control over Judea the high priesthood itself may have been at its nadir during the Hellenistic period. Antiochus III's charter for the temple-state (Josephus, *Ant.* 12.138–44) does not mention the high priest, but only the γερουσία, the priests, the scribes of the temple, and the temple singers. Insofar as γερουσία is a Greek term that corresponds to the Hebrew *sarim,* Antiochus's decree seems to confirm the priestly aristocracy as the "rulers" in the temple-state. (Its inclusion of the priests and scribes in positions of privilege also confirms the conclusion above that scribes such as Ben Sira worked for factions within the aristocracy.) But how do we understand the failure of Antiochus's decree to mention the "high priest"? Was he simply included in the γερουσία? Had the transition in imperial power simply caught Simon II off in exile as a result of the turmoil?

We must give credence to Ben Sira's celebration of Simon II for heading the repair of the temple and fortifications of Jerusalem (50:1–4), taking advantage of the funding provided in accordance with Antiochus III's charter. The limited, largely indirect evidence could be read either of two ways. On the one hand, that Simon II's successor Onias III could not exert sufficient power to prevent Simon the temple captain (προστάτης τοῦ ἱεροῦ) from appealing (successfully) over his head to the imperial governor Apollonius (Josephus, *Ant.* 12.224) suggests that the high priesthood remained fairly weak. On the other hand, particularly if the Seleucid regime treated the Jerusalem high priest as the local head of state and guarantor of its own revenues, the high priesthood would have been accordingly strengthened in its position in Jerusalem and Judea.[12] We thus have two possibilities for the power of the high priesthood precisely as the struggle among aristocratic factions came to a head in Jerusalem in the 170s, either of which could have led to factional struggle within the aristocracy. If it was relatively weak, the incumbent would have been more easily challenged by a Menelaus or a Jason and their supporters. If, on the other hand, the high priesthood had been strengthened by Seleucid imperial practice, it would have appeared as the greater prize for an ambitious usurper and/or a faction eager to seize power. The interest in "Westernization" in aristocratic circles that was gaining strength during these decades, of course, further complicated and exacerbated the power struggle in Jerusalem.

This general situation of rival factions in the aristocracy in interaction with the imperial regime (and its rival) sets up a number of complications

---

12. Patrick Tiller, "Sirach and the Politics of Seleucid Judea" (paper presented at the Annual Meeting of the New England Region of the SBL, Boston, 2002), 3–5.

for the relations between the wise/scribes and the rulers among whom they served. Rival scribal circles would understandably have been attached to rival aristocratic factions and critical of the opposing aristocratic faction. Given the scribes' sense of authority independent of their ruler-patrons, it is conceivable that a scribal circle could have taken a course independent of one or more dominant aristocratic factions, despite their economic dependency and political vulnerability. We appear to have examples of just such relationships between scribal circles and rival factions among the priestly aristocracy in Ben Sira and the scribes who produced the Enoch and Daniel literature.

Sirach

The book of Sirach is apparently a representative collection of materials cultivated and expounded by a Jerusalem scribe/sage and received by his audience toward the beginning of the second century B.C.E. The stated purpose of the grandson's translation (Prologue), that the book serve as an instructional and inspirational book for "those who love learning," is probably a good indication of the function of the materials included in Ben Sira's book. The audience for these instructions, admonitions, meditations, and hymns must have been others of the literate elite, that is, scribes-in-training. Since much of the content concerns the relationship between the addressees and the poor (peasants and urban workers) on the one side and the aristocratic rulers on the other, neither of them can be the audience. That much of Sirach is apparently instruction for scribes-in-training is a key difference from apocalyptic literature such as 1 *Enoch*. The latter also contains "sapiential" sayings and exhortation, but deploys them for purposes well beyond the instructional.

A further, more detailed review of the contents of the book may yield a more precise sense of who, in terms of social role and relations, comprise the producer and the audience of the wisdom of Ben Sira. Unlike Prov 10–29, Sirach is not simply a collection of proverbs and other sapiential sayings. The instructional meditations on wisdom offer reflections on wisdom's origin, character, and benefits (1:1–20, 25–27; 4:11–19; 6:18–31; 14:20–27; 15:1–10; 19:20–24). While "the fear of the Lord" is the beginning of wisdom and keeping the law is an important aspect of wisdom, only the laudatory hymn in Sir 24 explicitly identifies Wisdom with the law. Meditations on the order of (God's) creation draw implications for human sin and mortality; and heavenly observation (astronomical wisdom) grounds the lunar calendar, versus the solar, as authoritative (16:26–30; 17:1–24; 18:1–14; 39:16–35; 42:15–25; 43:1–33). On the other hand, Ben Sira rejects the validity of dreams and omens, that is, "mantic wisdom" (34:1–8) and simply forbids investigation of things that are "hidden," "too marvelous," or "too difficult" (speculation about the creation and/or the future? 3:21–24; see also 42:16, 19; 43:32–33).[13] Here are major factors by which Ben Sira differs from other scribes/sages such as those who produced 1 Enoch and Daniel.

As Ben Sira declares in the well-known and widely quoted discourse on the scribe/sage (38:24–39:11), the acquisition of wisdom depends on having the leisure necessary for study and reflection. In that connection, he lists as the sources for his wisdom, "the law of the Most High," "the wisdom of all the ancients," and "prophecies." That the wise scribe "preserves the sayings of the famous, penetrates the subtleties of parables, and seeks out the hidden meanings of proverbs ... and the obscurities of parables," that is, mainly traditional proverbial wisdom, is evident mainly in his poetic instructional discourses and admonitions. In the poetic meditations and reflections on creation is perhaps where he "pours forth words of wisdom of his own" (39:6).

Ben Sira occasionally refers to his activity as a teacher ("for all who seek instruction," 33:18; see also 24:32–33; 37:23), although the "house of instruction" in the epilogue may be metaphorical and does not attest a "school" in the modern sense. Far more prominent, in passing references laced throughout the materials, as well as in the discourse on the role of the scribe/sage, is the public political role he plays and reputation he builds. The scribes/sages that Ben Sira has in mind "are sought out for the council of the people, (and) attain eminence in the public assembly" (38:32–33). Indeed, besides serving on courts, the sage "serves among the great and appears before rulers" (38:33, 39:4). At the local level of the Jerusalem temple-state, Ben Sira's and his protégés' role was the same as that of their counterparts in the Egyptian, Babylonian, and Persian imperial courts, as advisers to the rulers. Perhaps we should take seriously the passing references to the scribe's travels in foreign lands, which may well have been connected with negotiations between imperial and local regimes (39:4; 34:9–13). Most impressive is Ben Sira's virtual obsession with the sage's role in the public assembly and the fame he achieves, which appears almost to be the purpose of learning wisdom (e.g., 6:33–34; 15:5–6; 21:17; 33:19; 37:22–24; 38:32–33; 39:10). And his proud references to serving among rulers takes on added credibility from his periodic admonitions to his protégés about watching their words and their step in dealing with their superiors (4:7; 8:1–2, 8–9; 11:1; 13:9; 23:14; 33:16–19; see also 4:15).

---

13. Benjamin G. Wright III, "'Fear the Lord and Honor the Priest': Ben Sira as Defender of the Jerusalem Priesthood," in *The Book of Ben Sira in Modern Research* (ed. P. C. Beentjes; BZAW 255; Berlin: de Gruyter, 1997), 208–14.

Ben Sira's satisfaction in serving among rulers and giving wise counsel in the public assembly fits handily with his admonition in 7:29–31 to "honor the priest and give him his portion," indeed to render up the offerings and sacrifices as commanded, presumably in the law, which he elaborates in 35:1–13.[14] Besides being required to fulfil the commandment of God, this payment of tithes, offerings, and sacrifices is parallel and virtually identical to "fearing the Lord with all your soul" (7:29).[15] Of course, it should not be surprising that scribes such as Ben Sira would encourage payment of offerings and sacrifices to God/the priest. They themselves must have been economically dependent on the priestly aristocracy, directly or indirectly. As noted, Ben Sira makes much of the fact that the scribe, unlike peasants and urban artisans, did not do manual labor, hence had leisure to study and appear in the assembly.

The most remarkable evidence of Ben Sira's and his colleagues' serving among rulers, of course, is the long paean of praise of the ancestral rulers and leaders. Some recent interpreters have found here a rehearsal of Israel's "epic history" and a sapiential development of a historical perspective on life.[16] That may be somewhat of an over-interpretation. This is hardly an epic history of Israel. It is too selective for that. And it focuses only on the leaders, indeed emphasizes rulers and ruling institutions. Tradition is being used here for contemporary purposes. The praise of ancestral heroes in Sir 44–50 has also often been taken somewhat at face value as a representation of the commonly accepted view of the high priesthood and its rootage in Israelite tradition. Now that a "hermeneutics of suspicion" is more commonly exercised, however, we can recognize that this hymn expresses not an already accepted view, but rather how its composers and users want the high priesthood to be understood. The lengthy hymn of praise in Sir 44–50 serves primarily to articulate a foundational ideology for the high priesthood in general and the incumbency of Simon II in particular, with whose praise the hymn concludes.

A closer examination of this long paean of praise, however, indicates that Ben Sira is not just a supporter of the "establishment" in general, but an advocate of a particular understanding of the high priesthood and a particular faction of priests. Not Moses or David, but Aaron and Phinehas are the principal ancestral rulers praised, the recipients of the eternal

---

14. See further Wright, "Fear the Lord and Honor the Priest."
15. See further Saul M. Olyan, "Ben Sira's Relationship to the Priesthood," *HTR* 80 (1987): 261–86.
16. Burton L. Mack, *Wisdom and Hebrew Epic: Ben Sira's Hymn in Praise of the Fathers* (Chicago: University of Chicago Press, 1985).

covenant of the priesthood. Moses plays an almost subordinate instrumental role, and David and his successors, while glorious in some respects, are hopelessly flawed and disqualified. Striking is not just the absence of any mention of the Levites but even more the absence of references to Zadok or of Simon II as a Zadokite, since the Zadokites had been the reigning priestly faction in the Judean temple-state. While honoring the Zadokite Simon II with the highest praise, Ben Sira is apparently pressing the claims of all Aaronid priests, not just Zadokites (and excluding the Levites), to the (high) priesthood, its authority, and its perks.[17] It is unclear whether the emphasis on the Aaronid priesthood along with a failure to mention Zadokites (when Simon II was a Zadokite) represents merely an attempt to include all Aaronid priests in the governing (high) priesthood, or also an implicit criticism of the exclusive claim of the Zadokites. In any case, it would have been an opportune time to press for a wider base for the priesthood. The Zadokite high priesthood of the incumbent Oniad family had been seriously weakened, first by the rise of the Tobiads to power in Judea and Palestine and then by the maneuvering and civil struggles entailed in the shift from the Ptolemaic to the Seleucid imperial regime.

For all his orientation to and cavorting with the high-and-mighty ruling aristocracy, however, Ben Sira insists that his fellow scribes/sages retain their mediating role in Judean society. Besides making a sharp criticism of sacrificing ill-gotten goods and an appeal to God on behalf of the humble, Ben Sira repeatedly exhorted his hearers to give special attention to the poor. Not only are they to give alms to the destitute and lend to a needy neighbor, but they should even use their positions to defend and "rescue the oppressed from the oppressor" (4:1–10; 7:32; 29:1–13; 42:2). Some of these exhortations explicitly identify this with observance of the law. Although most of Ben Sira's references to the law refer to studying and meditating on it, its observance as the beginning of wisdom was apparently more than mere sapiential piety. Modern scholars often emphasize that the scribes were the primary interpreters and teachers of the law. Yet references to teaching the law and actual citations of particular laws are rare in Ben Sira. The focus is rather observing the law, particularly in connection with mitigating the worst predatory practices of the powerful.

In sum, Ben Sira works creatively with traditional proverbial wisdom, cultivates astronomical lore and reflection on the created order, and composes meditations on the origin and character of wisdom, while

---

17. See further Olyan, "Ben Sira's Relationship to the Priesthood."

rejecting dreams and omens. He does all this primarily for the purpose of participating in the assembly and serving the incumbent high-priestly rulers of the Judean temple-state—and of course to maintain the respectable lifestyle appropriate to such an honorable position. Indeed, Wisdom, identical with the law, has made its home in Jerusalem where it endorses and supports the high priesthood and its current incumbents. Wisdom literature, at least in the principal example we have from mid-Second Temple history, is cultivated by scribes who support and are dependent on the currently established priestly rulers of the temple-state.

1 ENOCH

The four earlier sections of *1 Enoch* should be dealt with in their apparent respective historical contexts. The Book of Watchers (*1 En.* 1–36) and the Astronomical Book (*1 En.* 72–82) can both be dated to the third century B.C.E. The Epistle of Enoch, including the Apocalypse of Weeks (*1 En.* 92–105), seems to fit sometime prior to the Maccabean revolt. The Dream Visions, including the Animal Apocalypse (*1 En.* 83–90), dates after the beginning of the Maccabean revolt. That these various sections are "books" indicates that scribes produced them. In two sections of *1 Enoch*, moreover, the authors explicitly identify Enoch, the ostensible writer of the books, as a "scribe of righteousness," "scribe of truth" (*1 En.* 12:4, 15:1), and "(skilled) scribe" (92:1) and otherwise portray Enoch as writing and reading petitions, heavenly tablets, and books (13:3–7; 81:1–2; 82:1).

The content of Enoch's books or the revelations he obtains in visions can be generally characterized as wisdom. While Enoch's wisdom includes sapiential sayings like those in Sirach, most of his wisdom is of the kind that Ben Sira includes only cautiously, rejects as invalid, or forbids as dangerous. While Ben Sira includes some astronomical wisdom about the sun, moon, and stars, a point of which is to authorize a lunar calendar that controls the festivals (all important in a temple-state economy), Enoch has a whole book of astronomy which includes detailed treatment of a 364-day solar calendar, and passages that criticize those who do not follow it.[18] Similarly, much of the content of the Book of the Watchers is knowledge of the topography and patterns in the heavens. Enoch acquires much of his wisdom from dreams and visions (1:2; 13:8; 14:2, 8, 18–23; 19:3), which Ben Sira rejects. And two sections of *1 Enoch* include reviews of history focused on Israel/Judah, including a projection of fantastic events of judgment and restoration of the creation, which

---

18. Wright, "Fear the Lord and Honor the Priest," 204–8.

Ben Sira simply forbids as "too marvelous" and "too difficult" (although Sir 36 contains a psalmic appeal to God for the restoration of Israel, in very restrained language). All of the kinds of knowledge cultivated in the various books of Enoch, whether cultivated or rejected by Ben Sira, were standard in the repertoire of ancient Near Eastern scribes/sages working at various royal courts, whether in Egypt, Babylon, Ugarit, or later in Alexandria (Manetho) and Seleucid Babylon (Berossus).

Whereas Ben Sira tacitly accepts the imperial situation,[19] the producers of early Enoch literature view imperial rule as violent and oppressive. The overall purpose of the Book of the Watchers must be to explain the sinfulness and evil of imperial rule as caught up in the higher-level invasion of history by rebellious divine beings who generated the race of "giants," and to reassure "the chosen righteous ones" that God was still ultimately in control and would judge and punish the Watchers. If we were to read the Book of the Watchers as parallel in perspective to Dan 7, then the Hellenistic empires may have been particularly problematic and provocative (and Antiochus Epiphanes was not yet on the scene!). The Animal Apocalypse in *1 En.* 85–90 brings forward a far more comprehensive condemnation of rulers, domestic as well as imperial. All alien enemies and rulers are portrayed as vicious predatory birds or beasts of prey and both domestic rulers and "shepherds" of imperial nations are condemned for oppression and violence against the "sheep" with whose care they are charged and their judgment anticipated (89:59–90:27).

In contrast to Ben Sira, who spouts enthusiastic praise for the temple-state and its high-priestly incumbent, the two reviews of history included in *1 Enoch* both criticize the "Second Temple." In both, the symbol of "house (of the kingdom)" refers to the people (i.e., the kingdom of Israel/Judah and/or of God), or possibly to the ruling house in (or city of) Jerusalem as itself a synonym for the people, which will be restored in the glorious fulfillment of history (93:7, 8, 13; 89:39, 50, 66). The Apocalypse of Weeks, however, while mentioning the earlier tabernacle, pointedly omits any reference to the temple or its rebuilding, referring only to "a perverse generation" whose "deeds will be perverse" following the Babylonian conquest (93:9). The Animal Apocalypse does refer to the temple as a "tower built upon that house, ... [with] a full table" (89:50, 67). The rebuilt "tower," however, had "polluted" bread and the eyes of the sheep were blind, like those of their shepherds (89:73–74). In the eschatological fulfillment the Lord of the sheep is to bring a new house, but without a tower. Both of these "apocalypses" thus appear to

---

19. While Sir 36 expresses a hope for eventual restoration, Ben Sira praises Simon for rebuilding the temple, for which Antiochus III had recently provided imperial funding.

articulate not simply an alienation from particular incumbent high priests, but a virtual rejection of the postexilic temple and temple-state.

The Epistle is the only section of *1 Enoch* that provides enough information for us to discern more precisely what the relation may be between the scribes/sages who produced this literature and the high-priestly rulers on the one hand and the Judean people on the other. Through much of this literature, the principal division lies between "the (chosen) righteous" and the "sinners." Some have thought that the former must be a designation for the community or movement responsible for producing the literature. Closer analysis of the woes against the sinners in the Epistle, however, suggests that the relationship was more complex.[20] The authors of the woes have left a few "tracks" by which we may identify them vis-à-vis other actors in the drama. In the judgment, "the wise among men" who "will see the truth" appear to play a distinctive role among the righteous, holy, and pious who are to be vindicated by the Most High (100:5; similarly, "Enoch's" role is to provide wisdom to the chosen ones, in 5:8; 82:2–3). The righteous are a larger group among whom "the wise" have special knowledge and a special responsibility. The wealthy sinners, moreover, are addressed as "fools" precisely because they "do not listen to the wise," that is, their scribal opponents (98:9). In the Epistle, therefore, one scribe ("Enoch") appears to be addressing other (a circle of) scribes/wise, pronouncing woes of destruction in the divine judgment against the wealthy and powerful for oppressing the righteous/pious, who will finally be vindicated.

When we look for the reason that the wealthy are condemned we find the same portrayal of the wealthy and powerful oppressing the poor that Ben Sira articulated, with the difference that what are occasional observations in Sirach are the basis for an almost obsessive and uncompromising condemnation in the final divine judgment in the Epistle of Enoch. As in Ben Sira's discourses and almost any ancient agrarian society, the wealthy were those who held positions of political or political-religious power—which means the priestly aristocracy in ancient Judea. So in the "woes" pronounced by Enoch, the "mighty" gain great riches and an easy and luxurious lifestyle by exploiting the righteous (96:8; 97:2; 96:5–6 alluding to Amos 6:4–6). The lament of the lowly that "we were not masters of our labor ... and our enemies were our masters ... and to our enemies we bowed our necks" (103:3, 9, 11–12;

---

20. See the fuller analysis in Richard A. Horsley, "Social Relations and Social Conflict in the *Epistle of Enoch*," in *For a Later Generation: The Transformation of Tradition in Israel, Early Judaism, and Early Christianity* (ed. R. A. Argall et al.; Harrisburg, Pa.: Trinity Press International, 2000), esp. 111–15.

98:4) suggests that, against the covenantal norms of Judean society, the poor had been subjected to forced labor or debt-slavery by the wealthy. In this connection the repeated charge that the wealthy sinners "build their houses with sin" and "build their houses not with their own labors, (but) make the whole house of the stones and bricks of sin" (94:6–7; 99:13) similarly suggests some sort of servitude to which the poor have been subjected, probably because of their debts (Neh 5:1–12). That the rich sinners "lie awake to devise evil" (100:8), like the indictment in Mic 2:1–2, suggests that the wealthy are designing schemes to take over the labor or even the land of the poor, again probably on the pretext of their indebtedness. Such actions were a direct violation of covenantal commandments: they "plunder and sin and steal and get wealth" (102:9). Indeed, these series of woes frequently allude to the violation of Mosaic covenantal principles (97:6; 98:4, 7–8, 12; 99:2). The complaint that the wealthy "weigh out injustice" (95:6) resembles the prophet Amos's charge (2:6) that "they sell the righteous for silver," referring to their manipulation of the weights in measuring out grain or oil that the peasants were borrowing. And the charge that the rich and powerful "acquire gold and silver in judgment/unjustly" (94:7; 97:8, 10), like the classical prophets' similar indictments of the ruling elite, alludes to their manipulation of the courts to gain power over the powerless.

The scribes who produced 1 *Enoch*, like Ben Sira, saw themselves as socially and culturally superior to the poor Judean peasants. Whereas Ben Sira observed the exploitation of the poor by the rich in a relatively detached manner, however, the wise who produced the Enoch literature called down divine judgment against the wealthy, even saw themselves involved in retribution. They stood vehemently opposed to the wealthy, that is the aristocracy of the Judean temple-state, perhaps already in the late third century, but certainly in the early second century when the Epistle was produced.

Yet, however they may have imagined themselves in the special role of illuminating the chosen righteous at the judgment, they give no indication that they were engaged in forming a resistance movement, either among themselves or in the wider society. One has the sense that those who produced Enoch literature were simply a circle of scribes/sages who had for some time sharply opposed the incumbent high-priestly faction and perhaps the high priesthood as constituted by the prevailing imperial relations, however they might be manipulated. Nor do we find in Enoch literature implications of a scribal (priestly) movement that hopes to replace the incumbent rulers of the temple-state, as did the Qumran community later in the second century. In the latest of the early Enoch books, the Dream Visions, the Animal Apocalypse suggests that those behind that review of history did indeed form, or more likely joined, a resistance movement against Seleucid persecution (the lambs who began to open their eyes and resist before the ram, Judah the Maccabee, sprang into action, 90:6–14). In any case, this circle of scribes projected a future age of righteousness without sin, without oppression by the wealthy and powerful, without a temple and its high-priestly rulers.

In sum, the producers of the early Enoch literature were apparently a circle of scribes opposed to the temple-state as well as hostile to its incumbent rulers. Their "apocalyptic" literature was designed to explain how foreign and domestic oppression had become so severe in their society and to reassure themselves at least that God was still in control and would eventually execute judgment of the rulers and restoration of the people.

Daniel

As we have emerged from the previous dichotomization of "wisdom" and "apocalyptic," it has been noted that the portrayal of Daniel and his colleagues in the tales of Dan 1–6 closely resembles Ben Sira's reflection on the scribe/sage in Sir 39:1–11.[21] Well-born, these Judean lads are "versed in every branch of wisdom, endowed with knowledge and insight," and faithful to the Law, even active in prayer (Dan 1:4, 8–16,17, 20). They are trained in the language and literature of the Chaldeans (1:4, 17), just as Ben Sira's sage cultivates the wisdom of the (Judean) ancients. In the later visions (9:2), Daniel is "concerned with prophecies" as well, also like Ben Sira's scribe. Daniel "explains riddles and solves problems" (Dan 5:12), just as his counterpart penetrates subtleties, hidden meanings, and obscurities (Sir 39:2–3). Neither are portrayed much as teachers, certainly not as teachers and interpreters of the law. But Daniel and his "wise" colleagues serve at court, particularly in assemblies, just as Ben Sira's wise scribe serves among rulers and public assemblies. Daniel (1:5) states explicitly what Ben Sira indicates only indirectly, that such sages are economically supported by and dependent on the rulers they serve.

What differentiates Daniel and apparently the *maskilim* who recycled the tales and produced the visions is that their principal wisdom lies in dreams, visions, and their interpretation, which Ben Sira rejects (Dan 2; 7; 8; 10–12). With regard to "mantic" wisdom of dreams and their interpretation, Daniel resembles, while excelling, all the wise men of Babylon, all the "magicians, enchanters, sorcerers, and Chaldeans" (1:17, 20; 2:2, 10,

---

21. See Lawrence M. Wills, *The Jew in the Court of the Foreign King: Ancient Jewish Court Legends* (HDR 26; Minneapolis: Fortress, 1990).

12, 19, 27, 28; 4:6, 9; 5:7, 8, 11–12). A further difference from Ben Sira emerges in the visions and interpretations of Dan 7–12. While the *maskilim* still function as interpreters of dream visions in/for a ruler's court, it is now (as in *1 Enoch*) the divine ruler's court rather than a human ruler's court (as with Ben Sira). While still political in their functions, Daniel and the *maskilim* have moved up several notches in the scope of political jurisdiction with which their ruler-patron deals—from temple-state, past imperial, to the transimperial and transhistorical (Dan 2; 7; 10–12). Far from being uninterested in politics—in their obsession with purity and communion with the angels[22]—Daniel and the *maskilim* are focused on politics. Indeed, their wisdom (visions and interpretations) and the insights and activities entailed are completely focused on imperial politics and its implications for political-religious life in Judea.

Similar to both Sirach and *1 Enoch*, both the tales and the visions-and-interpretations in Daniel present a completely scribal ethos. Throughout the book everything significant is accomplished by writing: the young men receive literary training in chapter 1, a hand writes on the wall in chapter 5, Daniel writes down the dream and books are opened for judgment in chapter 7, prophetic books are interpreted in chapter 9, and the deliverance of people is written in the book and Daniel seals the book in chapter 12. The scribal ethos, moreover, is relatively self-centered, as communication within the scribal circle that produced the literature. Daniel's book is not for public consumption. The mysterious divine plan (*raz/mystērion*) revealed to Daniel and the *maskilim* in chapter 2 is only ostensibly communicated to the king. Although the tales in Dan 1–6 probably circulated orally prior to their inclusion in the book of Daniel, the visions in particular and the book as a whole were written for a literate audience, perhaps the *maskilim* themselves plus others (ordinary Judeans could not have read the written visions-plus-interpretation). And only the *maskilim* understood what was happening. They would "give understanding to many," but in oral communication and especially by their martyrdom in resistance to Antiochus Epiphanes's imperial program for Judea. Part of the secret wisdom to which they have become privy is that "the people (more generally) shall be delivered" (12:1), that "the people of the holy ones of the Most High" would be restored to (God's) sovereignty (7:27). When it comes to heroics of resistance and vindication for the martyrs, however, they are focused on themselves, on their own heroic role. The heroic *maskilim* who fall will be refined, purified, and cleansed, but apparently only as their own reward, since

---

22. See John J. Collins, "Daniel and His Social World," *Int* 39 (1985): 131–43, esp. 140.

nothing is said of benefit for or effect on the people generally (11:35). Half of the book focuses narrowly on the role of the faithful Judean sage at the foreign imperial court who refuses to compromise his loyalty to his God—and is vindicated.[23] And at the end of the book, the glorious vindication of shining like the stars was for "those who are wise ... and lead many to righteousness" (12:3). Daniel was produced by and for the circle of the *maskilim*.

While the *maskilim* receive revelation that the people generally will be restored and "shall give understanding to many," it would be going beyond anything suggested in the text to say that they are teachers or leaders of the people.[24] While the Epistle of Enoch envisages a future revelatory role for the wise vis-à-vis the righteous, no current or future leadership role appears for the *maskilim* in Daniel. They are almost exclusively the recipients of revelation, interpretation of the dream visions about what is happening under the suddenly super-oppressive imperial regime of Antiochus Epiphanes.

The *maskilim* who produced Daniel, however, have themselves moved into staunch resistance to the oppressive imperial forces. They, and apparently others "who are loyal to their God," are taking "action," albeit nonviolent, and to that extent they could be said to have formed, at least temporarily, a resistance movement. If the "little help" is indeed a reference to Judah the Maccabee, then it seems likely that "those who are loyal" may well be the more popular resistance movement already underway parallel but not directly linked with their own, apparently more individualized, nonviolent resistance. Their resistance to the imperial forces, moreover, means that they also stood in opposition to the incumbent high-priestly regime that Antiochus was supporting in its "reform," headed by the usurper Menelaus, who had replaced the previous usurper Jason. The *maskilim* who produced Daniel, however, appear to have opposed more than just the usurping incumbent high priesthood. They seem to be at least de-emphasizing the very institution of the temple and high priesthood. While the reviews of Antiochus's oppression and persecution view the actions against the temple building and the "burnt offering" as horrendous actions (8:13; 9:27; 11:31), the images of restoration do not include a temple or priestly leadership. The focus is on "the people (of the holy ones of the Most High)" (7:27; 12:1). Of course this might be due to how discredited the high priesthood had become in the previous decade of its purchase and (what they would have considered disgraceful) transformation in the "reform." Yet it

---

23. Wills, *Jew in the Court*, 151–52.
24. See Collins, "Daniel and His Social World," 132, 139.

seems evident from chapter 9 that they did not consider that the rebuilding of the temple after the exile had ended or overcome "the desolation of Jerusalem" (contrast 2 Chr 36:20–21, Zech 1:12–17). In the tales of Dan 1–6 the temple is conspicuous by its absence—after it was rebuilt precisely during the ostensible career of Daniel in the Babylonian court. At the end of the visions, finally, the sacrifices in the temple are apparently superfluous for the *maskilim,* since their own suffering and martyrdom have become the means of purification, at least for themselves.[25] We must conclude that the *maskilim* who produced Daniel were decisively alienated from the ruling high-priestly incumbents.

Conclusion

In and behind the book of Sirach, early Enoch literature, and the book of Daniel, we can discern different circles of scribes/sages. Each circle concentrated on developing particular aspects of the traditional ancient Near Eastern and Judahite scribal repertoire that ranges from proverbial and theological wisdom to astronomical and mantic wisdom.

What most differentiates these early Judean examples of apocalyptic literature and their scribal authors from Sirach is their extensive cultivation of visions and/or vision-interpretation, which Ben Sira simply rejected, and their inquiry into hidden prospects for the future, which Ben Sira forbade. A more subtle but nevertheless significant difference was their perspective on and review of Israelite and international history focused on the people as a whole, in contrast to Ben Sira's praise of ancestral leaders, particularly rulers.

What seems determinative for which aspects of the traditional repertoire a scribal circle cultivated and developed was its relation to the rival factions, particularly the dominant faction, in the struggle for power in the Jerusalem temple-state and the corresponding imperial power relations. Ben Sira and his protégés served among the incumbent priestly rulers in Jerusalem, while the Enochic and Danielic sages opposed them.

Ben Sira represents a nonpriestly scribal faction that supported the Oniad incumbents and propagandized for the authority of the Aaronids. He and his circle of scribes had adjusted to imperial rule and found an honorable life in service of the high priesthood sponsored by the imperial regime. Ben Sira lauded the Oniad priesthood as thoroughly grounded in a selectively chosen and characterized ancient Israelite lineage of royal

---

25. Philip R. Davies, "Reading Daniel Sociologically," in *The Book of Daniel in the Light of New Findings* (ed. A. S. van der Woude; BETL 106; Leuven: Leuven University Press/Peeters, 1993), 360.

and high-priestly rulers—simply ignoring the concrete imperial arrangement by which the temple-state and its incumbent rulers were established. Much of his wisdom accordingly consists of professional advice on serving among the high-priestly rulers, while also mitigating the worst effects of their (ab)use of power.

The wise scribes of Enoch literature and *maskilim* of Daniel, on the other hand, employed visions both to explain the debilitating circumstances of imperial rule and to imagine a judgment of the imperial rulers and restoration of the people's independence. Apparently well prior to a situation of persecution that followed upon the "Hellenizing" crisis of 175 B.C.E., the earliest Enoch literature sought to explain, indict, and anticipate the divine judgment of the imperial kings and by implication the high-priestly regime sponsored by them. The Apocalypse of Weeks questioned the validity of the temple-state, labeling the postexilic arrangement as "perverse." The Animal Apocalypse and the visions of Daniel reject not only the incumbent high priesthood, but they also appear to have questioned the very institution of the temple-state/high priesthood. The *maskilim* who produced Daniel, however, belonged to a different scribal circle from the one that produced Enoch literature. Both of these circles were apparently alienated from the Jerusalem high-priestly court. Of course, they may well also have been the clients of high-priestly patrons who had (temporarily) lost out in the struggle for power. But even if that were the case, their fantasies for the future restoration of the people and fulfillment of history tellingly lacked (or excluded) a temple and high priesthood.

Finally, yet another scribal circle (either priestly or allied with a faction of priests) appears to have preceded and then joined or helped form the Qumran community. The Qumran scribes/sages cultivated all of the various aspects of the conventional sapiential repertoire, including mantic and astronomical wisdom, and added to its scribal repertoire an intensive cultivation of legal traditions and concrete application of prophetic books to their own situation. The proto-Qumran scribes shared Ben Sira's positive attitude toward the temple-state and high priesthood as institutions. But like the Enoch scribes, they sharply opposed the incumbent high priesthood, the Hasmoneans. There must have been four different scribal circles in Jerusalem, therefore, in the early second century. But that should not be surprising given the different and shifting factions in the aristocracy maneuvering for position in the unstable imperial situation during these decades.

PART 3:
WISDOM AND APOCALYPTICISM IN EARLY CHRISTIANITY

"WHO IS WISE AND UNDERSTANDING AMONG YOU?" (JAMES 3:13): AN ANALYSIS OF WISDOM, ESCHATOLOGY, AND APOCALYPTICISM IN THE LETTER OF JAMES*

Patrick J. Hartin

Much recent research has focused on wisdom, eschatology, and apocalypticism, especially as they relate to genre.[1] These examinations have argued that such terms cannot be used to differentiate neatly defined types of discourse as was once thought. Instead, their interrelationship has been the subject of much investigation.[2] This present effort focuses on the Letter of James and examines its relationship to wisdom, eschatology, and apocalyptic. Can this letter shed any light upon the relationships between these different types of discourse? Reference will also be made to the Epistle of Enoch (*1 En.* 92–105) as a help to identify these relationships.

1. TRADITIONS REFLECTED IN THE LETTER OF JAMES

1.1. WISDOM TRADITIONS REFLECTED IN THE TEXT

Israelite wisdom traditions give evidence of a twofold area of concern, namely, the presentation of ethical admonitions and advice as well as an attempt to reflect upon the nature of wisdom. This wisdom tradition shows that Israel is a daughter of the Middle East, for it binds her to her neighbors in the use of forms, structure, and even content. This tradi-

---

*This paper is a shortened version of the original that was published in *HvTSt* 53 (1997): 969–99. It has been reproduced with the kind permission of the editor, Professor Andries van Aarde.

1. See George W. E. Nickelsburg, "Wisdom and Apocalypticism in Early Judaism: Some Points for Discussion," in this volume.

2. John J. Collins, "Wisdom, Apocalypticism, and Generic Compatibility," in *In Search of Wisdom: Essays in Memory of John G. Gammie* (ed. L. G. Perdue et al.; Louisville: Westminster John Knox, 1993), 165–85.

tion continues in the period between the two Testaments and accounts for many of the writings preserved from this period. A twofold development can be observed within Israelite wisdom thinking.[3] The first stage revolved around the notion that the fear of the Lord was the beginning of wisdom. The path to acquiring wisdom is through the acceptance of God and adherence to the covenant faith. The second stage engages the question of how knowledge, derived from the realm of human wisdom, can be given the quality of truth. To bridge the gap between the divine and the human, the wise postulated the personified figure of wisdom. This heavenly figure dwells in their midst and is responsible for enlightening the minds of the wise.[4] These two aspects of wisdom form the focus of attention throughout the wisdom thinking of the Hebrew writings, namely the ethical way of life demanded by wisdom (fear of the Lord) and the personification of wisdom itself. The Letter of James is to be viewed against this two-stage development of wisdom. Attention will be given to both dimensions mentioned above, namely, the relationship of wisdom and ethics, and the nature of wisdom.

Some wisdom literature, in particular the books of Proverbs, Qoheleth, and Sirach, aim at providing instruction for the art of living, or the mastery of life itself. The ethical teaching of the wisdom writings has as its goal the leading of a happy existence under God's sovereignty. This provides the context for James's[5] ethical teaching, and its character as a wisdom writing can only be fully appreciated and understood against this background. In James the ethical is expressed by means of specific forms that owe their origin to the Hebrew tradition. Among these forms in which the wisdom advice is presented are the following:

1.1.1. Wisdom Sayings

Wisdom sayings arise from experience and draw conclusions from this experience. Very often they entail giving advice on how to lead one's life. James contains numerous examples of such wisdom sayings. For example: "For judgment will be without mercy to anyone who has shown no mercy; mercy triumphs over judgment" (Jas 2:13).[6] Most often these

---

3. James L. Crenshaw, *Studies in Ancient Israelite Wisdom: Selected with a Prolegomenon by James L. Crenshaw* (New York: Ktav, 1976), 24–26.
4. Sirach takes the personification a step forward when Wisdom is seen to dwell above all in Israel. This is achieved through the identification of Wisdom and Torah (Crenshaw, *Studies in Ancient Israelite Wisdom*, 25).
5. For the sake of brevity, I shall refer to the Letter of James simply as James. By using this designation "James," I do not mean to imply anything about the identity of the author.
6. Martin Dibelius (*James: A Commentary on the Epistle of James* [trans. M. A. Williams; Philadelphia: Fortress, 1975], 147) argues that this is "an isolated saying" that has no

wisdom statements conclude a pericope by reinforcing the argument. For example: "And a harvest of righteousness is sown in peace for those who make peace" (3:18).[7] This saying brings together the thought development in this pericope: the gift of wisdom produces the gift of righteousness, which is illustrated by peace. At the same time this saying bridges the gap to the next pericope. Chapter 3 concludes with a reference to peace, while chapter 4 opens with a question about the origins of conflicts: "These conflicts and disputes among you, where do they come from?" (4:1).

1.1.2. Wisdom Admonitions

Admonitions lay emphasis on the didactic element and call for obedience to and implementation of the advice. Usually a reason is added to support the admonitions. They are eminently suited to the wisdom style that offers practical advice to its readers. James finds this form to be the most appropriate way to express his paraenetical advice, as shown in the following examples. (1) James 1:2 ("My brothers and sisters, whenever you face trials of any kind, consider it nothing but joy") continues with numerous other admonitions: "And let endurance have its full effect, so that you may be mature and complete, lacking in nothing" (1:4); "If any of you is lacking in wisdom, ask God, who gives to all generously and ungrudgingly, and it will be given you" (1:5); "But ask in faith, never doubting, for the one who doubts is like a wave of the sea, driven and tossed by the wind" (1:6). (2) James 1:19–27 contains a series of admonitions that revolve around the threefold saying: "Let everyone be quick to listen, slow to speak, slow to anger" (1:19).[8] This pericope considers each one of these phrases, which give rise to admonitions. (3) James 4:7–10 contains ten imperatives that include related admonitions: "Submit yourselves therefore to God.... Humble yourselves before the Lord, and he will exalt you." All the admonitions are contained between these parallel admonitions to submit to God. (4) The Letter of James ends with various admonitions on such themes as not taking oaths, the exhortation to prayer, and finally concluding with the admonition: "You should know that whoever brings back a sinner from wandering will save the sinner's

---

connection with the themes of the section preceding it. A close examination of this passage, however, shows that this verse does form an essential part of the context where it summarizes the main argument of the pericope, namely not to show partiality in one's actions.

7. Other similar sayings are: "For just as the body without the spirit is dead, so faith without works is also dead" (2:26); "For where there is envy and selfish ambition, there will also be disorder and wickedness of every kind" (3:16).

8. Dibelius (*James*, 109–10) has argued that this three-part saying is constituted from traditional wisdom sayings.

soul from death and will cover a multitude of sins" (5:20). By following these admonitions and the way of life that this letter outlines, the reader can hope for salvation.

A twofold perspective emerges in these admonitions. A focus on the present shows the readers the type of life they are to lead now. Secondly, it opens up a vision onto the future attainment of salvation. The worldview of wisdom has been broadened to include the eschatological dimension.

1.1.3. Beatitudes

The beatitude is a common form in wisdom literature. In comparing the form of the beatitude in the Hebrew Bible[9] with that in the New Testament, one striking difference emerges. In the New Testament the perspective has changed from the blessing conferred in the present, to one that awaits a fulfillment in the future eschatological age.[10] There are two occasions where the beatitude is found in James.

In 1:12 ("Blessed [μακάριος] is anyone who endures temptation. Such a one has stood the test and will receive the crown of life that the Lord has promised to those who love him")[11] the eschatological dimension dominates and transforms this wisdom form. The wisdom statement is referred to the future, producing a definite contrast between present and future. An eschatological correlative is evident here: the blessedness projected onto the future stands in opposite correlation to what is experienced in the present. The promise is made to those who endure trial now that they will inherit "the crown of life." This is close to the expression of the beatitudes in the Sayings Gospel Q as well as in the book of Revelation, where they occur within an eschatological framework.[12]

The word μακάριος occurs again in 1:25 ("But those who look into the perfect law, the law of liberty, and persevere, being not hearers who forget but doers who act—they will be blessed [μακάριος] in their

---

9. Although the literary form of a beatitude has been shown to be at home in both the Jewish and the Greek worlds (see Friedrich Hauck, "Μακάριος," *TDNT* 4:362-64), it is really in the world of the writings of the Hebrew Bible and Second Temple period that the closest analogies are found.

10. For example, in Sir 26:1 the blessing is clearly upon the present: "Happy is the husband of a good wife; the number of his days will be doubled" (see also Prov 14:21). The New Testament envisages the blessing largely for the future: "Blessed are you who are poor, for yours is the kingdom of God" (Luke 6:20).

11. The structure here conforms to the normal New Testament way of expressing the beatitude. See, for example, the beatitudes in Matt 5:2-12 and Luke 6:20-23: μακάριος appears first, followed by the person who is considered blessed, and then the reason for the blessedness is expressed (Hauck "Μακάριος," 367).

12. Ibid., 367-70.

doing"), but this time it is used not in the form of a beatitude but rather as an adjectival description. The blessing refers to the future: one's present actions bring the promise of future blessings. Again the perspective is that of the eschatological correlative.[13]

These two occurrences of μακάριος demonstrate the eschatological correlation between present and future. The promise of blessedness is reserved for the future, to be attained as a consequence of what one does now. The eschatological provides the motivation for the present way of life. The wisdom advice and ethical exhortations are all governed by the eschatological perspective. The traditional wisdom worldview has now been injected with an eschatological worldview that provides the overlay and the motivation for present actions.

1.1.4. Woes

This literary form is evident in both the prophetic and wisdom traditions. The Letter of James has brought it into harmony with the wisdom tradition. Two examples are evident in the letter.

James 4:13–17 addresses a condemnation against false confidence. He opens this address with a call: "Come now!" ("Ἄγε νῦν).[14] He operated in the same way in which the prophets of the Hebrew Bible presented their message.[15] They often directed their attacks outside the

---

13. Hauck (ibid., 369) comments on Jas 1:12 and 1:25, "Similarly, those who stand fast are called blessed in Jas 1:12, for their earthly endurance brings them eternal salvation. The thought of a sure reward is also present when the righteous doer is called blessed in Jas 1:25. In all these verses the light of future glory shines over the sorry present position of the righteous. Thus the New Testament beatitudes are not just intimations of the future or consolations in relation to it. They see the present in the light of the future."

14. A phrase not found elsewhere in the New Testament, apart from the beginning of the next chapter (Jas 5:1–6). It is found elsewhere in Greek literature, for example, in the diatribe, Epictetus 1.2.20; 1.6.37; 3.24.40; as well as in *Sib. Or.* 3:562.

15. In the prophetic literature the criticisms are sharp. For example, "Can I tolerate wicked scales and a bag of dishonest weights?" (Mic 6:11); "Hear this, you that trample on the needy, and bring to ruin the poor of the land, saying, 'When will the new moon be over so that we may sell grain; and the sabbath, so that we may offer wheat for sale? We will make the ephah small and the shekel great, and practice deceit with false balances, buying the poor for silver, and the needy for a pair of sandals, and selling the sweepings of the wheat" (Amos 8:4–6). Ezekiel singles out the great trading city of Tyre for condemnation: "Now you, mortal, raise a lamentation over Tyre, and say to Tyre, which sits at the entrance to the sea, merchant of the peoples on many coastlands" (27:1–36).

In the wisdom literature the accusations are equally forceful: "Differing weights are an abomination to the Lord; and false scales are not good" (Prov 20:23). Sirach devotes a series of chapters to the temptations that come from commerce (26:29–29:28). He criticizes very sharply the way of life of the trader: "A merchant can hardly keep from wrongdoing, nor is a tradesman innocent of sin" (26:29).

community of Israel with no real expectation that the nations whom they addressed would in fact turn from their ways. Instead, these attacks operate as a call for the people of Israel to heed the warnings and correct their way of life. James provides his readers with a teaching that calls for faith to be carried out in action. By putting their trust entirely in themselves, they reject God. *First Enoch* exhibits a similar manner of address in the context of a series of woes. In 94:1 Enoch speaks to his "sons," then in 94:8 he changes his address to embrace the rich: "Woe to you rich," and he continues with this second person address.[16] As in the Letter of James, so here in *1 Enoch*, a distinction is drawn between the community and those rich outside the community. While James is not attacking a specific incident, he is warning the community in prophetic style against an attitude evident within the world, which they are to avoid. Faith and action are not to be separated.

A second woe ("Ἄγε νῦν, Jas 5:1–6) follows immediately on the previous condemnation of those who fail to put their trust in God. This pericope illustrates how the rich place their trust, not in God, but in their riches. The eschatological references are much more specific and intense. In language that bears close similarities to the prophets, this pericope opens with a reference to "the miseries that are coming to you" (5:1) and continues with reference to "the last days" (5:3), which are graphically depicted as "a day of slaughter" (5:5). In contrast to the attitude of the rich stands the attitude of the righteous one who offers no resistance. The implication given is that the righteous will be justified in the eschatological age.[17]

In James wisdom emerges as a strategy wherein advice is offered to the hearer on how best to lead one's life. Faithful to this strategy, James uses not just the wisdom tradition, but other types of discourse as well, namely the eschatological and the prophetic. By incorporating the eschatological and the prophetic worldviews within the wisdom perspective, the call to a specific way of life becomes all the more urgent. The eschatological provides the motivation—judgment in the future depends upon the way one leads one's life here and now. The use of prophetic imagery and terminology reinforces this urgency: "You have

---

The book of Revelation continues this tradition of condemning merchants in its criticisms against Babylon: "And the merchants of the earth weep and mourn for her, since no one buys their cargo anymore, cargo of gold, silver, jewels, and pearls, fine linen, purple, silk, and scarlet, all kinds of scented wood, all articles of ivory, all articles of costly wood, bronze, iron, and marble, cinnamon, spice, incense, myrrh, frankincense" (18:11–13).

16. The same change of address is observable between 95:3 and 96:1–3. In these passages the audience envisaged is the righteous and the suffering. But within the same context an address is made to the rich and sinners: 95:1, 2, 4–7; 96:4–8; 97:2–10.

17. The same promise is made to the righteous in *1 En.* 92–105.

lived on the earth in luxury and in pleasure; you have fattened your hearts in a day of slaughter" (5:5).

1.1.5. Wisdom Forms of Comparison
The use of different forms of comparison is characteristic of all wisdom writing. The reader is actively involved in the processes of discovering the relationship intended by the speaker. The Letter of James makes use of different types of comparison, among which three are to be noted: (1) The *simple contrast* calls the reader to adopt a specific action, such as, "But ask in faith, never doubting" (1:6).[18] (2) *Explicit comparisons* such as similes or metaphors are characteristic of James's style of writing, as in, "[F]or the one who doubts is like a wave of the sea, driven and tossed by the wind" (1:6).[19] (3) Like the Gospels, the Letter of James also uses the *parabolic method of comparison and instruction*. Again the reader becomes actively involved in discovering the intended meaning: "For if any are hearers of the word and not doers, they are like those who look at themselves in a mirror; for they look at themselves and, on going away, immediately forget what they were like" (Jas 1:23–24). The comparison illustrates the need to put into action what has been heard: to be a doer of the word.

These wisdom forms (sayings, admonitions, beatitudes, woes, and forms of comparison) all demonstrate James's firm roots in the wisdom tradition. At the same time, wisdom functions as a strategy that integrates aspects taken from the prophetic and eschatological traditions in order to show how faith must give direction to action.

1.2. THE NATURE OF WISDOM

The wisdom tradition going back to the book of Proverbs (ch. 8) also demonstrates a reflection upon the nature of wisdom itself, a speculation that would ultimately lead to a personification of wisdom. An aspect of this tradition is evident in two pericopes in James (1:5–8; 3:13–18), although it is not as prominent as the practical dimension of wisdom.

1.2.1. Wisdom as a Gift from God (1:5–8)
James reflects the Jewish wisdom tradition that sees God as the giver of all wisdom, "generously and ungrudgingly" (1:5); "all wisdom is from

---

18. See also "But be doers of the word, and not merely hearers who deceive themselves" (1:22); "Adulterers! Do you not know that friendship with the world is enmity with God?" (4:4).

19. See also "[T]he rich will disappear like a flower in the field" (1:10); "It is the same with the rich; in the midst of a busy life, they will wither away" (1:11).

the Lord, and with him it remains forever" (Sir 1:1).[20] The book of Wisdom also develops this perspective: "Therefore I prayed, and understanding was given me; I called on God, and the spirit of wisdom came to me" (Wis 7:7).[21] James also relies upon the Jewish wisdom tradition that encourages constant prayer: "The prayer of the righteous is powerful and effective" (Jas 5:16).

1.2.2. Wisdom from Above (3:13–18)

This passage contains the most direct reflection on wisdom. A striking connection with the previous pericope (3:1–12)[22] appears through the parallelism in the opening of each pericope; Jas 3:1 deals with the teacher, διδάσκαλος, while 3:13 considers the wise person, σοφός. Διδάσκαλος and σοφός stand in parallel to each other. The true teacher is the wise person—the διδάσκαλος becomes the σοφός.[23] This passage unfolds in three parts.

James 3:13 presents the criterion for true wisdom and asks the question: "Who is wise and understanding?"[24] James argues that whoever makes a claim to be a leader in the church (διδάσκαλος σοφός) must lead a life that demonstrates faith in action. In addition to the specific actions that are performed, the truly wise person will demonstrate a life led "with gentleness born of wisdom." The believer is challenged to see the cardinal virtue for life as consisting in "meekness" (especially in situations of strife).[25] This sentence operates as a topic sentence for the rest of the vices and virtues that follow, and it acts as a guiding force for each list.[26]

---

20. See also Sir 1:26; 17:11; 24:2; 39:6.

21. See also 8:21; 9:4.

22. This is contrary to the position of Dibelius (*James*, 207), who states: "There is no indication of a connection with the preceding section, and the interpretation will reveal that there is no connection in thought either."

23. Franz Mussner, *Der Jakobusbrief: Auslegung* (4th ed.; Fribourg: Herder, 1981), 168–69, shows that this shift from διδάσκαλος to σοφός reflects the world of the first century C.E, where the two concepts were used interchangeably. As Mussner says, "Weil im Spätjudentum der Lehrer (Rabbi) und der Weise fast identisch sind" (168–69).

24. While the phrase "wise and understanding" (σοφὸς καὶ ἐπιστήμων) does not occur in the rest of the New Testament, it is found frequently in the Septuagint. See, for example, Deut 1:13; 4:6; Sir 21:15; and Dan 1:4 (Peter H. Davids, *The Epistle of James: A Commentary on the Greek Text* [NIGTC; Grand Rapids: Eerdmans, 1982], 150.).

25. See Davids, *Epistle of James*, 150. This is a characteristic Christian virtue, as can be seen from its appearance in almost every tradition of the New Testament (Gal 6:1; Eph 4:2; 2 Tim 2:25; Tit 3:2; 1 Pet 3:16; Jas 1:21).

26. There is a striking parallel to this verse in Sir 3:17: "My child, perform your tasks with humility; then you will be loved by those whom God accepts." Again James demonstrates that he lies close to the wisdom world view of Sirach that sees one's life directed by virtues such as meekness.

James 3:14–16 gives a negative definition of a lifestyle led without wisdom. In this and the next section James contrasts two lifestyles: one led without wisdom (3:14–16) and one led with wisdom (3:17–18). The proper lifestyle of one who is wise excludes all "bitter envy and selfish ambition." One cannot possess God's wisdom if at the same time one is full of jealousy and causes dissensions.

James 3:17–18 presents a positive definition of wisdom in describing the true wisdom from above. James 1:17 helps to shed light upon the understanding of this text. Wisdom is that great gift that comes down from above[27] resulting in the person receiving the word of truth, becoming "a kind of firstfruits of his creatures" (1:18) and receiving rebirth.[28] With this as the wider context to 3:17, the wisdom from above is directed not simply toward a specific moral type of life, but toward regeneration and rebirth. The eschatological has already begun in that believers are promised the gift of wisdom that works regeneration and makes of them "firstfruits." The audience to whom James writes already participates in the eschatological age announced by the prophets of old. The promise of the fruit of righteousness for those who work for peace (3:18) is part of the promise of this wisdom from above. All the ethical admonitions in this section are directed towards this eschatological gift of righteousness. The one who has lived by the qualities of wisdom will possess the fullness of the gift of righteousness in the life to come.

Characteristic of James's application of the wisdom tradition is the fact that he has consistently broadened the perspective to incorporate an eschatological perspective. Attention will now be given to this significance of broadening the wisdom tradition within the Letter of James.

1.3. The Function of the Eschatological in the Letter of James

Eschatology provides the context for the teaching of this writing. James shares a common apocalyptic worldview with his hearers/readers and presupposes it. The letter opens with the address: "To the twelve tribes of the Dispersion" (1:1). While the exact meaning of the phrase is

---

27. On a number of occasions James teaches that true wisdom comes down from heaven (Jas 1:5, 17; 3:17). In the Jewish wisdom tradition it was tantamount to an axiom that all true wisdom is divine in origin and comes down from heaven (Prov 2:6; 8:22–31; Sir 1:1–4; 24:1–12; Wis 7:24–27; 9:4, 6, 9–18).

28. As Davids (*Epistle of James*, 95) says, "Thus the God who regenerates (begets) the Christian by the word of truth will save him by the same word implanted in him if he receives it."

disputed,[29] I think the best approach is to understand it in the context of the hope in the restoration of the twelve-tribe kingdom of Israel. Nathan the prophet promised King David that his kingdom would not end: "Your house and your kingdom shall be made sure forever before me; your throne shall be established forever" (2 Sam 7:16). The belief arose that the twelve-tribe kingdom would continue forever. This belief survived despite the destruction of both the northern and southern parts of the land of Israel. During the exile the prophets began to proclaim the return of the people and the restoration of the destroyed twelve-tribe kingdom (e.g., Ezek 37:19-24; Jer 3:18; Sir 36:13). This became a central conviction of Jewish eschatology and apocalyptic literature. The literature specific to the Qumran community also presupposes the restoration of the twelve-tribe kingdom. It even plans the organization of the Qumran community, its battle order and the temple, as if it were already a fact.

This belief in the coming of the kingdom provided the motive for John the Baptist's call to repentance: "In those days, John the Baptist appeared in the wilderness of Judea proclaiming, 'Repent, for the kingdom of heaven has come near'" (Matt 3:1-2). In the context of the ever intensifying kingdom eschatology, the first-generation Judean church must have held views similar to those expressed by John. They, as well as John, were preparing the people for the dawn of a restored twelve-tribe kingdom. It is for this purpose that the Gospel writers present Jesus appointing a group of twelve. In the tradition of Matthew's Gospel the importance of the twelve tribes emerges even more forcefully. Jesus has the exclusive task of reconstituting the twelve tribes of Israel. In Matt 15:24 Jesus counters the woman from Tyre and Sidon with the statement: "I was sent only to the lost sheep of the house of Israel." This passage conveys the belief that Matthew's community saw the gathering-in of the lost sheep of the house of Israel as Jesus' task. When Jesus in turn commissioned the twelve, he was in effect delegating this same task to them, namely, of gathering together the lost tribes.

In addressing his readers in this way, James is exercising the role of gathering in the twelve tribes of Israel. James sees the Jewish Christians as the true Israel. In them the eschatological hope of Israel's past reaches fulfillment. The beginning of the end time occurs with this Jewish Christian community, which is the twelve-tribe people. Those who belong to

---

29. See, e.g., the different perspectives adopted by Dibelius (*James*, 66-68); Sophie Laws (*A Commentary on the Epistle of James* [BNTC; London: Black, 1980], 47-49); Mussner (*Jakobusbrief*, 11-12); Davids (*Epistle of James*, 63-64); and Luke Timothy Johnson (*The Letter of James: A New Translation with Introduction and Commentary* [AB 37A; New York: Doubleday, 1995], 169).

this new Israel, the twelve tribes, are described as "the firstfruits of God's creatures" (1:18). The language of creation permeates this verse and the preceding one. Without doubt James has in mind the eschatological creation in which Jewish Christians are consciously conceived of as the firstfruits (ἀπαρχή) of God's creatures. God's redemptive activity claims Jewish Christians as the firstfruits of God's creatures (κτισμάτων).[30] The previous verse referred to God as the "Father of lights" (1:17), which also has creation in mind: God is the creator of sun and moon.[31] As creator of the lights of heaven, God is different from creatures in that in God "there is no variation or shadow due to change" (1:17).

While using terminology related to creation, James has in mind the new creation that brings about rebirth. The starting point for God's new creative activity lies with Jewish Christians, but it is not intended to end there. It is meant to embrace ultimately all humanity.[32] "Firstfruits" implies that others will follow. Addressed to those who are the firstfruits of this eschatological age, the letter also looks forward to a future where this will be brought to fulfillment. Creation imagery is used to give further understanding to this eschatology. The present is on the threshold of the end of history. The new age has begun to break in, which causes a tension between this world and the world to come.[33] James 5:7–11 is rich in traditional eschatological images: "The coming of the Lord is near" (5:8). The reader is exhorted to have patience in this intervening period before the Lord's coming, which will usher in a period of judgment, for the "Judge is standing at the doors!" (5:9). Images such as "the coming of the Lord" and the "Judge" belong to an eschatological worldview.

The context of this passage focuses especially upon the judgment of the rich who have not recognized the imminent judgment. James 5:1–6 condemns the rich in true prophetic fashion for their behavior. They "have laid up treasure for the last days" (5:3); they have amassed fortunes and have behaved as if they will last forever; they have not realized that the "last days" have broken upon the world; they have "fattened (their) hearts in a day of slaughter" (5:5).[34] This is the closest that

---

30. The word κτίσμα is often used in wisdom literature to refer to God's creatures (e.g. Wis 9:2; 13:5; 14:11; Sir 36:20).

31. Genesis 1:14–15 speaks of the lights of the heavens: "Let there be lights in the dome of the sky to separate the day from the night, and let them be for signs and for seasons and for days and years, and let them be lights in the dome of the sky to give light upon earth."

32. Mussner, *Jakobusbrief*, 96.

33. Davids, *Epistle of James*, 38.

34. This phrase "a day of slaughter" (5:5) belongs to that prophetic tradition where God's judgment is viewed as a day of slaughter for God's enemies (for example: Isa 34:5–8; Jer 46:10). What is also significant is that Enoch explicitly connects the judgment of the rich

James comes to the use of apocalyptic language. He uses it without emphasis and does not develop the characteristic apocalyptic descriptions. In the same context (5:17) James refers to another symbol that appears in the eschatological worldview, namely, Elijah. According to the tradition, Elijah is due to return before the end of the world. James focuses not on the eschatological, but on Elijah as a "human being like us" (5:17). The biblical picture had presented Elijah as a man of prayer, a man whose prayer had powerful effects (1 Kgs 18:36–40). James turns away from apocalyptic speculations to focus upon a human quality that speaks more vividly to his readers.

The awaited "coming of the Lord" brings both judgment and salvation: judgment against those who have failed to follow the right path (chief among these are the rich) and salvation for those who are patient (chief among these are the poor). The themes of judgment and salvation run like threads throughout the letter. Negatively, the theme of judgment sees the rich fading away like the flowers in the field (1:10); in the middle of life they wither away (1:11). Positively, this letter promises a "crown of life" (1:12) for those who love God. It promises as well to those who are poor that they will be "heirs of the kingdom" (2:5). James shows that the believer's life is oriented toward a future with an eschatological end resulting in either salvation (life) or judgment (condemnation).

1.4. Eschatology and Ethics

James has used the eschatological perspective as the motivation for his wisdom advice. All the ethical instructions within the letter are embraced by the eschatological. On the negative side, judgment acts as a caution. The teacher is warned: "[F]or you know that we who teach will be judged with greater strictness" (3:1). Believers are cautioned against acting as a judge of their neighbor in the present, because this will fuel their own judgment in the future: "There is one lawgiver and judge who is able to save and to destroy. So who, then, are you to judge your neighbor?" (4:12).[35] On the positive side, the eschatological motivation provides certain promises:

✦ Those who withstand temptation are promised "the crown of life" (1:12).

---

to such a day: "You ... have become ready for the day of slaughter, and the day of darkness and the day of the great judgment" (1 En. 94:9; 97:8–10; 99:15).

35. Correct use of the tongue is also stressed (3:5–10), as is the correct usage of the taking of oaths "that you may not fall under condemnation" (5:12).

- Those who persevere "will be blessed in their doing" (1:25).
- Those who are "the poor in the world" will be "heirs of the kingdom that he has promised to those who love him" (2:5).
- Those who put faith into action will be justified: "You see a person is justified by works and not by faith alone" (2:24).
- Those who bring back "a sinner from wandering will save the sinner's soul from death and will cover a multitude of sins" (5:20).

1.5. AN APOCALYPTIC ESCHATOLOGY?

By encouraging people to persevere amidst trials and temptations (1:12), James does not give any detailed description of what the trials actually are.[36] James 1:27 refers to the affliction of widows and orphans using the term θλῖψις ("affliction"), a technical term occurring in apocalyptic literature for the sufferings of the eschatological age.[37] In the New Testament, the same term is adopted with theological significance to refer to sufferings now endured by the Christian church in the eschatological age.[38] James's usage of θλῖψις does not focus upon its possible apocalyptic setting. He deliberately reinterprets the tradition in order to show that present events are signs of the coming end. James reinterprets everyday sufferings of those most abandoned in society as signs that the end is rapidly approaching.[39] Without doubt James is aware of the apocalyptic imagination since it is part of the thought patterns that he shares with his contemporaries and in particular with his readers. However, James tends to distance himself from apocalyptic thinking in two ways. In the first instance, James is convinced that the eschatological age has arrived since the "Judge is standing at the doors" (5:9); yet, those formal elements that

---

36. Laws, *Commentary*, 28.

37. Heinrich Schlier ("θλίβω," *TDNT* 3:139-48) argued that this term in the Septuagint had acquired a "theological significance from the fact that it predominantly denotes the oppression and affliction of the people of Israel or of the righteous who represent Israel" (142).

38. Attention is drawn in the New Testament usage of this term especially to the sufferings that occur prior to the Parousia. The book of Revelation sees the sufferings and tribulations of the present as already being experienced and marking the beginning of the end: "I, John, your brother who share with you in Jesus the persecution (θλίψει) and the kingdom" (1:9).

39. Laws (*Commentary*, 90) examines the reason for this shift in the usage of the term θλῖψις, and she suggests two possible reasons for this change: "It could be that he is trying to dispense with the old eschatological ideas, finding them no longer appropriate.... Alternatively James may be trying to keep the expectation alive and real in a situation where the traditional 'signs' are conspicuously lacking, and in that attempt he carries out a deliberate reinterpretation of the nature of the signs."

belong to a truly apocalyptic discourse are absent. This leads James to reinterpret the apocalyptic signs. The ordinary sufferings of the present are reinterpreted as signs of the end, such as the tribulations afflicting the widow and orphan, as well as the trials faced by every brother and sister (1:2). Second, despite the view that the coming age brings judgment, the ethos of the whole letter is that this coming age is to be approached not with fear and trepidation, but with joy and happiness: "Count it all as joy" [1:2]). Adopting James's wisdom exhortations will bring hope, joy, peace, and perfection. The focus rests on the future hope, "the Lord of glory" (2:1) who provides the "crown of life" (1:12), rather than on dread and fear of judgment.

2. The Epistle of Enoch and the Letter of James

The Epistle of Enoch (1 En. 92–105)[40] bears a number of similarities to the Letter of James. An examination of these similarities may help to specify James's relationship to the traditions of wisdom, prophecy, eschatology, and apocalypticism. The Epistle of Enoch is presented as a letter addressed from the ancient "patriarch" Enoch to "all the offspring that dwell upon the earth, and for the latter generations which uphold uprightness and peace" (1 En. 92:1).[41] This bears some resemblance to the Letter of James, which is addressed from James, a "patriarch" in early Christianity, to "the twelve tribes in the dispersion." In a sense the addressees are analogous: while Enoch is addressed to all his spiritual descendants throughout time and the world,[42] James is addressed to Jewish Christians, the spiritual descendants of Israel throughout the world. Throughout both texts lies the contrast between the righteous and sinners and the respective judgments that await them in the future: "Now, my children, I say to you, 'Love righteousness and walk therein!

---

40. *1 Enoch* is an interesting literary collection developing over a long period of time. George W. E. Nickelsburg ("The Apocalyptic Construction of Reality in *1 Enoch*," in *Mysteries and Revelations: Apocalyptic Studies since the Uppsala Colloquium* [ed. J. J. Collins and J. H. Charlesworth; JSPSup 9; Sheffield: Sheffield Academic Press, 1991], 51) estimates that it spanned more than three centuries. Not only is it a collection of different texts, but it is also a collection of different traditions that have been forged into a unity: "Nonetheless, *1 Enoch* is a consciously shaped compilation of traditions and texts, and it is appropriate to search for internal points of commonality (apart from Enochic attribution in most cases) in which the compilers and editors saw the potential for a unity comprised of diversity" (52). In particular it provides a good example of the development of traditions, forms, and genres during the Second Temple period as no extant piece of literature does. In this sense it occupies a unique position.

41. The translation of *1 Enoch* is that of Ephraim Isaac in *OTP* 1:5–89.

42. George W. E. Nickelsburg, "First Book of Enoch," *ABD* 2:511.

For the ways of righteousness are worthy of being embraced; (but) the ways of wickedness shall soon perish and diminish'" (*1 En.* 94:1). Likewise James states: "You do well if you really fulfill the royal law according to the scripture, 'You shall love your neighbor as yourself.' But if you show partiality, you commit sin and are convicted by the law as transgressors" (Jas 2:8–9). While James refers to judgment, there is no detailed description of the judgment as occurs in *1 En.* 92–105.

The major similarity between *1 En.* 92–105 and the Letter of James is that they both employ many of the same literary forms in their composition, namely woes, exhortations and judgment.[43]

2.1. WOES

The form of woes presents the charge of evil against sinners as well as the impending judgment they can expect. For example, "Woe unto those who build oppression and injustice! Who lay foundations for deceit. They shall soon be demolished" (*1 En.* 94:6). While some of the woes are directed against those who abandon the teachings of the Torah, the majority concerns those who fail in social demands.[44] A particular concern is expressed for the way in which the rich abuse the poor. In condemning the rich, James and *1 En.* 92–105 share some close similarities. James 5:5 condemns the rich for having "fattened your hearts in a day of slaughter"; *1 Enoch* uses similar imagery: "Woe unto you, O rich people.... In the days of your affluence, you committed oppression, you have become ready for death, and for the day of darkness and the day of great judgment" (*1 En.* 94:8–9).

2.2. EXHORTATIONS

The righteous are exhorted to persevere in the life of courage and peace that they are leading. "Be hopeful, you righteous ones, for the sinners shall soon perish from before your presence. You shall be given authority upon them, such (authority) as you may wish to have" (*1 En.* 96:1). The Letter of James is essentially a series of admonitions on how to lead one's life. While James prefers exhortations over woes, *1 En.* 92–105 is the opposite; it contains far more woes than exhortations.

---

43. George Nickelsburg has shown that *1 En.* 92–105 uses three major literary forms throughout (*Jewish Literature between the Bible and the Mishnah* [Philadelphia: Fortress, 1981], 146–48). I shall compare James to these three literary forms.
44. Ibid,, 147.

2.3. Descriptions of Judgment

James and the Epistle of Enoch both utilize prophetic forms of speech, but not in exactly the same way. In *1 En.* 92–105 we find passages of judgment that are very similar to what is found in the prophets.[45] For example, "In those days, the prayers of the righteous ones shall reach unto the Lord; but for all of you, your days shall arrive. He shall read aloud regarding every aspect of your mischief, in the presence of the Great Holy One. Then your faces shall be covered with shame, and he will cast out every deed that is built upon oppression" (*1 En.* 97:5–6). James, on the other hand, does not enter into descriptions of judgment. Instead James focuses on the present and issues warnings to sinners, rather than giving detailed descriptions of what punishments are ahead.

The Epistle of Enoch and James use traditional material that is at home both in the prophetic and in the wisdom traditions, yet they use them in different ways and in different degrees. *First Enoch* gave more emphasis to the woes, while James made more use of the form of the exhortation and admonitions. Both give evidence that a clear distinction between prophetic and wisdom traditions was not observed by all authors in this period.[46] The major difference between the Epistle of Enoch and the Letter of James lies in the focus the former places on the revelation of the future that acts as a comfort for those suffering now. The imminent future day of judgment is the revealed message that *1 En.* 92–105 communicates to the readers, a day that will overcome injustice and bring the righteous to happiness (*1 En.* 102:1; 103:1–3). This revealed message shines through both the prophetic and wisdom traditions used by the Epistle of Enoch and in turn brings it into the orbit of the apocalyptic genre. It is especially the claim to the revelation of the heavenly realm and the future that cements this connection (*1 En.* 97:6).[47] Belief in a

---

45. Ibid., 148.
46. George W. E. Nickelsburg, "The Apocalyptic Message of *1 Enoch* 92–105," *CBQ* 39 (1977): 327.
47. The genre apocalypse becomes more obvious from the context in which *1 En.* 92–105 occurs. The Apocalypse of Weeks (93:1–10; 91:11–17) appears within this section (92–105), while the visions of the other world in chs. 1–36 provide further justification for the revelatory message that Enoch proclaims. As Nickelsburg (*Jewish Literature*, 149) says: "The epistle of Enoch is similar to other apocalyptic writings in the kind of situation it presumes, the message it conveys, and the purpose for which it was written. The author exhorts his readers to steadfastness on the basis of a revealed message about an imminent judgment that will remove oppression and adjudicate injustice. This work shares with the apocalypses the claim that it is an ancient writing intended for latter-day readers. It differs from them in form. Although it contains a brief, sketchy apocalypse, as a whole it is not an ordered account of events to come."

future judgment operates in James as an explanation for the way in which one should conduct life now in the immediate expectation of the "coming of the Lord." However, in comparing references to judgment in James and 1 En. 92–105, James does not describe this future judgment that will befall the righteous and the sinner. The most noteworthy difference, then, between the Epistle of Enoch and James is that revelation, so central to the former, is absent from the latter. The aspect of "revelatory literature" separates the Letter of James from the apocalyptic genre apocalypse. Essential to the definition of apocalyptic literature is the notion that "revelation" is the distinguishing mark of this type of writing.[48] Instead, James directs attention to the present. No narrative framework is given to the letter, nor is any supernatural being present to mediate the transcendent world.

This is not to deny that the future does operate in James as a call to the present. To paraphrase Nickelsburg, one can say, "In the Letter of James the future calls the oppressed community to faith, courage, and joy in the present."[49] However, there is no "revelation of God's unseen world" as there is in the Epistle of Enoch. The coming of the Lord is imminent, but there is no description of that coming, or of what the world will be like after it. It is presented as an event in the immediate future, but James does not speculate on it, nor does he give information about it. While the context of the audience of James does include situations of oppression and affliction, the exhortations and wisdom comparisons give a picture of a community that needs to be reminded of the importance of putting faith into action, of fulfilling the law of love, of bridling the tongue, and so forth.

On the other hand, one cannot claim that James is not influenced by apocalyptic discourse. While the imagery of Daniel or Revelation is lacking in James, the world of James is a world that is dominated by evil to the extent that James defines religion as keeping oneself "unstained by the world" (1:27). The future does operate as the motivation for the way one leads one's life in the present. The future proclaims the imminent coming of the Lord, as the "Judge standing at the doors!" (5:9).

---

48. The definition of the genre of an apocalypse, as given by John J. Collins, is worth noting as further support for showing that James does not conform: "An apocalypse is defined as: a genre of revelatory literature with a narrative framework, in which a revelation is mediated by an otherworldly being to a human recipient, disclosing a transcendent reality which is both temporal, insofar as it envisages eschatological salvation, and spatial insofar as it involves another, supernatural world" (*The Apocalyptic Imagination* [New York: Crossroad, 1992], 4).

49. Nickelsburg, "Apocalyptic Message," 326.

3. Conclusion

3.1. Genre and Traditions

The Letter of James belongs to that wisdom tradition that offers practical advice and instruction on the art of leading one's life. Two aspects of wisdom material are evident, namely wisdom instruction or exhortations and reflection upon wisdom, upon its origin with God.[50] The issue of genre shows that the nature of the Letter of James is wider than just one category. Both the prophetic and eschatological play a decided influence in determining the nature of the letter. Prophetic forms are used in order to give expression to the wisdom advice. At the same time, eschatology plays a vital role in providing motivation for the wisdom teaching that is offered. For James the future holds sway over the present. The coming of the Lord acts as the motivation for the way one leads one's life in the present. It gives meaning to all the ethical advice.

Like the Epistle of Enoch, James utilized prophetic woes and admonitions. Eschatology also played a dominant role in each text by providing the motivation for the present. James and Enoch are heirs to traditions that they used in different ways. In *1 En.* 92–105 the apocalyptic revelatory genre unites the wisdom, prophetic and eschatological material together. In James, wisdom provides the overarching genre that brings together the prophetic and eschatological material, while the author retains some distance from full-blown apocalyptic motifs.

3.2. Worldview

The revelation of the future is not a focus for the writer of James as it is with apocalyptic texts. Neither is James couched in dreams, visions, or revelations by means of angels. However, James does seem to share aspects of some thought patterns present in an apocalyptic worldview. He knows that there is a world of devils (2:19); that the world of future judgment brings about a separation between the righteous and the sinner (5:1–11); and that there is a "crown of life" (1:12) in store for those who show their love of God. While James shares these thought patterns with his contemporaries, they do not displace his focus of providing exhortations and advice to the readers about how they are to lead their lives in

---

50. This corresponds to the first two categories of wisdom material that Collins ("Wisdom, Apocalypticism, and Generic Compatibility," 168) identifies within Israelite traditions, namely wisdom sayings and theological wisdom. The other three categories, nature wisdom, mantic wisdom, and higher wisdom through revelation, are absent from James.

the present. James does not work out a comprehensive worldview whereby this world is understood only in relation to the heavenly world. In this sense, then, James is not apocalyptic.

Reflection on the Torah, so characteristic of the wisdom writings of the Hebrew Bible as well as the Second Temple period, has continued in the Letter of James. Certainly the Torah provided the foundation against which one can judge the practical advice that is given for the way to lead one's life. The Letter of James has given this reflection on the Torah a particular focus with a centrality assigned to the law of love: "You shall love your neighbor as yourself" (also identified as the "royal law" [2:8], and the "law of liberty" [2:12]). This law of love provides impetus for the ethical advice that becomes a specific illustration of this law in action, whether it be "caring for widows and orphans," or showing no partiality with regard to rich and poor (2:1–7), or even the bridling of one's tongue (3:5–10).

3.3. COMMUNITY

The community presupposed by the Letter of James is the wider Jewish-Christian community outside Palestine ("the twelve tribes in the Dispersion" 1:1). In the very designation, "the twelve tribes in the Dispersion," the author reminds the readers of their eschatological position in the plan of God. They are the reconstituted people of Israel expected in the eschatological age. While the community that the letter envisages does experience sufferings and persecutions, these emanate chiefly from the hands of the rich against the poor. The sufferings are not the apocalyptic cataclysmic destructions of Revelation and Daniel. Yet, the same technical language is used to refer to the sufferings and afflictions of the present moment, such as those endured by widows and orphans (1:27). Tensions emerge within the community when it discriminates against the poor in favor of the rich (2:12). As a wisdom teacher, James aims at transmitting, not knowledge, but ethical exhortations in line with the way Sirach presented his teaching.[51] The author does not present his teaching as directly revealed or inspired. Yet, his reflection on the nature of wisdom shows that he views it as a gift that comes down from above (3:13–18). As a teacher, James must share this wisdom with his readers. No specific situations can be identified, however, which are seen to give rise to the letter's ethical advice. This does not mean that the ethical advice is presented in a vacuum; many of the admonitions must emerge

---

51. Nickelsburg, "Wisdom and Apocalypticism in Early Judaism," 725.

from the background of events that have taken place (such as discriminations against the poor [2:1–12] or the oppression of the poor by the rich [5:1–6]).

This examination of the Letter of James shows a writing emerging from the world of early Christianity that is home to wisdom, prophetic, apocalyptic, and eschatological discourses. James challenges scholarship to discard the focus upon "pure" traditions as a confusion that does not do justice to the evidence. Classifications such as apocalyptic, eschatological, wisdom, and prophetic are heuristic tools that remain such—tools that help scholars to enter into the reality of the past. They are not the reality itself. To try to classify a text solely in one category produces a distortion of the evidence. James is in fact a hybrid, which brings many different traditions together, as did 1 En. 92–105, and as such provides a possible example for the way other traditions operated in the New Testament world. Wisdom, eschatology, and apocalypticism are not to be seen in opposition, but as James and the Epistle of Enoch show, they exist in a relationship as part of the same social world.

THE RICH AND POOR IN JAMES:
AN APOCALYPTIC ETHIC*

Patrick A. Tiller

INTRODUCTION

In a previous meeting of the Wisdom and Apocalyptic Consultation, Patrick Hartin[1] and Matt Jackson-McCabe[2] wrote about wisdom, apocalyptic, and eschatology in the Letter of James. Jackson-McCabe concluded that James is better characterized as "moral exhortation rather than as a 'wisdom writing.'"[3] He further argued that James's apocalyptic worldview was "distinguished primarily by the increased importance attached to supernatural agents and a world beyond this one, and by the hope for judgment and vindication beyond death."[4] Hartin examined the Wisdom traditions reflected in James and the function of eschatology in the epistle. He concluded that James is not pure wisdom but uses both wisdom and prophetic forms and contains apocalyptic patterns of thought, which, however, "do not displace his focus on pro-

---

*This is a revised, abbreviated version of a paper that was presented at the annual meeting of the SBL, Orlando, FL, 24 November 1998 and published in *Society of Biblical Literature 1998 Seminar Papers* (2 vols.; SBLSP 37; Atlanta: Scholars Press, 1998), 2:909–20. It is given here in essentially the same form in which it was originally presented in order to provide the reader with a sense of the state of the discussion at that time. No attempt has been made to update it in the light of later discussions or publications.

1. Patrick J. Hartin, "'Who is Wise and Understanding Among You?' (James 3:13). An Analysis of Wisdom, Eschatology and Apocalypticism in the Epistle of James," in *Society of Biblical Literature 1996 Seminar Papers* (SBLSP 35; Atlanta: Scholars Press, 1996), 483–503 [published in this volume in a revised form, pp. 149–68].

2. Matt A. Jackson-McCabe, "A Letter to the Twelve Tribes in the Diaspora: Wisdom and 'Apocalyptic' Eschatology in the Letter of James," in *Society of Biblical Literature 1996 Seminar Papers*, 504–17.

3. Ibid., 507.

4. Ibid., 508, quoting from John J. Collins, "Wisdom, Apocalypticism, and Generic Compatibility," in *In Search of Wisdom: Essays in Memory of John G. Gammie* (ed. L. G. Perdue et al.; Louisville: Westminster John Knox, 1993), 170.

viding exhortations and advice to the readers about how they are to lead their lives in the present."[5]

My purpose is to deal with the same sort of questions as they,[6] but with a more narrow focus on the question of the rich and the poor and social status in general. It is clear that James[7] appropriates motifs, ideas, and forms that are at home in both older Hebrew wisdom, apocalyptic, and prophetic literature and more recent Hellenistic moral literature.[8] The mere application of these scholarly categories to James, however, does not advance our understanding of the epistle very far.

James's Appropriation of Sayings of Jesus

The tradition that informs James's theology most significantly is early Jesus proclamation, especially as it is otherwise preserved in the Sermon on the Mount/Plain. The parallels between James and the Synoptic Gospels have often been catalogued and studied.[9] In this study I will examine one such parallel in order to discover how James appropriated the teaching of Jesus.

> Ούχ ὁ θεὸς ἐξελέξατο τοὺς πτωχοὺς τῷ κόσμῳ πλουσίους ἐν πίστει καὶ κληρονόμους τῆς βασιλείας ἧς ἐπηγγείλατο τοῖς ἀγαπῶσιν αὐτόν.
> Has not God chosen those who are poor from the world's point of view to be rich in faith and to be heirs of the kingdom that he has promised to those who love him? (James 2:5b)

James's rebuke of those who show favoritism toward the rich represents a conflation of at least two traditions: that God has chosen the poor and that he has promised that the poor will inherit the kingdom. The first

---

5. Hartin, "Who is Wise," 499.

6. Other writers have treated James with similar interests and observations, e.g., Todd C. Penner, *The Epistle of James and Eschatology: Re-reading an Ancient Christian Letter* (JSNTSup 121; Sheffield: Sheffield Academic Press, 1996).

7. The question of the authorship of the letter remains unsolved. None of the proposed solutions (James the Lord's brother, some lesser-known James, or a pseudonymous author) is entirely persuasive.

8. See, e.g., the discussion of Luke Timothy Johnson, *The Letter of James: A New Translation with Introduction and Commentary* (AB 37A; New York: Doubleday, 1995), 16–24, 27–29.

9. See, e.g., Patrick J. Hartin, *James and the Q Sayings of Jesus* (JSNTSup, 47; Sheffield: JSOT Press, 1991). For a convenient table of the parallels, see Peter H. Davids, *The Epistle of James: A Commentary on the Greek Text* (NIGTC; Grand Rapids: Eerdmans, 1982), 47–48. For an intentionally shorter list of parallels, see Helmut Koester, *Ancient Christian Gospels: Their History and Development* (London: SCM, 1990), 72–73.

is reflected also in 1 Cor 1:27: "God has chosen the foolish things of the world to shame the wise, and God has chosen the weak things of the world to put the strong things to shame." Both Paul and James independently preserve the tradition that God chooses those who are despised in this world.

The second tradition overlaps with the first beatitude in both canonical versions. All versions of the beatitude include both of the key words of the saying in James: πτωχοί (poor) and βασιλεία (kingdom).

> Matt 5:3: Μακάριοι οἱ <u>πτωχοὶ</u> τῷ πνεύματι, ὅτι αὐτῶν ἐστιν ἡ <u>βασιλεία</u> τῶν οὐρανῶν.
> Blessed are the poor in spirit because the kingdom of heaven is theirs.

> Luke 6:20: Μακάριοι οἱ <u>πτωχοί</u>, ὅτι ὑμετέρα ἐστὶν ἡ <u>βασιλεία</u> τοῦ θεοῦ.
> Blessed are you poor because the kingdom of God is yours.

> Gos. Thom. 54: ⲡⲉϫⲉ ⲓ̅ⲥ̅ ϫⲉ ⲛ̅-ⲙⲁⲕⲁⲣⲓⲟⲥ ⲛⲉ ⲛ̅ϩⲏⲕⲉ ϫⲉ ⲧⲱⲧⲛ̅ ⲧⲉ ⲧⲙⲛ̅ⲧⲉⲣⲟ ⲛⲙ̅ⲡⲏⲩⲉ
> Jesus said, "Blessed are you poor because the kingdom of heaven is yours."

> Pol. Phil. 2.3d: Μακάριοι οἱ πτωχοὶ καὶ οἱ διωκόμενοι ἕνεκεν δικαιοσύνης, ὅτι αὐτῶν ἐστίν ἡ βασιλεία τοῦ θεοῦ.
> Blessed are the poor and those who are persecuted on account of righteousness because the kingdom of God is theirs.

James expands on the beatitude in several ways. The addition of the phrase τῷ κόσμῳ has a function similar to that of Matthew's τῷ πνεύματι. Both restrict the characterization of "poor" by specifying a particular point of view. James is talking about those who are poor from the world's point of view. This restriction implies the possibility of a different, more correct point of view. The addition of "to be rich in faith" has a similar function. Though someone may be poor from the world's point of view, from the (correct) standpoint of faith, they can be rich. The addition of κληρονόμοι (heirs) may have been imported from one of the other beatitudes in the Matthean version of the collection: μακάριοι οἱ πραεῖς, ὅτι αὐτοὶ κληρονομήσουσιν τὴν γῆν ("Blessed are the meek for they shall inherit the earth," Matt 5:5).[10] James's final expansion is the addition of

---

10. See also Did. 3.7: ἴσθι δὲ πραΰς ἐπεὶ οἱ πραεῖς κληρονομήσουσι τὴν γῆν ("Be meek because the meek will inherit the earth").

"which he promised to those who love him." Here James makes explicit his identification of the poor with those who love God.

The reference to the "royal law" (or more properly, the "king's law" [νόμον βασιλικόν]) of 2:8 and the kingdom promised to the poor in 2:5 imply the existence of a kingdom and a king. The adjective "royal" does not mean "fit for a king" but "of the king" and must mean that the law is understood by James as the law that governs the kingdom promised by Jesus to the poor. As far as James is concerned, it is the King's law that commands him to "love your neighbor as yourself."[11]

Thus, James has taken a beatitude of Jesus, conflated it (slightly) with another from the same collection (that the meek would *inherit* the earth), and applied it to his teaching on the treatment of the poor. The most obvious difference between James's allusion and the older collection of beatitudes is that the traditional pronouncement of blessing has become the basis for a rebuke. If Jesus has pronounced the poor blessed, then one ought not to dishonor the poor (v. 6), but honor them. This is in marked distinction to the treatment of the poor and rich that might normally be expected in "polite society" and that James has (to his dismay) observed. It is here that we may observe how James's theology controls his ethics.

The Implied Social Setting

Several previous studies have dealt with the social situation that serves as the context for Jas 2:1–7.[12] All agree that this passage is an exhortation to impartiality in reference to socioeconomic status using judicial language. The exhortation itself is traditional and parallels may be found throughout Jewish and Christian literature. But James thinks of much more than a particularly low level of material wealth and social status when he speaks of the poor or the rich. These are not simply terms that describe a socioeconomic status, but also ethical categories. Indeed, in spite of the fact that James must indirectly admit that there are "rich" people among his "twelve tribes of the dispersion" (1:1), he

---

11. I find the argument of Luke Timothy Johnson that the quotation of Lev 19:18 in Jas 2:8 is but one piece of an elaborate complex of references to Lev 19 less than totally convincing ("The Use of Leviticus 19 in the Letter of James," *JBL* 101 [1982]: 391–401). In any case, James understands the law in terms of the promised kingdom, not in terms of Moses.

12. See, e.g., Martin Dibelius, *James* (rev. H. Greeven; trans. M. A. Williams; Hermeneia; Philadelphia: Fortress, 1976), 128–32; Roy Bowen Ward, "Partiality in the Assembly: James 2:2–4," *HTR* 62 (1969): 87–97; François Vouga, *L'Épitre de Saint Jacques* (CNT 13a; Geneva: Labor et Fides, 1984), 72; and Johnson, *Letter of James*, 220.

systematically avoids calling them "brothers."[13] This reluctance may have originated in the social condition of most early Christians, but it has also become a theological conviction. Thus the implied social setting has little to do with social entities, but rather with theological constructions of reality.

The Theological Basis

Part of the reason for James's antipathy toward rich people is undoubtedly based on experience. In 2:6–7 James catalogues three offenses committed by rich people: (1) they oppress the addressees; (2) they "drag" the addressees into court; and (3) they blaspheme the name of Jesus.[14] The first two have sometimes been understood in terms of persecution of Christians. Dibelius argues that these should be understood not as an actual "Christian persecution," but as economic and legal action taken by the rich against Christians for economic reasons similar to those in Acts 16:19 or 19:24 or because of irritation with Christian propaganda.[15] As Johnson correctly observes, however, there need not be any anti-Christian activity alluded to at all, since "[i]t is universal enough a characteristic of the world's rich to oppress and humiliate the poor by 'legal' means."[16] While the charge of blasphemy is directed against religious opponents, the other charges are not criticisms of religious competitors; they address social exploitation. This observation is important because James's theological position is based not on religious competition, but on competition between two very different understandings of social ethics. The exploitative actions of the rich are not offensive because they are directed against Christians in particular, but because they represent the norms of a demonic society.

James has similar criticisms of rich people in the two parallel passages, 4:13–17 and 5:1–6. The passages are held together by their content

---

13. This has often been noted and is probably due to the fact that for James πλούσιος ("rich") is a boundary marker that excludes the rich from the Christian community. Vouga notes further the movement from the third person to second person (*Saint Jacques*, 25). Though James's real audience surely included people of relative wealth, his implied audience seems to exclude them.

14. In each case the subject ("the rich," "they," "they") is emphatic, either by position or by the use of the emphatic pronoun. For parallels to "the fair name which is called over you" from the DSS, see 4Q418 81 i 12, (ו)וכול הנקרא לשמ<ו> קודש ("And everyone who is called by his name"), and 4Q285 1 9–10, ושם קודשו נקרא ע[ליכם ("And his holy name is called ov[er you").

15. Dibelius, *James*, 139–40.

16. Johnson, *James*, 226.

(criticisms of actions characteristic of rich people) and introductory particles ("Come now" plus vocative). The first is directed against "those who say" that they will travel and make a profit by buying and selling, and it criticizes them for failing to recognize their temporality and for their pretentious, evil boasting. They are advised to change their attitude to one of submission to what "the Lord wills." This advice is in marked contrast with the far more severe advice in the next passage addressed to "the rich" who are advised to weep and wail because of their impending doom. They are condemned because of economic exploitation (they have withheld the rightful wages of their agricultural workers) and because they have condemned and murdered the righteous.[17] If, as was suggested above (n. 13), πλούσιος ("rich") is a boundary marker, then we may conclude that pretentiousness, while sinful, does not exclude one from the community upon which the name of Jesus is named (2:7). The blatant injustice named in 5:1–6, however, does merit the label "rich" and marks those who practice it as bound for judgment.

James's condemnation of economic exploitation is apparently based on the Deuteronomic obligation to act toward the needy with justice and kindness, based on God's justice and love for the poor. According to Deut 10:18–19, God is one "who executes justice for the orphan and the widow, and who loves the strangers, providing them food and clothing. You shall also love the stranger, for you were strangers in the land of Egypt." A similar ethic is found in the Psalms, which occasionally discuss God's care for the poor. According to Ps 72:12–13, for example, "He delivers the needy when they call, the poor and those who have no helper. He has pity on the weak and the needy, and saves the lives of the needy." Job echoes this sentiment in his final defense where he affirms the impropriety of failing to feed and clothe the poor, the orphan, and the widow or of acting unjustly toward them (Job 31:16–23). This is apparently also in imitation of God's treatment of the poor: "But he saves the needy from the sword of their [the wicked's] mouth, from the hand of the mighty. So the poor have hope, and injustice shuts its mouth" (Job 5:15–16). Ben Sira's advice to his readers explicitly mentions kindness to the poor as a form of imitation of God.

> My child, do not cheat the poor of their living, and do not keep needy eyes waiting. Do not grieve the hungry, or anger one in need.... Give a hearing to the poor, and return his greeting with deference. Deliver the oppressed from his oppressors; let not right judgment be repugnant to

---

17. Presumably the charge of murder is due to the fact that one who lacks an income runs the risk of starvation (cf. Sir 34:21–22).

you. To the fatherless be as a father, help the widows in their husbands' stead; then God will call you a son of his, and he will be more tender to you than a mother. (Sir 4:1–10 NRSV)

The prophets contain similar criticism for those who oppress the poor. Amos proclaims judgment for those who "trample on the needy and bring to ruin the poor of the land" (Amos 8.4) along with those who are impatient at not being able to do business on the Sabbath and those who use false weights (v. 5). Many other examples could be cited.

The Epistle of Enoch contains extremely harsh criticisms of the rich:

> Woe to you, you rich, for you have trusted in your riches, and from your riches you will be parted, because you have not remembered the Most High in the days of your riches. You have committed blasphemy and unrighteousness and have become ready for the day of slaughter and for the day of darkness and for the day of the great judgment. (1 En. 94.8–9)[18]

The precise nature of their unrighteousness, however, is not always clear. In only one case is it clear that oppression of the poor is one of the crimes of the rich:

> Woe unto you, you sinners, for your riches make you appear righteous, but your hearts convict you of being sinners, and this word shall be a testimony against you for a memorial of your evil deeds. Woe to you who eat the finest of the wheat and drink new wine, the choicest of the wine and tread underfoot the poor in your might. (1 En. 96.4–5)

In this passage one of the actions that belies the appearance of righteousness is the oppression of the poor. More often, however, it is the persecution of the righteous for which the rich are condemned (1 En. 95.7). Thus 1 Enoch may differ from the other examples cited in that its real concern is not so much with economic exploitation of the poor as with social dominance by those who are deemed unrighteous by the Enochic writer.

James's acceptance of the attitude displayed in these traditions is clear in 5:1–6, where the rich are advised to weep and lament in view of their impending judgment. Their injustice has been noted by God and will be judged. In this passage God is the arbiter of injustice done by the rich; the implication is that God's care for the poor is grounds for the

---

18. All translations of *1 Enoch* are taken from Matthew Black, *The Book of Enoch or I Enoch: A New English Edition* (SVTP 7; Leiden: Brill, 1985).

judgment of those who oppress the poor. In the light of this assurance, James advises his readers to be patient "because the Lord's coming is near" (Jas 5:8).

James has also another theological vantage point for developing his ethics of wealth and poverty. The occasional use of the term עֲנָוִים ("humble/poor/pious") in some of the Psalms has apparently led to a similar use of the term "poor" in some of the *Psalms of Solomon*.[19] The term is apparently used as a self-designation in certain of the sectarian Qumran texts, possibly because the writers may have identified their piety with a lack of desired social status. This is especially clear in Pesher Habakkuk and the pesher on Ps 37.

> The interpretation of the word concerns the Wicked Priest, to pay him the reward for what he did to the poor.... God will sentence him to destruction, exactly as he intended to destroy the poor. (1QpHab 12.2–6)

> And the poor shall inherit the land and enjoy peace in plenty. Its interpretation concerns the congregation of the poor who will tolerate the period of distress and will be rescued from all the snares of Belial. (4QpPs37 2.9–11)[20]

What is distinctive about James's exhortation to impartiality is not simply that he adopts the identification of poverty and piety (which he seems to do in part), but that he applies his apocalyptic interpretation of the contours of reality to the problem. The eschatology of James is relatively conventional. He appeals to eschatology in order to encourage the pious and to threaten the wicked. Eschatology, however, does not provide the theological foundation for the statements of chapter 2. That foundation is provided by the apocalyptic division of the cosmos into above and below (3:15), God and this world (4:4), God and the devil (4:7; 3:15), and the contrast between desire, which leads to sin, and the word of truth, which gives "us" birth (1:14–18; cf. 4:1–4). James objects to far more than simple acts of exploitation. He objects to a whole cosmic structure that is in open conflict with God and that determines the false and evil social structure in which humans live.

---

19. For example, "And the devout shall give thanks in the assembly of the people, and God will be merciful to the poor to the joy of Israel" (*Pss. Sol.* 10:6; see also 15:1; 18:2). Translations of the *Psalms of Solomon* are from Robert B. Wright, "Psalms of Solomon," *OTP* 2:639–70.

20. Translations of the Dead Sea Scrolls are from Florentino García Martínez, *The Dead Sea Scrolls Translated: The Qumran Texts in English* (trans. W. G. E. Watson; Leiden: Brill, 1994).

Dibelius is typical in his explanation of apocalypticism as the reason for Jesus' convictions regarding the poor (which have influenced James).

> If the proclaimer of this message and those who followed him lived in poverty, it was not because of thoroughgoing asceticism or strict proletarian consciousness, for Jesus consents to support from others and to being invited as a guest. The decisive element, again, is the apocalyptic expectation. He lives apart from active involvement in the economic functions of the world because he foresees the end of this world. Thanks to the situation in Galilee and the hospitality of his followers, this life of poverty never becomes penurious and proletarian.[21]

He is correct that apocalypticism has influenced this thinking, but he is not correct in emphasizing the "apocalyptic expectation." It was not merely the expectation of certain future events that influenced these attitudes, but more fundamentally it was the apocalyptic way of understanding the present.

James's appropriation of Jesus' beatitude contains a critical window onto his understanding of the meaning of poverty—James's addition of the little phrase τῷ κόσμῳ ("in the world's point of view"). Unlike Matthew, whose addition of τῷ πνεύματι ("in spirit") limits the scope of the word "poor" to poverty that cannot be measured in material terms, James adds a modifier that accepts the material sense of the word, but at the same time he criticizes it as false. The conventional use of the word "poor" is inauthentic because it assumes the social order of the world in which the rich (those who have social as well as economic status) are honored and the poor are dishonored and exploited. The fact that God has chosen the poor and dishonored of this world to be rich in faith and to inherit the kingdom is proof that the conventional criteria for assigning honor are false and in need of reversal. The importance of this view for James is evident also in his exhortation to the "lowly" brother (ὁ ἀδελφὸς ὁ ταπεινός) to boast in his exalted position, while the rich man (not "brother") should "boast" in his humiliation in view of the fact that he is about to perish (1:9–10). These verses are a clear declaration of the reversal of values that James believes is in force within the Christian community. Thus the addition of τῷ κόσμῳ clearly connects James' ethics concerning the poor with his wider conviction of the dualism of heaven and earth with its concomitant ethic of social reversal.

One other passage confirms James's negative evaluation of the world. In 3:13–4:10 James contrasts two kinds of wisdom and the consequences

---

21. Dibelius, *James*, 43.

of living by one or the other. According to 3:15, one kind of wisdom is "earthly, unspiritual, and demonic" (ἐπίγειος ψυχική δαιμονιώδης); the other "comes down from above" (ἄνωθεν κατερχομένη). The latter characterization should be understood in the context of 1:17 which proclaims that "every good and perfect gift is from above (ἄνωθεν), coming down (καταβαῖνον) from the Father of lights." Commentators have rightly understood this characterization of wisdom in the light of the traditional Jewish understanding of wisdom as a gift of God, the one who created wisdom and who is truly wise.[22] It is possible, however, that "coming down from above" is an allusion to a more concrete tradition of the descent of wisdom from heaven to earth to dwell among those who were to receive her (Sir 24:1–12; denied in *1 En.* 42:1–2).

James presses this contrast even more forcefully in the discussion of the opposition of the world to God that follows his characterization of wisdom. In his criticism of those who want to have things that they can squander on their own pleasures (4:3), James says that friendship with the world (κόσμος) is hatred toward God (4:4) and that God resists the proud but exalts the lowly (4:6, 10). The readers are accused of being "double-minded" (δίψυχοι) precisely because of their failed attempt to bring this diabolic cosmos (4:7) into harmony with God.

Conclusion

Moral exhortation (how one ought to live in this world) has probably always been one of the functions of apocalyptic literature. Our fascination with the temporal, eschatological aspects of apocalyptic texts and their outlandish descriptions of future judgment and heavenly journeys may sometimes blind us to the function of these mythical descriptions as symbols for an ethical system that involves the rejection of experienced social realities. The scholarly emphasis on the bizarre elements of apocalyptic may have also helped to obscure the fundamental concern with the "here and now" of all apocalyptic texts insofar as they seek to explain and redefine experienced reality and the moral obligations of those who live in that reality. The literary function of the mythical elements is to create an imaginative interpretation of the structure of the cosmos. Texts, such as James, that deemphasize the geographic contours of heaven and hell and the details of future judgment, but that adopt the dualistic definition of reality that is characteristic of apocalyptic literature should not be excluded from the category of apocalyptic. Some texts (those that belong to

---

22. E.g., Dibelius, *James*, 212; Johnson, *James*, 272; Vouga, *Saint Jacques*, 105; Davids, *James*, 152.

the genre of apocalyptic) are characterized by descriptions of the apocalyptic construction of reality. Others, such as James, adopt that construction but focus on understanding one's rightful place within the apocalyptically defined cosmos. By interpreting Jesus' teachings within the context of an apocalyptic construction of reality, James has created a powerful social critique and a positive foundation for granting honor to those who otherwise lack it.

CITY VISIONS, FEMININE FIGURES AND ECONOMIC CRITIQUE: A SAPIENTIAL *TOPOS* IN THE APOCALYPSE

Barbara R. Rossing

Wealth, poverty, and imperial critique are central to the book of Revelation, climaxing in the vivid contrast between Babylon and New Jerusalem as competing political economies. While Revelation's apocalyptic city visions have been widely analyzed for their use of material from the Hebrew prophets, Revelation also draws on wisdom traditions to structure the ethical contrast between Babylon and New Jerusalem. Specifically, Revelation introduces the two cities first as "women" or feminine figures dressed in contrasting clothing in order to invoke recognition of a "two-women" ethical *topos* that was well-known in Jewish, pagan, and early Christian contexts. The topos furnished a structure for exhorting the audience to shun the evil alternative (Babylon/Rome) and embrace the good (New Jerusalem). Revelation thus offers an example of the interplay of wisdom and apocalyptic traditions in the service of hard-hitting economic and political critique.

The first part of the paper will introduce the sapiential two-women *topos* and its wide-ranging use in ancient texts. Indeed, I will propose that this two-women *topos* is so prevalent in ancient Jewish, pagan, and early Christian texts that the nomenclature of what has been called the "two-ways" tradition should be expanded to include "two women." In the second part of the paper, I will analyze Revelation's transformation of the two-women tradition out of the realm of wisdom and personal morals into the realm of political and economic critique. Revelation fills out the feminine figures not as Vice and Virtue nor wisdom and folly, as in the tradition of Proverbs and the moralists, but as two powerful empires—God's empire and Babylon—with their contrasting economies, ideologies, and citizenships. In analyzing how Revelation employs the two-women tradition to construct a comprehensive indictment of Rome and a vision of citizenship in God's alternative empire (New Jerusalem), I will focus on the element of economic critique. The gold and jewelry that adorn the evil prostitute in chapter 17 furnish a "bridge image" to more sweeping economic critique of the Roman Empire in chapter 18. The author uses the two-women *topos* to exhort the audience to "come out" of the unjust economy of Babylon/Rome in order to participate in God's New Jerusalem, where the essentials of life are given to everyone "without cost" (δωρεάν).

Revelation's Feminine Figures: Are The "Women" Modeled on Prophetic Traditions?

Separately, the images of both a new Jerusalem and an evil Babylon appear frequently in Jewish literature of the Second Temple period, as a description of the future blessing of God's people and as a critique of the Roman Empire.[1] Revelation is unique, however, in juxtaposing Jerusalem and Babylon as contrasting cities with the exhortation to the audience to "Come out" (ἐξελθεῖν, Rev 18:4) of the one city in order to be eligible to enter into (εἰσελθεῖν, Rev 21:27, 22:14) the other.[2] Also unique to Revelation is the introduction of both cities as "women" (γυνή, Rev 17:4, 19:7), distinguishable in terms of their contrasting clothing, jewelry and physical appearances. Revelation portrays evil Babylon as a woman "arrayed in purple and scarlet, and bedecked with gold jewels and pearls" (Rev 17:4), while her counterpart, the lamb's wife/woman,[3] is "clothed with fine linen, bright and pure" (Rev 19:8).

Many scholars seek to explain Revelation's labeling of evil Babylon as the garish "prostitute" in terms of the Hebrew prophets' labeling of cities as prostitutes (see Jer 4:30; Isa 23:15–18, Ezek 16:13; Nah 3:4). M.-E. Boismard, Albert Vanhoye, Jean-Pierre Ruiz, and others have argued that the harlot's purple, scarlet, gold, jewels, and pearls are modeled on Ezek 16 and 23,[4] while John Court has proposed Jer 4:30 as a source.[5] But such

---

1. Jerusalem: *4 Ezra* 9–10; *2 Bar.* 4; *Sib. Or.* 5.420–27; Tob 13–14; Gal 4:26; Heb 12:22; Babylon: *4 Ezra* 3:1–2, 28–31; *2 Bar.* 10:1; 11:1; 67:7; *Sib. Or.* 5.143, 159; 1 Pet 5:13.

2. A number of literary features establish the two city visions' close parallelism, especially in the opening and closing verses. In both visions the same angel of the bowl plagues extends the invitation, "Come, I will show you" and carries the author "in the spirit" to a location where he is shown a city (Rev 17:1, 21:9). Both visions portray the city as a feminine figure. Both visions are followed by identical prohibitive commands not to worship the angel, who is a "fellow servant," but rather to worship God (Rev 19:10, 22:9).

3. The reading γυνή ("woman") is much better attested than νύμφη ("bride") in the manuscript evidence for Rev 19:7. It is unfortunate that both the RSV and NRSV translate γυνή as "bride" rather than "woman" in Rev 19:7, thereby obscuring the parallelism of this figure with the "woman" of Rev 17:4.

4. Albert Vanhoye, "L'utilisation du livre d'Ézéchiel dans L'Apocalypse," *Bib* 43 (1962): 436–76; M.-E. Boismard, "'l'Apocalypse' ou 'les apocalypses' de S. Jean," *RB* 56 (1949): 507–41; Jean-Pierre Ruiz, *Ezekiel in the Apocalypse: The Transformation of Prophetic Language in Revelation 16:17–19:10* (European University Studies 23/376; Frankfurt: Lang, 1989).

prophetic parallels do not fully explain the attention to the prostitute's dress or other unique features of Revelation's personification.[6] Likewise, while the bridal woman's radiant clothing, adornment, and jewelry, and the call to rejoice in Rev 19:7 may link her to Isa 61:10, as Jan Fekkes has proposed, even Fekkes is forced to concede the lack of "close dictional correspondence" between Rev 19:8 and the Isaiah text.[7]

More importantly, Revelation structures the rhetorical appeal of its city visions very differently from that of Ezekiel or Jeremiah. Ezekiel and Jeremiah accuse the audience itself—God's people, "Jerusalem"—of playing the harlot (compare the accusations addressed to "you" in Ezek 16:13, Jer 4:30). By contrast, Rev 17–18 scripts the audience not in the role of the harlot city but rather as potential victims who must resist her seductions, a significant shift in terms of rhetorical appeal. Revelation's urgent warning to the audience to "Come out" of Babylon (Rev 18:4) is closer to Proverbs' warning to resist the strange woman than to Ezekiel's or Jeremiah's indictments of the audience as a harlot.

I propose that Prov 1–9 and the sapiential/moralist "two-women" tradition furnished an important model on which the author of Revelation also drew, both for the physical descriptions of the prostitute and bride, and for the overall "either-or" rhetorical structure of the Babylon/New Jerusalem ethical polarity. Such a two-women tradition would have been familiar to ancient audiences both from the Jewish wisdom tradition and from the broad popular moralist tradition, including the story of Heracles' choice.

THE MORALISTS' VERSION OF THE "TWO-WOMEN" OR "TWO-CHOICE" TRADITION: HERACLES' CHOICE

The story of the choice of Heracles was a stock moral *topos* in the ancient world, employed by pagan, Jewish, and Christian authors to represent ethical "either-or" choices of various sorts. Philostratus summarizes the story in his sketch of the philosopher Prodicus, who first composed the tale:

---

5. John Court, *Myth and History in the Book of Revelation* (Atlanta: John Knox, 1979), 141.
6. Of the five elements in Revelation's description—purple, scarlet, gold, jewels, and pearls—only "gold" appears in Ezek 16:13, and only "scarlet" and "gold" appear in Jer 4:30.
7. Jan Fekkes, "His Bride Has Prepared Herself: Revelation 12–21 and Isaian Nuptial Imagery," *JBL* 109 (1990): 273; see also idem, *Isaiah and Prophetic Traditions in the Book of Revelation: Visionary Antecedents and Their Development* (JSNTSup 93; Sheffield: JSOT Press, 1994), 236.

Prodicus of Ceos composed a certain pleasant fable in which Virtue (Ἀρετή) and Vice (Κακία) came to Heracles in the shape of women, one of them dressed in seductive and multi-colored attire, the other with no care for effect. And to Heracles, who was still young, Vice offered idleness and sensuous pleasures, while Virtue offered squalor and toil on toil. For this story Prodicus wrote a rather long epilogue, and then he toured the cities and gave recitations of the story in public, for hire, and charmed them.[8]

The story appears in endless variations in numerous ancient texts, over many centuries, to exhort a variety of actions. The widespread familiarity of the Heracles topos is evident from the citations and allusions to it among a range of authors, including Christian authors. [9]

The central element of the Heracles *topos* is the visual contrast of two women, distinguishable in terms of their clothing and physical appearance. The stereotypical "evil woman" wears bright colors, make-up, and gold jewelry, and may be seductive, ugly, or otherwise "false" in her appearance. The "good woman" figure is typically radiant, simple, elegant, and dressed in white or linen garments. The second essential element of the Heracles *topos* is the exhortation to the audience to choose between the two women. In some texts the two women themselves make competing speeches, while in other texts a guide or narrator exhorts the choice. The exhortation to choose may also be accomplished simply by the visual contrast or *synkrisis* between two women.

Using this framework—a visual contrast between two feminine figures and an exhortation to choose one and reject the other—ancient authors could fill out the ethical contrast with a whole range of ethical topics. Vice and Virtue are the most common topics, but the *topos* also worked for contrasting other ethical or political opposites such as Peace and War (Silius Italicus), Strife and Concord (Aelius Aristides), or Flattery and Friendship (Maximus of Tyre). Lucian employs a version of the *topos* to explain his rejection of a career in Sculpture (scripted as the "evil woman") in favor of the pursuit of a career in Rhetoric (scripted as the

---

8. Philostratus, *Lives of the Sophists* 482–483 (trans. W. C. Wright; LCL; London: Heinemann, 1922). See also §496: "Even Xenophon did not disdain to relate the fable (μῦθος) of Prodicus called *The Choice of Heracles*." Philostratus adapted the story to represent Apollonius's choice for the feminine figure of "wisdom" in *Life of Apollonius* 6.10.

9. See Xenophon, *Mem.* 2.1.21–22; Maximus of Tyre, *Or.* 14.1; Dio Chrysostom, *Or.* 1.66–84; Lucian, *The Dream* 6; *Double Indictment* 21; *On Salaried Posts in Great Houses*; *A Professor of Public Speaking*; *Hermotimus*; Julian, *Or.* 2.57; Philo, *Sacrifices* 20–35; Cicero, *Off.* 1.32.118; Athenaeus, *Deipnosophistae* 12.510; Silius Italicus, *Pun.* 15.1–132; *Tabula of Cebes*; Justin Martyr, *Second Apology* 11; Clement of Alexandria, *Paed.* 2.10.110.

"good woman").¹⁰ Dio Chrysostom uses the Heracles story politically, casting the good woman as Royalty (Βασιλεία) and the evil woman as Tyranny (Τυραννίδα) in order to appeal to the emperor Trajan to rule benevolently rather than tyrannically. Clement of Alexandria uses it to exhort Christian women to dress modestly, while Justin Martyr uses it to applaud Christians' fearlessness in the face of death. Whatever the topic, audiences familiar with the topos would recognize the two women from their visual description and the contrasting "either-or" parallelism by which they are introduced.

The Jewish Wisdom "Two Women" Tradition: Philo of Alexandria; 4Q184, 4Q185

If Revelation drew on the two-women *topos* in structuring the two-city contrast, as I argue, it is probable that the author was familiar from this *topos* not directly from the Heracles story or the moralists, but from the broad stream of Jewish wisdom traditions. Proverbs 1–9 provides the paradigm, with its contrasting feminine figures of Wisdom and the evil woman who compete for men's allegiance. Wearing the dress of a prostitute, the evil woman of Proverbs woos young men with seductive speech (Prov 5:3; 7:21), while Wisdom offers a table of bread and wine and bestows gifts of life, honor, wealth, a good name, and a crown. The reader is urged to choose Wisdom: "Say to wisdom, 'You are my sister,' and call insight your intimate friend, that they may keep you from the loose woman, from the adulteress with her smooth words" (Prov 7:4–5).

The use of the Proverbs *topos* by Philo of Alexandria shows how the personified feminine figures could be elaborated and modified in light of the Heracles story. In *On the Sacrifices of Abel and Cain,* Philo does not explicitly mention either Proverbs or the Heracles story, but his basic structure resembles the familiar portraits:¹¹

> For each of us is mated with two wives, who hate and loathe each other, and they fill the house of the soul with their jealous contentions. And one of these we love, because we find her winning and gentle, and we

---

10. See Lucian, *Dream* 6. Cicero is another author who uses the *topos* to discuss a choice of careers (*Off.* 1.32.118).

11. Jean LaPorte, "Philo in the Tradition of Biblical Wisdom Literature," in *Aspects of Wisdom in Judaism and Early Christianity* (ed. R. L. Wilken; University of Notre Dame Center for the Study of Judaism and Christianity in Antiquity 1; South Bend, Ind.: University of Notre Dame Press, 1975), 112, argues that although Philo is familiar with the two-women *topos* from biblical tradition, his use of it is more akin to the classical tradition. He "develops it according to the Greek example of Heracles at the crossing."

think her our nearest and dearest. Her name is Pleasure ('Ηδονή). The
other we hate; we think her rough, ungentle, crabbed and our bitter
enemy. Her name is virtue ('Αρετή). So Pleasure comes languishing in
the guise of a harlot or courtesan (πόρνη).... [T]he lascivious roll of her
eyes is a bait to entice the souls of the young. (Philo, *Sacrifices* 20–21)

Philo's Pleasure is a shameless figure, wearing gold and jewels, with braided hair, excessive make-up, false beauty, and artificial scents. She promises freedom from punishment and a coffer of blessings. Upon hearing Pleasure's seductive speech, the plain-clad figure of Virtue steps forward to warn that Pleasure's beauties are "mere nets and snares to take you as her prey." Philo concludes this allegory with a call to resist the ways of Pleasure and a warning of some one hundred and fifty vices that will befall the person who succumbs to the easy way of Pleasure.

The two-woman/two-way tradition was also at home in the sectarian Jewish setting of Qumran. "The Wiles of the Wicked Woman" (4Q184) is a vivid portrayal of an evil seductress, in the tradition of Prov 1–9.[12] The text describes in lurid detail the body, garments, and dwelling of an evil woman who leads people astray:

[...] speaks vanity and [...] errors. She is ever prompt to oil her words.
... her eyes are defiled with iniquity; her hands have seized hold of the
Pit; her legs go down to work wickedness, and to walk in wrong-doings.
Her [...] are foundations of darkness, and a multitude of sins is in her
skirts. Her [...] are darkness of night, and her garments [...] Her clothes
are shades of twilight, and her ornaments plagues of corruption.[13]

Most scholars identify the seductress of 4Q184 as the familiar figure of "Folly" or the "Strange Woman" from Proverbs.[14] The text does not confine itself to the Proverbs description, however, but adds specifics about her dress and body and expands the language of darkness, dualism, election, and punishment for those seduced by her.[15] Although 4Q184 does

---

12. John Allegro, "The Wiles of the Wicked Woman: A Sapiential Work from Qumran's Fourth Cave," *PEQ* 96 (1964): 53.

13. 4Q184 1–7; trans. Geza Vermes, *The Complete Dead Sea Scrolls in English* (London: Penguin, 1997), 395. The full seductress text is seventeen lines.

14. So Daniel Harrington, *Wisdom Texts from Qumran* (The Literature of the Dead Sea Scrolls; London: Routledge, 1996), 33; see also Rick Moore, "Personification of the Seduction of Evil: 'The Wiles of the Wicked Woman,'" *RevQ* 10 (1981): 505–19.

15. So Harrington (*Wisdom Texts from Qumran*, 33): "In this respect—the theme of the eternal rewards for following Lady Wisdom and the eternal punishment for following Lady Folly, the Qumran text goes beyond what appears in its biblical model, Proverbs 1–9." Harrington pairs 4Q184 with 4Q185, a Wisdom counterpart to the seductress text.

not explicitly mention a second woman, Wisdom, as the positive counterpart to the evil figure, many scholars pair 4Q184 with 4Q185, a composition about Wisdom as a positive feminine figure. Even without the second woman, Daniel Harrington reads an implicit two-way structure in 4Q184 and an appeal to the audience to make a choice:

> The poem has created a harshly negative portrait that is intended to warn the readers against the enticements of Lady Folly. The readers have to make a choice between the way of Wisdom and the way of Folly. The intellectual presupposition of the text is the dualism of the "two ways" found in Proverbs and in the Qumran sectarian writings (the classic example of which is Community Rule 3:13–4:26).[16]

This linking of the dualism of 4Q184 to a broader tradition is important, although I will question Harrington's labeling the dualistic tradition as the "two ways" (see below).

Reviewing the Question: Two Women or Two Ways?

To summarize, an ethical *topos* of two personified "women" figures— one evil, one good, both wooing seekers—was well-known in pagan and Jewish wisdom literature. Elaborations on the two feminine figures abound both in Hellenized wisdom settings, with influence from the Heracles tradition, and also in the more sectarian and apocalyptic setting of Qumran.[17] In considering whether and how the author of Revelation might have used this sapiential two-women *topos*, two points are important:

First, while the structure is similar to what has been called the "two ways" tradition, the word "way" (ὁδός) was not a necessity for invoking the "either-or" ethical *topos*. "Ways" and "women" could be used almost interchangeably. In Prov 1–9, as in the original Heracles story of Xenophon, the motifs of "two ways" and "two women" are closely linked, though not identical.[18] The relative importance of "ways" and

---

16. Ibid., 34–35.
17. For the characterization of the Qumran community as "apocalyptic," see John J. Collins, "Was the Dead Sea Sect an Apocalyptic Movement?" in *Archaeology and History in the Dead Sea Scrolls: The New York University Conference in Memory of Yigael Yadin* (ed. L. Schiffman; JSPSup 8; JSOT/ASOR Monograph Series 2; Sheffield: JSOT Press, 1990), 25–52.
18. Klaus Berger ("Hellenistische Gattungen im Neuen Testament," *ANRW* 25.2:1091) suggests that the role of the women as "guides" or "companions" in the Heracles tradition is different from the standard function of the "two ways": "Die Frauen sind daher nicht (nur) Personifikationen der beiden Wege, sie sind vielmehr Gefährtinnen und Führerinnen. In der gesamten Heraklestradition liegt eine ausgeführte Zwei-Wege-Lehre nicht vor."

"women" in the imagery of Prov 1–9 and in the broader wisdom tradition is a matter of debate. Norman Habel argues that "way" is the primary or "nuclear symbol," while the feminine figures are "satellite symbols."[19] Claudia Camp points to the *inclusio* of female imagery framing the book of Proverbs (chs. 1–9 and 31) to counter that Woman Wisdom is the book's "root metaphor."[20] Raymond Van Leeuwen rejects such attempts to reduce the tradition to one single root metaphor of either ways or women. Together, the "roads" and "women" are both root metaphors that "embody different, though related aspects of one underlying" view.[21]

The implications of this "way *versus* woman" argument are broader than Prov 1–9. At stake is the claim to the tradition that New Testament scholars have almost universally labeled as the "two ways" tradition. To the degree that this "two ways" label carries with it the implication that all other two-choice ethical imagery is somehow derivative from or subordinate to "ways," this label should be challenged. The assumption of primacy for "ways" may fit some Christian texts (*Didache, Barnabas*, Matt 7:13–14) but it does not reflect the complexity of the biblical or early Christian tradition (for example, *Shepherd of Hermas*) in which "two women" and other images may be equally foundational.

Robert Kraft has proposed expanding the two-ways terminology to speak of a "basic binary form" that can be manifested in a variety of pairs of ethical opposites, including life/death (*Didache*), light/darkness (*Barnabas*), angels or spirits of righteousness/iniquity (*Barnabas*, 1QS), truth/error (1QS, *Testaments of the Twelve Patriarchs*), good/evil, law of the Lord/works of Belial, straight/crooked, and right hand/left hand.[22] Indeed, the Hebrew Bible itself contains at least two separate strands of two-choice imagery, a covenantal strand in Deut 30:15–20 in addition to the wisdom strand in Prov 1–9. A whole range of biblical and classical texts appeal to the same general "two-choice" ethical structure, which may have arisen independently in several different forms, and which

---

19. Norman Habel, "The Symbolism of Wisdom in Proverbs 1–9," *Int* 26 (1972): 133.

20. Camp adds the word "woman" to her translation of Prov 1:20 ("Wisdom Is a *Woman* Who Cries Aloud in the Street," in *Wisdom and the Feminine in the Book of Proverbs* [Bible and Literature 11; Sheffield: Almond, 1985], 73). See also idem, "Woman Wisdom as Root Metaphor: A Theological Consideration," in *The Listening Heart: Essays in Wisdom and the Psalms in Honor of Roland Murphy* (ed. K. Hoglund et al.; JSOTSup 58; Sheffield: JSOT Press, 1987), 45–76.

21. Raymond Van Leeuwen, "Liminality and Worldview in Proverbs 1–9," *Semeia* 50 (1990): 113–14.

22. Robert Kraft, "Early Developments of the 'Two-Ways Tradition(s),' in Retrospect" in *For a Later Generation: The Transformation of Tradition in Israel, Early Judaism and Early Christianity* (ed. R. A. Argall et al.; Harrisburg, Pa.: Trinity Press International, 2000), 137–38.

could be elaborated in a number of possible directions by focusing on ways, women, or other imagery.[23]

The absence of the word "way" (ὁδός) from Revelation's city visions does not preclude the use of this two-choice tradition, if the ethical "either-or" *topos* structure is established instead by contrasting feminine figures. Other authors such as Clement, Aristides, Philostratus, and Philo also do not use the word "way," yet the presence of the topos in their work is unmistakable. The "basic binary form" (Kraft's language) of Virtue/Vice or Wisdom/Evil Woman offered imagery that could be elaborated in several different directions—with or without the women, and with or without the ways—while still making the same ethical appeal to the audience to choose between contrasting alternatives.

Second, while Revelation's language world is apocalyptic, this does not preclude the use of wisdom imagery in constructing the text's ethical appeal. The argument for the use of a sapiential *topos* in Revelation becomes more plausible in light of the evidence from the Qumran and other texts that there was no strict separation between apocalyptic and wisdom genres in Hellenistic Jewish literature. Other Jewish texts with apocalyptic frameworks and language also make extensive use of wisdom elements.

Indeed, the whole division between wisdom and apocalyptic genres in Hellenistic Jewish texts is being called into question in this SBL Group. George Nickelsburg has identified apocalyptic elements in so-called wisdom texts (Tobit, Sirach, Baruch) and a comparable number of wisdom elements in Jewish apocalypses (Daniel, 2 *Baruch*, 4 *Ezra*). Hybrid "texts that complicate the categories" (Wisdom of Solomon, 1QS 3:13–4:26) employ both wisdom and apocalyptic elements. Given such overlapping imagery, Nickelsburg concluded that "the entities usually defined as sapiential and apocalyptic often cannot be cleanly separated from one another."[24] John Collins came to similar genre-bending conclusions in a 1993 study,[25] arguing that wisdom forms (macarisms, woes) and ethical admonitions are frequent in apocalyptic literature. Testamen-

---

23. Berger calls the tradition one of an "Entscheidung zwischen zwei Möglichkeiten" that can be represented equally well by either ways or women ("Hellenistische Gattungen," 1091).

24. George W. E. Nickelsburg, "Wisdom and Apocalypticism in Early Judaism," reprinted in this volume. Among the features Nickelsburg identifies as common to both sapiential and apocalyptic texts are "wisdom forms; and interest in Torah and prophets; prediction of future events; ethical admonitions; claims of revelation" (p. 20).

25. John J. Collins, "Wisdom, Apocalypticism, and Genre Compatibility," in *In Search of Wisdom: Essays in Memory of John G. Gammie* (ed. L. G. Perdue et al.; Philadelphia: Westminster, 1993), 165–85.

tary literature is another genre in which a hybrid of sapiential material (primarily ethical exhortation) is embedded in an apocalyptic worldview. For the *Testaments of the Twelve Patriarchs*, "The wisdom tradition provides the ethical focus of the testament; the apocalyptic traditions provide the explanatory frame, the larger context of meaning."[26]

Such a description of a "sapiential ethical focus within an apocalyptic context of meaning" may also be helpful for characterizing the genre of Revelation. The book of Revelation combines a large number of apocalyptic and prophetic elements in an epistolary frame. A strong ethical dualism, reminiscent of the wisdom tradition, runs throughout Revelation.[27] In addition to the "two women" *topos* that I have identified, wisdom influence can also be seen in the book's calls for "Sophia" on the part of the reader (Rev 13:18; 17:9), in the use of wisdom forms such as macarisms and vice lists,[28] and in imagery such as the descent of God's σκηνή (compare Sir 24) in the New Jerusalem vision.[29] Sapiential traditions are more important to the language world of Revelation than has been recognized.

Revelation's Transformation of the Two Women

When the two feminine city figures first appear in Rev 17–21, each one initially fits the visual pattern of the sapiential two-women *topos*. Attired in purple and scarlet, with jewelry of gold and pearls, Babylon looks more like the stereotypical "evil woman" seductress from the Heracles story than any figure from the Hebrew prophets.[30] Her golden "cup," full of abominations and the impurities of her fornications (Rev 17:4), may be another link to the moralist tradition, recalling the identifying objects that a number of the moralists place in the hands of their evil woman figures.[31] Similarly, when the bride appears for her marriage to

---

26. Collins, "Wisdom, Apocalypticism and Generic Compatibility," 179.

27. See Elisabeth Schüssler Fiorenza's observation that "Revelation engages in a radical ethical dualism that places before the audience an either-or decision" (*Revelation: Vision of a Just World* [Proclamation Commentaries; Minneapolis: Fortress, 1991], 130).

28. Seven macarisms are employed in Revelation: 1:3; 14:15; 16:15; 19:9; 20:6; 22:7; 22:14. Vice lists: Rev 9:21; 21:8, 27; 22:15.

29. See my *The Choice between Two Cities: Whore, Bride and Empire in the Apocalypse* (HTS 48; Harrisburg, Pa.: Trinity Press International, 1999).

30. Her dress resembles Philostratus's figure of Vice, "adorned with gold and necklaces and with purple raiment ... and she also wears golden slippers" (*Life of Apollonius* 6.10). Silius Italicus's evil figure of Pleasure wears a robe of Tyrian purple, embroidered with gold (*Pun.* 15.25); Dio Chrysostom's Tyranny wears a dress of "purple, scarlet, and saffron" (*Or.* 1.79).

31. Jacobus Wettstein, Pierre Prigent, and others note the similarity of Revelation's Babylon's cup to the opening scene of the *Tabula of Cebes*, in which a young seeker receives a

the Lamb immediately following Babylon's fall (Rev 19:7-9), her pure bright linen and her radiant appearance resemble the dress of the stereotypical "good woman." "Bright" and "pure" (λαμπρός and καθαρός) are attributes of the "good woman" for Dio Chrysostom, Xenophon, and Clement, and also for the Wisdom of Solomon (6:12).

What is striking in Revelation is that once the visual presentations of the two stereotypical "women" have served to invoke the familiar "either-or" ethical *topos*, the embodied aspects of the "women" recede from prominence. From the naming of the harlot as Babylon in Rev 17:5 through the end of the Babylon vision, imagery of empire or *polis* takes over. The bridal woman, too, quickly disappears into a spacious bridal city in chapters 21-22. The author's interest is clearly not in women but in cities.

Revelation's genius comes in transforming the two-women topos out of the realm of wisdom and personal morals into the realm of economic and political critique. The familiar sapiential two-women *topos* provides the structure for the ethical contrast of the Babylon/Jerusalem polarity, but Revelation does not fill out the contrasting figures in a sapiential way. The two women of Revelation are not Virtue and Vice (the original figures in Prodicus's story of Heracles), nor Wisdom and Folly (Prov 1-9) nor even contrasting models of ruling (Dio Chrysostom's Tyranny and Royalty). They are two mighty cities—two powerful empires—the one demonic and the other divine. Revelation uses the *topos* not to exhort the audience to "live wisely" or "control your passions," as in the sages and moralists, but to exhort the audience to undertake an exodus out of an evil empire.

Revelation accomplishes this fundamental transformation of the two-women ethical tradition into the realm of political and economic critique by drawing on the Hebrew prophets and their personification of cities as feminine figures. By means of Jeremiah's cup of wrath, Revelation politicizes the cup of fornications that evil Babylon holds in her hand so that the golden cup itself becomes a symbol of judgment against the Roman Empire, foretelling its imminent destruction. Likewise, while "purple, scarlet, gold, jewels, and pearls" first appear as the stereotypical attire of the "evil woman" prostitute from Proverbs and the moralists in Rev 17:4,

---

drink from a woman seated on a throne who holds a "cup" in her hand. The overlapping vocabulary of the two texts is so striking that Prigent calls the similarity "unmistakable." See Jacobus Wettstein, *Novum Testamentum Graecum* (2 vols.; Amsterdam: Ex Officina Dommeriana, 1751), 2:820; Pierre Prigent *l'Apocalypse de Saint Jean* (2nd ed.; Geneva: Labor et Fides, 1988), 258. Jewish wisdom texts also portray the stereotypical evil woman as using wine to tempt or compel seekers; see *T. Jud.* 13:4-5; *T. Reu.* 3:13.

these elements become much more important over the course of Revelation's economic critique of Babylon/Rome in chapter 18. Drawing on Ezekiel's model of the shipwreck of Tyre's global trading economy (Ezek 25–27), Revelation attacks Rome's entire exploitive political economy, focusing on the merchants and their "growing rich" (πλουτέω, Rev 18:3, 18:19). Babylon's attire of purple, scarlet, gold, jewels, and pearls functions as a bridge-image, linking the critique of the prostitute to critique of the merchants' global trade in chapter 18. These same commodities of "purple, scarlet, gold, jewels, and pearls" head the list of the unjust cargoes of the merchants' doomed ship in Rev 18:12 and are the object of the merchants' lament as they weep over their great loss in 18:16:

> Alas, alas, the great city, clothed in fine linen and purple and scarlet, and gilded with gold and jewels and pearls. In one hour all this wealth has been laid waste. (Rev 18:16)

Such a transformation of "purple, scarlet, gold, jewels, and pearls" first from a feminine figure, then to a merchant ship's cargo list and finally to an entire imperial economy, has no precedent in the literature of the moralists or Proverbs. This transformation demonstrates the all-encompassing nature of Revelation's critique of Babylon/Rome as a seductive and dangerous prostitute, an evil economy, and an unjust empire.

Revelation's Social Location

One of the questions this Group is considering is how the critique of wealth may shed light on issues of Revelation's audience and social location. This is currently a topic of debate among Revelation scholars, partly due to differing views on the relationship between the polemic of the seven opening letters and the anti-Roman polemic of the rest of the book. Revelation addresses issues of wealth and poverty already in these letters (Rev 2–3). Smyrna lives in poverty but is said to be "rich" (πλοῦτος, Rev 2:9), while Laodicea—the wealthiest and proudest of the seven churches—is declared to be poor and is threatened with retribution for its excessive wealth and boasts of invincibility. Three instances of the adjective "rich" (πλούσιος) and verb "grow rich" (πλουτέω) in the letter to the Laodiceans underscore the centrality of wealth to the critique:

> You say, "I am rich, I have grown rich, and I need nothing." You do not realize that you are wretched, pitiable, poor, blind, and naked. Therefore I counsel you to buy from me gold refined by fire so that you may be rich. (Rev 3:17–18)

Yet the repetition of the same verb "grow rich" later in the book, in the critique of Babylon's/Rome's merchants and their global trade in Rev 18, underscores the political and imperial dimension of wealth and poverty for the author. In light of Rev 18, Rev 2–3 cannot be read as addressing economic issues at merely an individual or church level. The warning to the Laodicean church leads into the broader warning against the seductions of the entire imperial economy that will become the central polemic of Revelation.

I do not share the view of several recent scholars who have proposed locating the primary object of the Babylon polemic not externally (in the Roman Empire) but internally, as a polemic against other Christians such as the Laodiceans. Leonard Thompson, for example, understands Revelation as a "minority report on how Christians relate to the larger Roman society."[32] In his view, John's major challenge "comes not from outside the church but from Christians who are open to living in the world"[33]—from those seeking to assimilate socially and economically. In his view, the strong anti-Roman polemic is largely a generic convention of apocalypses, not a clue to the social location of Revelation.

My own position is more akin to that of Richard Bauckham, who interprets the Babylon vision primarily as an external critique of Rome, but who also points to the element of "deception" and "seduction" in Revelation's Babylon vision. The vast majority of Revelation's audience members were certainly poor. Bauckham suggests, however, that among those people deceived by the harlot may be a few members of the very Christian communities to which John is writing—Christian merchants or shippers involved them in the Roman economic system.[34] Addressing the issue of why the author of Revelation narrates the fall of Babylon from the perspective of those who mourn over Babylon (the kings, merchants, and seafarers, Rev 18:9–19), Bauckham suggests that the laments function as a kind of "hermeneutical trap" for those readers who may have collaborated, or are tempted to collaborate, with the Roman economy: "Any readers who find themselves sharing the perspective of Rome's mourners—viewing the prospect of the fall of Rome with dismay—should thereby discover, with a shock, where they stand, and the peril in which they stand."[35] In Bauckham's view, the command to "Come out" of

---

32. Leonard Thompson, *The Book of Revelation: Apocalypse and Empire* (Oxford: Oxford University Press, 1990), 132.

33. Ibid., 195.

34. Richard Bauckham, "Economic Critique of Rome in Revelation 18," in *Images of Empire* (ed. L. Alexander; JSOTSup 122; Sheffield: JSOT Press, 1991), 84.

35. Ibid.

Babylon (Rev 18:4) may be addressed also to some readers who "find themselves, with a salutary shock of recognition, among 'the merchants of the earth (who) have grown rich with the wealth of (Babylon's) wantonness' (18:3)."[36]

The Exhortation to "Come Out"

The call to "Come out" of Babylon in Rev 18:4 is a rhetorical key to the entire Babylon vision.[37] This call to "come out" has been the subject of widely differing interpretations, as scholars debate whether the command is to be read literally or metaphorically, as an appeal to the audience to withdraw from economic interaction with Babylon,[38] to cease participation in the imperial cult,[39] or to withdraw spiritually from participation in evil.[40] This exhortation links Revelation to the exodus tradition and also to the ethical two-choice tradition. Audience members are not cast merely as spectators in Revelation's two-city drama, watching as Babylon sinks into the sea and New Jerusalem descends from heaven. Rather, like Heracles, they stand at an ethical crossroads. The audience of Revelation is called to choose to undertake an exodus "out" from Babylon as a preparation for entry "into" God's new Jerusalem. Revelation 18:4 sets in motion the "either-or" choice that the audience must make.[41]

The macarism of Rev 19:9, "Blessed are those who are invited into the marriage supper of the Lamb," invites readers "into" the bridal woman's

---

36. Ibid., 86.
37. This call is modeled on Jer 51:45, "Come out of her, my people!" Similar exhortations to flee Babylon are issued in Jer 50:8; 51:6, 9, 50 and Isa 48:20; 52:11.
38. In 1977 Adela Yarbro Collins ("The Political Perspective of the Revelation to John," *JBL* 96 [1977]: 241–56) argued that Revelation's perspective is similar to that of the Zealots in advocating "refusal to use Roman coins." In 1984, however, she embraced a more psychological interpretation of the call to withdraw from Babylon as an example of Revelation's "turning aggression inward" in advocating strict social exclusivism (*Crisis and Catharsis: The Power of the Apocalypse* [Philadelphia: Westminster, 1984], 157).
39. J. Nelson Kraybill, *Imperial Cult and John's Apocalypse* (JSNTSup 132; Sheffield: Sheffield Academic Press, 1996). Kraybill views the primary polemic as against imperial cult participation, an idolatrous and unavoidable aspect of commerce in the late first century.
40. Augustine's spiritual interpretation is widely quoted: "This prophetic instruction is spiritually interpreted as meaning that we should escape from the city of this world (which is, of course, the society of wicked angels and of wicked men)" (*City of God* 18.18 [trans. H. Bettenson; New York: Penguin, 1972], 782).
41. Pablo Richard's interpretation of the meaning of "Come out" as a comprehensive economic, social, political, and spiritual resistance is convincing: "This departure from Rome is not understood in the physical sense.... the idea is to resist, to refuse to participate, to create alternatives" (*Apocalypse: A People's Commentary on the Book of Revelation* [Maryknoll, N.Y.: Orbis, 1995], 135).

marriage feast. No actual marriage takes place, however, since chapters 21–22 transform the bridal woman into a splendid and welcoming city. Guided by an angel, the audience takes a tour of this bridal city, culminating in God's voice speaking from the throne to offer an inheritance to those who conquer. Every detail of the city's evocative architecture, beauty, radiant stones, waters, and open gates invites the audience to enter as heirs and citizens. Terrifying threats of being left outside the city (Rev 21:8, 27) heighten the urgency of participation in this beloved city.

The tour of the city culminates in an irresistible description of the river and healing tree of life, followed by another macarism inviting the audience to enter: "Blessed are those who wash their robes that they may have the right to the tree of life and may enter into (εἰσελθεῖν) the city by the gates" (Rev 22:14). This invitation completes the exhortation to "Come out" from Rev 18:4. Readers who undertook an exodus out of Babylon are now called to "enter into" God's alternative empire of justice and well-being. The bridal woman herself repeats the invitation to "come" in Rev 22:17, echoing what may have been a familiar liturgical dialogue in the churches of Revelation: "The spirit and the bride say 'Come.' And let everyone who hears say 'Come.' And let the one who is thirsty come. Let anyone who is thirsty receive the water of life without payment" (δωρεάν). This bridal invitation recalls Wisdom's invitation to "Come" from the Proverbs tradition (see also Sir 24:19, "Come all you who desire me"). The economic image of water given free of charge, "without payment," may be based on Isa 55:1, a text that itself harks back to wisdom traditions.[42] Such economic aspects of New Jerusalem are very much a part of its appeal, perhaps because of the hunger and poverty of most of Revelation's communities.

As Elisabeth Schüssler Fiorenza points out, early apocalyptic language could function in two ways, either to control the behavior of individuals or to provide an alternative vision and encouragement of new community structures in the face of oppression.[43] Her distinction can apply also to the function of the two-women *topos*. The classical moralists

---

42. So Richard Clifford, "Isaiah 55: Invitation to a Feast," in *The Word of the Lord Shall Go Forth: Essays in Honor of David Noel Freedman in Honor of His Sixtieth Birthday* (ed. C. L. Meyers and J. Murphy-O'Connor; Winona Lake, Ind.: Eisenbrauns, 1983), 27. See also James Muilenberg ("The Book of Isaiah, Chapters 40–66," IB 5:642) for the argument that Isa 55:1 employs the "literary form of the wisdom writers of wisdom's invitation to a banquet (Prov 9:5–6, Sir 24:19–21, Matt 11:28–29)."

43. Elisabeth Schüssler Fiorenza, "The Phenomenon of Early Christian Apocalyptic: Some Reflections on Method" in *Apocalypticism in the Mediterranean World and the Near East: Proceedings of the International Colloquium on Apocalypticism, Uppsala, 1979* (ed. D. Hellholm; Tubingen: Mohr Siebeck, 1989), 313.

and many other authors employed the two-women *topos* moralistically, to influence the behavior of individuals. By contrast, the Apocalypse employs the *topos* politically, for encouragement of an alternative community, envisioned as citizenship in God's realm. The "evil woman," Babylon, represents Rome's entire unjust political economy and military empire. The bridal "good woman" represents God's visionary political economy—a *polis* of justice and healing in which the gifts of God are given to everyone, "without payment," even to those who have no money.

"THE *BASILEIA* OF JESUS IS ON THE WOOD": THE *EPISTLE OF BARNABAS* AND THE IDEOLOGY OF RULE

Ellen Bradshaw Aitken

INTRODUCTION

In the *Epistle of Barnabas,* the audience is addressed as the heirs of the covenant, as the inhabitants of the promised land, and as those who have been made new in God's new creation. This identity, according to *Barnabas,* is linked to Jesus' reign (βασιλεία) and results in the capacity to "rule" (κυριεύω). These ways of speaking about the community to whom this treatise is addressed, however, are set within an understanding of "the present time" as one in which the "worker of evil" is in power (*Barn.* 2:1). Thus in *Barnabas* we encounter the language of rule and governance within the basic framework for conceiving of the identity of the members of the inscribed community and the world in which they live. In this essay, I attempt to bring to the foreground questions of the exercise of ruling authority as I examine the world that this text constructs. I do so in order to understand how an ideology of rule informs the particular strategies of community formation and legitimization visible in *Barnabas,* as well as how this construction of an early second-century Christian community takes place with reference to the exercise of Roman imperial power.

After a consideration of the possible date and geographical provenance of *Barnabas,* the essay turns to an examination of how the author assesses the present situation of the inscribed community and thus also of the basic assumptions and perspectives at work in this text (principally in chs. 1–17 and thus not including the Two Ways material in chs. 18–20). This analysis provides the groundwork for considering the ritual, narrative, ethical, and interpretive practices by which the community is to constitute itself as participating in Jesus' reign. It will then be possible to see how *Barnabas*'s conception of the *basileia* of Jesus is closely linked to the practices and strategies of community formation. Thus it is important to speak not only of an "ideology" of rule, but also of the complex of rituals and narratives in which rule is embodied and expressed. On this basis it will then be possible to see how *Barnabas* locates its own practices in relation to the other practices and ideologies of rule, namely, those of covenantal Judaism (to which *Barnabas* refers simply as "they")[1] and the Roman *imperium*. Inquiring into the historical setting for these rhetorical strategies assists in understanding how *Barnabas* responds to the political situation of its time. Throughout this examination it will be evident how traditions or interpretive practices that can be parsed as either apocalyptic or sapiential work together within this text.

The principal argument of this essay is that *Barnabas* constructs an ideology of rule in which the *basileia* of Jesus is defined through the narrative of Jesus' passion. The paraenetic and polemic material in *Barnabas* is grounded, moreover, in the premise that the community gains access to this reign by means of baptism, specifically a baptism that is shaped by the process of remembering Jesus' suffering and death. Thus, the inscribed audience of this text is constituted as rulers and participants in Jesus' reign.

The Date and Provenance of the *Epistle of Barnabas*

The date and provenance of *Barnabas* are notoriously vexed questions. The issue of date, however, has a direct impact on our assessment of rule in *Barnabas*, because of the implications for the text's relation to Roman imperial activity in Jerusalem and with regard to the Jews. Discussion of the dating has centered on two passages in *Barnabas*, namely, 4:3–5 and 16:1–4. The first of these portrays the present situation in terms of an apocalyptic timetable of rulers:

> The final scandal is at hand, concerning which it is written, as Enoch says. For the master has cut short the times and the days for this reason, that his beloved may make haste and come into his inheritance. And the prophet speaks thus, "Ten kingdoms will reign on earth, and afterwards there will arise a little king, who will humiliate three of the kingdoms under one [or, at the same time, ὑφ' ἕν]." Likewise, Daniel says concerning the same one, "And I saw the fourth beast, evil and powerful and

---

1. The proper terms to categorize the identity of the other ("they") in *Barnabas* are elusive; clearly *Barnabas* is writing in opposition to a form of Israelite, covenantal religion that maintains the importance of the ritual prescriptions of Torah, including the sacrifices of the Jerusalem temple, but which is not refracted through the memory of Jesus. *Barnabas* claims the covenant for its own community ("we"), over against the claims of others, but this covenant is the "covenant of the beloved" (i.e., Jesus). *Barnabas* does not use language of "Jews" or "Christians."

more dangerous than all the beasts of the sea; and how ten horns rose up from him, and from them a little horn budded, and how it humiliated three of the great horns under one [or, at the same time]." Therefore, you ought to understand! (*Barn.* 4:3–5)[2]

The second passage, which needs to be taken together with the timetable of rulers, refers to the rebuilding of a temple in Jerusalem:

> And now, concerning the temple also, I will tell you how those miserable ones, erring, placed their hope in the building and not on their God who made them, as though it were a house of God. For, roughly speaking, they consecrated him by means of the temple, as the nations do. But how does the Lord speak when he abolishes it? Learn! "Who measured the heavens with a span, or the earth with a hand? Was it not I, says the Lord? The heaven is my throne, and the earth is a stool for my feet. What sort of house will you build for me, or what is the place of my rest?" You knew that their hope was vain. Furthermore, he says again, "Behold, those who tore down this temple will themselves build it." It is happening. For because of their warring it was torn down by the enemies, and now the servants (ὑπηρέται) of the enemies will themselves rebuild it. (*Barn.* 16:1–4)

On the basis of these two passages, a number of possibilities in the period between the two Jewish Wars, from 70 to 135 C.E. have been proposed: roughly 130–132 C.E. in reaction to Roman plans to rebuild the temple in Jerusalem under Hadrian as Aelia Capitolina;[3] a date toward the end of the reign of Trajan, approximately 115–117 C.E.;[4] the period in which

---

2. Translations of *Barnabas* are my own, based upon the Greek text of Robert A. Kraft in Pierre Prigent and Robert A. Kraft, *Épître de Barnabé* (SC 172; Paris: Cerf, 1971), and following at many points Kraft's English translation in Robert A. Kraft, *Barnabas and the Didache* (vol. 3 of *The Apostolic Fathers: A New Translation and Commentary*; ed. R. M. Grant; New York: Nelson, 1964).

3. John J. Gunther, "The Epistle of Barnabas and the Final Rebuilding of the Temple," *JJS* 7 (1976): 143–51; Leslie W. Barnard, "The 'Epistle of Barnabas' and Its Contemporary Setting," *ANRW* 27.1:180; and, most recently, Ferdinand R. Prostmeier, *Der Barnabasbrief* (Kommentar zu den Apostolischen Vätern; Göttingen: Vandenhoeck & Ruprecht, 1999), 118–19. Prigent and Kraft (*Épître de Barnabé*, 26–27) speak broadly of a date anywhere between 70 and the end of the second century but suggest the plausibility of a date in the second quarter of the second century. Similarly, Kraft (*Barnabas and the Didache*, 42–43) is reluctant to date the text precisely but also points out that, since *Barnabas* makes extensive use of source material, the age of these materials should be distinguished from the date of the final editing of the epistle.

4. This view is summarized, but not accepted, in Peter Richardson and Martin B. Shukster, "Barnabas, Nerva, and the Yavnean Rabbis," *JTS* NS 34 (1983): 33.

Vespasian shared his reign with his sons, Titus and Domitian, 70–79 C.E.;[5] and during or immediately after the reign of Nerva, 96–98 C.E.[6]

Without rehearsing all of the arguments here,[7] I take as a working premise Peter Richardson and Martin Shukster's argument that *Barnabas* dates from the reign of Nerva. They argue that this date alone makes the best sense of both pieces of internal evidence, that is, the rise of a fourth king over the preceding three, and the rebuilding of the temple by the servants of the enemy. Either Vespasian or Nerva makes the most sense out of the sequence of rulers, yet Nerva, as an unpredictable choice for emperor after the assassination of Domitian, best fits the description of "a little horn" that grows out of the preceding three (i.e., the three Flavian rulers).[8] The keystone of their argument, however, is the evidence for a change in imperial policy toward Judea and the Jews under Nerva, namely, the coin issue with the inscription, *fisci Iudaici calumnia sublata*.[9] They interpret this inscription as referring not to the abolition of the *fiscus Iudaicus*, imposed on all Jews in the empire by Vespasian in 70 C.E.,[10] but rather to a reform whereby the *fiscus* was directed toward a proposed rebuilding of the Jerusalem temple, instead of to Jupiter Capitolinus or the rebuilding of the Capitoline temple in Rome (as under Domitian). Although full evidence for such a change in policy is lacking, this interpretation makes good sense of the word *calumnia* ("pretense" or "trickery") on the coins and also of the contrast between this coin issue and the earlier *Iudaea capta* issues of the Flavians.[11] Thus, Richardson and

---

5. John A. T. Robinson, *Redating the New Testament* (London: SCM, 1976), 313–19.

6. Richardson and Shukster, "Barnabas, Nerva, and the Yavnean Rabbis," 53–55 followed by James Carleton Paget, *The Epistle of Barnabas: Outlook and Background* (WUNT 2/64; Tübingen: Mohr Siebeck, 1994), 42–45. Prostmeier, *Barnabasbrief*, does not appear to know Richardson and Shukster's argument or to consider the numismatic and rabbinic evidence that they adduce.

7. An excellent summary and analysis are provided in Carleton Paget, *Epistle of Barnabas*, 9–30.

8. Richardson and Shukster ("Barnabas, Nerva, and the Yavnean Rabbis," 40) assert that the figure of "ten" kingdoms is simply carried over from Daniel into *Barnabas* and does not have particular contemporary valence for *Barnabas*. Carleton Paget (*Epistle of Barnabas*, 28) suggests that *Barnabas* here may be adapting to the reign of Nerva a text that originally referred to Vespasian.

9. Richardson and Shukster, "Barnabas, Nerva, and the Yavnean Rabbis," 41. On this coin issue, they cite, among others, I. A. F. Bruce, "Nerva and the *Fiscus Iudaicus*," *PEQ* 96 (1964): 34–45.

10. They point out that if this were the case the inscription should read *fiscus Iudaicus sublatus* (Richardson and Shukster, "Barnabas, Nerva, and the Yavnean Rabbis," 42).

11. Richardson and Shukster (ibid., 42–43) are arguing for a different interpretation of Nerva's actions from that put forward by E. Mary Smallwood, *The Jews under Roman Rule: From Pompey to Diocletian* (SJLA 20; Leiden: Brill, 1976), 376–85, who takes *calumnia* as "false

Shukster reconstruct a situation under Nerva in which Jewish hopes for the rebuilding of the Jerusalem temple, as a Jewish temple, are kindled, and Jews throughout the empire look forward to participating in the rebuilding of the temple through the *fiscus Iudaicus,* even with a continued Roman presence in Jerusalem. This cooperation then makes sense of the reference in *Barn.* 16:4 that the "servants of the enemies" are rebuilding the temple.[12]

This dating for *Barnabas* locates the text firmly in the nexus of Roman imperial rule. *Barnabas*'s depiction of the current situation is thereby closely connected to changes in the power relations between the Roman rulers and Jews throughout the empire and particularly in Jerusalem and Judea. It is arguable that, under Nerva, Roman rule is perceived by Jewish communities as less oppressive and possibly by some as beneficial. Thus, for example, James Carleton Paget offers as a proposed reconstruction of the historical context for *Barnabas*'s vehement anti-Judaism a situation, in light of the perception of a more pro-Jewish policy under Nerva, in which "Christians may have felt moved to assert their confraternity with their Jewish neighbors."[13] It may then be against this "ecumenical" spirit that *Barnabas* is written, in the attempt to draw sharper boundaries between its own community and Jews.[14]

The question of the geographical provenance for *Barnabas* also has implications for the relation of this text to the local expressions of imperial rule. The three regions usually put forward for *Barnabas*'s composition are Egypt (usually Alexandria),[15] Syria-Palestine,[16] and west-

---

charge or accusation" and understands Nerva's actions as limiting the tax to "self-confessed Jews and proselytes" (p. 385). A similar interpretation is found in Martin Goodman, "Nerva, the Fiscus Judaicus and Jewish Identity," *JRS* 79 (1989): 40–44, without consideration of Richardson and Shukster's argument.

12. Richardson and Shukster, "Barnabas, Nerva, and the Yavnean Rabbis," 42–43, 54–55. They also adduce evidence from early rabbinic sources indicating a Yavnean embassy to Rome at the beginning of Nerva's reign and a pattern of cooperation between the Yavnean rabbis and the Roman government. This suggests a tendency toward accommodation with the Romans, whereby *Barnabas* can call the Jews "the servants of the enemies."

13. Carleton Paget, *Epistle of Barnabas,* 69.

14. It is debatable whether the community to which *Barnabas* is addressed would itself have been subject to the *fiscus Iudaicus.* I suspect that from the Roman point of view it would have been but that many of the text's strategies for delineating boundaries were important for distinguishing this community from Jewish communities and thus also may have part of an endeavor to remove this community from inclusion in the *fiscus Iudaicus.*

15. See Barnard, "Epistle of Barnabas," 161–207; and more cautiously, Carleton Paget, *Epistle of Barnabas,* 42. An Alexandrian setting is usually argued on the basis of purported similarities with Philo, as well as because of the early use of *Barnabas* as authoritative by Clement of Alexandria.

16. Prigent and Kraft, *Épître de Barnabé,* 22–24.

ern Asia Minor.[17] Although the *fiscus Iudaicus* would apply to Jews throughout the empire, we should expect the perceptions of Roman rule, together with the vagaries of local exercise of Roman government, to vary from province to province. I am not prepared at this point to explore the implication of provenance for *Barnabas*'s attitudes toward governing rule. I would, however, argue that *Barnabas* most likely originates in a Syrian context, based on its affinities with Qumran texts, early rabbinic Judaism, the writings of Justin Martyr, and particularly the *Odes of Solomon*[18]—all of which have a closer connection to Syria-Palestine than to Egypt or Asia Minor.[19] In addition, *Barnabas*'s witness to the early narrative and ritual traditions centered around Jesus' passion is also more explicable in a Syrian setting.[20]

The widely recognized homiletic character of *Barnabas* is important for our purposes in that it permits us to locate the text's arguments in a context of constituting and forming a community.[21] Moreover, it permits us to investigate *Barnabas* as a text closely connected to the cultic life of a

---

17. See Klaus Wengst, *Tradition und Theologie des Barnabasbrief* (Arbeiten zur Kirchengeschichte 42; Berlin: de Gruyter, 1971), 114–18; idem, *Didache (Apostellehre), Barnabasbrief, Zweiter Klemensbrief, Schrift an Diognet* (Schriften des Urchristentums; Munich: Kösel, 1984), 117–18. Wengst sees *Barnabas* concerned with similar issues as are found in Ignatius's letter to the Philadelphians and in the Pastoral Epistles. Prostmeier (*Barnabasbrief*, 127–28) follows Wengst.

18. We might add to this list also the *Oracles of Hystaspes*, which John C. Reeves has discussed in relation to the Enochic citation and the apocalyptic traditions in *Barn.* 4:3, noting also certain similarities in diction (especially the epithet, "the beloved") with the *Cologne Mani Codex*. See "An Enochic Citation in *Barnabas* 4.3 and the *Oracles of Hystaspes*," in *Pursuing the Text: Studies in Honor of Ben Zion Wacholder on the Occasion of His Seventieth Birthday* (ed. J. C. Reeves and J. Kampen; JSOTSup 184; Sheffield: Sheffield Academic Press, 1994), 260–77.

19. This is also the position of Prigent in Prigent and Kraft, *Épître de Barnabé*, 20–24. Kraft (*Barnabas and the Didache*, 55–56) offers a judicious hypothesis that also takes into account the early familiarity of *Barnabas* in Alexandrian circles (e.g., Clement of Alexandria): *Barnabas* comes from northeastern Egypt and is the work of a teacher "whose thought was oriented toward Alexandria" and who was trained not in the Philonic tradition but perhaps in a "Christianized offspring of a Qumranlike Judaism in Greek dress."

20. See Ellen Bradshaw Aitken, *Jesus' Death in Early Christian Memory: The Poetics of the Passion* (NTOA/SUNT 53; Göttingen: Vandenhoeck & Ruprecht, 2004), 88–129.

21. See, e.g., Klaus Baltzer, *The Covenant Formulary in Old Testament, Jewish, and Early Christian Writings* (trans. D. E. Green; Philadelphia: Fortress, 1971), 123–27; Lawrence Wills, "The Form of the Sermon in Hellenistic Judaism and Early Christianity," *HTR* 77 (1984): 277–99; Leslie W. Barnard, "The Epistle of Barnabas—A Paschal Homily?" *VC* 15 (1961): 9–10. Reider Hvalvik (*The Stuggle for Scripture and Covenant: The Purpose of the* Epistle of Barnabas *and Jewish Christian Competition in the Second Century* [Oslo: Det Teologiske Menighetsfakultet, 1994], 74–75) emphasizes the epistolary context but notes nevertheless the pervasive use of "material earlier employed in oral teaching/preaching."

community. In other words, even though it is highly unlikely that *Barnabas* represents an actual homily, it nevertheless draws upon the narrative and ritual experiences of a community setting, as well as upon the audience's expectations as they are established within the context of those experiences. Thus, as we examine how *Barnabas* depicts the reign of Jesus, it is possible to find in the text indications of the ritual experiences and other practices by which the community gains access to this *basileia*.

The Construction of the Audience's Situation

From the outset *Barnabas* offers a view of the world that encompasses past, present, and future; indeed this panoramic view is what has been disclosed or given by God: "For the master (ὁ δεσπότης) has made known to us through the prophets what has already come to pass and what is now occurring, and he has given us the first fruits (ἀπαρχάς) of what is about to happen" (*Barn.* 1:11). This threefold division of salvation history recurs at *Barn.* 5:3, where it is clear that the audience not only has been given the knowledge (γνῶσις) necessary for understanding what has happened and is happening, but is also equipped to understand what is about to happen. The primary focus in *Barnabas*, however, is on the proper understanding of the present situation, including how to interpret the scriptures of Israel and the experiences of Israel so that they are appropriately actualized in the here and now of the community's life. That is, *Barnabas* shows little interest in depicting future events, but emphasizes rather the correct reading of the past in accordance with the present definition of the community as the heirs of the covenant, sealed in Jesus. The hortatory or paraenetic thrust of the text is directed chiefly toward the practices of the community in the present time. Nevertheless, this emphasis occurs within a discourse of totality, that is, one that seeks to comprehend all time. This discourse frames what *Barnabas* has to say about rule and so marks it as having universal or eternal import.

We may observe the various ways in which *Barnabas* characterizes the present time, the here and now of the community: "the present days are evil and the worker of evil himself holds sway (ἔχοντος τὴν ἐξουσίαν)" (*Barn.* 2:1);[22] the "evil one" is capable of "slipping in among us and hurling us away from our life" (*Barn.* 2:10); these are the "last times" (*Barn.* 6:13). The "evil one" is also identified as "Satan" (*Barn.* 18:1), the "black one" (*Barn.* 4:10; 20:1), and the "evil ruler" (ὁ πονηρὸς ἄρχων; *Barn.* 4:13). It is important to note the language of rule in this characterization,

---

22. The Latin manuscript (L) interprets this "worker of evil" as the "adversary": *et contratius habeat huius saeculi potestatem*. See Prigent and Kraft, *Épître de Barnabé*, 79.

specifically, "holding sway" and "ruler." Through the use of prophetic timetables for the last days, *Barnabas* is able to place the events of history within this divine history. The text encourages the audience "to inquire earnestly into the present things and to seek those things which are able to save us" (*Barn.* 4:1). The present times, which the audience already knows are evil, are further established as the time when "the final scandal is at hand" (*Barn.* 4:3), the times which "the master has cut short" (*Barn.* 4:3), and the period of the reign of the king foretold by "the prophet" and Daniel. We have seen already how *Barn.* 4 is central to arguments concerning the date of composition. It is also, however, just as important to observe that the prophecies employed here, regardless of their relation to external history, are directed toward the point that the prophets have foretold as a time critical for the unfolding of salvation, namely, the present time. Kraft, although unwilling to press these passages for historical reference, posits that here the author is making use of "a living apocalyptic tradition based on Dan 7:7–8, 19–24."[23] This apocalyptic chronology, moreover, is structured in terms of reigns and rulers. *Barnabas* is, in effect, using a "king list" to define the here and now of the audience as the time of culmination. There are thus at least three motifs at work in *Barnabas*'s diagnosis of the present time: the designation that it is an evil time (presumably in contrast to an ideal "good" or "righteous" time); an apocalyptic timetable; and the persistent reference to kingship or rule.

Out of *Barnabas*'s diagnosis of the here and now emerges much of the rest of the theological and paraenetic "work" of the text. That is, the author uses this characterization of the present time as the reason why the audience should undertake certain actions and attitudes. This is immediately apparent in *Barn.* 2:1, where the characterization of the days as evil and as the time when the evil one holds sway provides the basis for the statement, "We ought, attending to ourselves, to seek out the ordinances of the Lord." "Attending" and "seeking out the ordinances of the Lord" are the catchall categories for the interpretive activities that follow in the subsequent chapters. This stance, in the face of the present situation, is then further characterized first by the virtues of fear, endurance, long-suffering, and continence, and second by "wisdom, understanding, knowledge, and gnosis" (σοφία, σύνεσις, ἐπιστήμη, γνῶσις; *Barn.* 2:2–3). In other words, the orientation of the audience is to be distinguished precisely by those capacities with which the author goes on to mark the proper interpretations of scripture and the proper practices of the

---

23. Kraft, *Barnabas and the Didache*, 88.

community. Thus equipped, the audience will be able to negotiate its way in the present situation.[24]

A second passage programmatic for apprehending the implications of "the present time" emerges in *Barn.* 4 out of the apocalyptic prophecies and the discussion of the covenant:

> Therefore, let us attend in the last days, for the whole time our faith will profit us nothing, unless now in the lawless time and in the scandals that are to come, we resist, as is proper for the sons of God, so that the black one may not have a deceitful entrance. (*Barn.* 4:9)

Here again "attending" (προσέχω) sums up the proper behavior for the last time, but it is supplemented here by "resisting" (ἀνθίστημι), activity that is redolent of battle and contests. The response is thus conceptualized both in intellectual terms ("attending," "seeking out") and in agonistic terms ("resisting"). The text then specifies what one is to do: flee vanity, hate the deeds of wickedness, do not live apart, but come together and seek the common good. The ethic of *Barnabas* results from a particular interpretation of the "ordinances of the Lord," that is, from a certain intellectual stance that redefines covenantal practices, but it is also an ethic of "resistance" for the last times.

In this same passage, the implication of living this ethic, moreover, is expressed in the language of rule:

> Let us attend, lest we ever slumber in our sins, by coming to rest as those who have been called, and the evil ruler, by taking the authority over us, thrust us out of the *basileia* of the Lord. (*Barn.* 4:13)

Here the contrast between the "*basileia* of the Lord" and the evil ruler is portrayed in terms of who has authority (ἐξουσία) over the community addressed. This competition between reigning authorities is, I suggest, foundational to the ethic espoused in *Barnabas*.

Throughout *Barnabas* there are markers of the intellectual and interpretive stance that the audience needs for living in the last times, the stance that the text sums up under the categories of "wisdom, understanding, knowledge, and gnosis" (*Barn.* 2:3) or by the exhortation to "attend." Kraft supplies a full list of these markers, which he labels "gnostic-parenetic terminology."[25] For example, the audience is "to perceive"

---

24. Kraft (ibid., 83) notes that this passage, *Barn.* 2:1–3, "sets the stage" for chs. 2–16, "since the idea of eschatological warfare permeates the epistle."

25. Ibid., 24–27. I do not attempt to repeat here Kraft's entire list or the many references.

(αἰσθάνομαι), "to hear" (ἀκούω), "to see" (βλέπω), "to know" (γινώσκω), "to discover" (εὑρίσκω), "to meditate" (μελετάω), and "to understand" (νοέω or συνίημι). God or scripture "makes known" (γνωρίζω), "makes clear" (φανερόω, δηλόω), "says" (λέγω), and "shows" (δείκνυμι). It is important to observe, however, that throughout the text these refer to getting the "right" meaning out of scripture. This "right" meaning, of course, for *Barnabas* derives from the possession of the covenant. It is thus regularly contrasted with the misinterpretation of scripture or what "they" do. The community's intellectual and ethical capacity or practice suitable for the last times must therefore include properly recognizing who the people of the covenant are.

This logic makes sense of why the apocalyptic prophecies in *Barn.* 4 flow immediately into a discussion of the covenant. The quotation of Dan 7:7–8 in *Barn.* 4:5 is followed by a retelling of the story of the broken tablets of the covenant whereby, according to *Barnabas,* the wilderness generation and all of Israel irrevocably lost the covenant. The present situation of the audience members, however, is defined by their inheritance of the "covenant of Jesus, the beloved," a covenant which is "sealed" in their hearts (*Barn.* 4:6–8). This retelling is repeated in *Barn.* 14 but introduced in *Barn.* 13:1: "Let us see whether this people or the first people is the heir, and whether the covenant is for us or for them." Reider Hvalvik has argued that the chief matter of contention in the text is the question to whom the scriptures and their promises belong.[26] Certainly *Barnabas*'s claim is that the people of the covenant (i.e., the covenant of Jesus) alone have the capacity to interpret scripture rightly. *Barnabas*'s interpretations of scripture, including the commandments of Torah, regularly issue in prescriptions for the ethical and ritual practice of the community. For example, the interpretation of the food laws in *Barn.* 10 in which the prescriptions against eating certain animals are taken to refer no longer to food but to interpersonal and inter-group relations thus foregrounds the social aspects of covenantal behavior. Because practice is so much at the center of *Barnabas*'s argument, I would maintain that the practices of the community (ethical, ritual, narrative, and interpretive) are the chief matters of contention. The explicit question of who possesses the covenant and the scriptures is in this way ancillary to concerns about the community's practices.

In the here and now of the community, as portrayed by *Barnabas,* the practices that result from its possession of the covenant are its means to negotiate the last times. Within the context of *Barn.* 4, the covenantal

---

26. Hvalvik, *Struggle for Scripture and Covenant,* 142.

practices, including the interpretation of scripture and the capacity for right recognition, are the community's means for resisting the authority of the evil ruler and remaining within the "*basileia* of the Lord." Chief among these practices is the proper identification of the covenant people (*Barn.* 4:6–8); thus, one of the results of *Barnabas*'s understanding of the present situation, as marked by the activity of the evil ruler and as coded by the apocalyptic prophecies, is the creation of a text and a set of practices aimed at drawing very sharp community boundaries between "us" and "them." In other words, the present time is a time of sifting and discernment, effected through the practices of the community. In this respect, *Barnabas* presents covenantal behavior as a response to rule and competing rulers.

The *Basileia* of Jesus and the People of the Covenant as the Rulers of the Land

Barnabas seeks to shape the audience's response to the present situation by interpreting the stories of the scriptures of Israel in such a way that they are actualized or reenacted in the narratives and practices of the community. In *Barn.* 5–8, the story of creation and the account of the Israelites' entry into the promised land are central to this process. In the course of *Barnabas*'s argument, both narrative experiences are used to shape the identity of the community and their constitutive practices, including the practice of baptism and their narrative of Jesus' suffering and death. To anticipate, we might say that these scriptural stories and their resulting practices permit the members of the community to constitute themselves as "rulers of the land" and to participate in the *basileia* of Jesus. Furthermore, they permit the definition of this *basileia* through the narrative of Jesus' passion. It is also important to recognize that this central section of *Barnabas* is, in effect, the fleshing out of the ethical stance of "attending" and "resisting," which in chapter 4 articulates the response to the activity of the evil ruler in the present. So, although chapter 5 would appear to begin a new section, we should recognize its rhetorical connection to what has immediately preceded it:

> For it was for this reason that the Lord endured to hand over the flesh to corruption, so that we might be sanctified by the remission of sins, that is, in the blood of his sprinkling. (*Barn.* 5:1)

"The reason" for Jesus' passion, namely, the sanctification by the sprinkling of blood, itself connects back to the preceding discussion of covenant, since the sprinkling of blood is involved in the making and renewing of the Sinai covenant; here this blood (i.e., Jesus' death) effectively ratifies the covenant of the beloved. The link back to stances articulated in chapter 4 underscores that the audience must claim the ethical consequences of Jesus' death and of their covenantal identity.

The scriptures of Israel are refracted through the lens of Jesus' suffering and death throughout this section. The creation story from Gen 1 is explicitly invoked in *Barn.* 5:6 as the basis for saying that Jesus is "the Lord of all the world" (παντὸς τοῦ κόσμου κύριος). We may note here the claim of universal lordship for Jesus, similar to claims for imperial rule. The creation story, however, is not in the foreground again until *Barn.* 6:12 where it is brought to bear upon the identity of the audience:

> For the scripture says concerning us, as it says to the son, "Let us make the human according to our image and likeness, and let him rule (ἄρχω) over the beasts of the earth and the birds of the air and the fish of the sea." (*Barn.* 6:12)

As in Genesis, creation is here linked to governance. Because this "scripture," Gen 1:26, is explicitly interpreted with reference the community, it serves to define the community as those who are to rule.

Between the invocations of the Genesis creation story in *Barn.* 5:6 and 6:12, the story of the people's entrance into the land "flowing with milk and honey" is introduced (*Barn.* 6.8). Barnabas undertakes a complex interpretation of this story, linking it to Jesus' suffering and ultimately to the identification of the community. Submerged in this process of interpretation, but essential to the moves that it makes, is reference to the community's practice of baptism. We see indications of baptismal "renewal" in the statement that links the land of promise to the creation story:

> Since then, having made us anew (ἀνακαινίζω) in the forgiveness of sins, he made us another type, so that we had the soul of a child, as it were indeed that he was fashioning us (ἀναπλάσσω) anew. (*Barn.* 6:11)

The reference to "milk and honey" may, in this context, provide another link to the community's baptismal practice.[27] Through baptism, the community not only "enters the land" (thus reenacting the story of the conquest) but is also "created anew" (thus reenacting the story of creation).

---

27. Compare *Odes Sol.*19:1–4; 40:1. See Nils A. Dahl, "*La terre où coulent le lait et le miel,* selon Barnabé 6.8–19," in *Aux sources de la tradition chrétienne: Mélanges offerts à M. Maurice Goguel à l'occasion de son soixante-dixième anniversaire* (Bibliothèque Théologique; Neuchâtel: Delachaux & Niestlé, 1950), 70; Aitken, *Jesus' Death,* 122–26, where I examine the several references to baptism in *Barnabas.*

What links the two stories in this instance is the reference to the "land" or "earth" (ἡ γῆ).

The two stories are further linked in *Barn.* 6:13 by the allusion to the promise to the Israelites that they would enter the land:

> Again, I will show you how he speaks to us. In the last [days] he made a second creation; and the Lord says, "Behold, I make the last things as the first." For this reason, then, the prophet proclaimed, "Enter into a land flowing with milk and honey and exercise lordship (κατακυριεύω) over it." See then, we have been fashioned anew. (*Barn.* 6:13–14a)

This is a crucial text for understanding how *Barnabas* constructs an ideology and practice of rule. Although the promise that the people will enter and inherit the land flowing with milk and honey is common in the wilderness narratives (e.g., Exod 33:1, 3; Lev 20:24), it is not explicitly linked with "exercising lordship" (κατακυριεύω) over it.[28] Rather, "ruling" is introduced into this "quotation" from Gen 1:28 and the command to the first human to "exercise lordship" (κατακυριεύω) over the earth.

There are a number of important features to this passage. First, the combination, by means of the shared word γῆ, of the entrance into the land with the command to rule over the earth from Genesis has the effect of broadening the mandate to the community. Not only are they to rule over the land of promise, but in effect the land of promise is redefined as the whole earth. Second, the new identity of the people as the rulers takes place "in the last times" (ἐπ' ἐσχάτων); the refashioning is explicitly set in an eschatological context. From what has already been said in *Barnabas*, however, the inscribed audience has come to know that they live in the last times. Therefore, their baptismal refashioning and renewal constitutes them specifically in and for these times. Moreover, baptism has constituted them *as rulers*. This link between baptism and rule is reinforced a few sentences later in *Barn.* 6:16–17:

> Therefore we are those whom he leads into the good land. What then is the "milk" and the "honey"? Because the infant is made alive (ζωοποιέω) first by honey, then by milk. Thus then, we too who are made alive (ζωοποιέω) by faith in the promise and by the word, we will live exercising lordship (κατακυριεύω) over the land.

Rule or lordship is then defined in *Barn.* 6:18, with reference to Gen 1:28, in terms of giving commandments. "For we ought to perceive that 'to rule'

---

28. On "ruling" the land, see Num 21:24; 32:22, 29.

implies authority, so that one may exercise lordship by commanding" (αἰσθάνεσθαι γὰρ ὀφείλομεν, ὅτι τὸ ἄρχειν ἐξουσίας ἐστίν, ἵνα ἐπιτάξας κυριεύσῃ). In the larger context of *Barnabas* we can see that the interpretive work of seeking out, understanding, and implementing the "ordinances" of God, particularly in terms of a social, interpersonal covenantal ethic, is the work of "ruling" and "exercising lordship."

Barnabas 6:19 recognizes the tension between the present "historical" situation and the present situation as it is portrayed through the interpretation of scripture in this text, "If then this is not the present situation (νῦν), then he has told us when it will be—when we ourselves will be perfected as heirs of the covenant of the Lord." I would suggest that this statement is an attempt to mediate the historical situation of a ruled people with a vision of a future in which they rule the whole earth. Indeed, because ritual often enacts realities not possible outside of ritual time and space, the status of the community as "rulers" could indeed be actual in the ritual practices of the community, even though outside those practices, they live under Roman rule.

Barnabas 7 and 8 continue the process of reflection, through the medium of scripture, upon Jesus' suffering and death. In doing so, the text makes considerable use of the ritual of the scapegoat from Yom Kippur (Lev 16) and also of the ritual of the red heifer (Num 19). The "matter" of these rituals (scarlet wool, thorns, wood, water) are central to the rituals' interpretation as actualized in the remembrance of Jesus' passion. Thus, for example, the scarlet wool wrapped around the head of the scapegoat and then found on the thorn bush indicates, according to *Barnabas*:

> the type (τύπος) of Jesus in the church, since whoever wishes to take the scarlet wool must suffer much because the thorn is terrible and must master (κυριεύω) it through affliction. In such a way, he says, those who wish to see me and to take hold of my *basileia* must receive me through affliction and suffering. (*Barn.* 7:11)

This is the first indication we have that *Barnabas* is explicitly linking Jesus' suffering with the concept of kingship or reign. Through similar interpretive moves, *Barnabas* connects the scarlet wool bound upon the sticks in the ceremony of the red heifer with Jesus' cross and then with his reign:

> And the fact that the wool is on the wood signifies that the *basileia* of Jesus is on the wood, and that those who hope in him will live for ever. (*Barn.* 8:5)

The "wood" of the cross is, I would contend, the feature that draws in the material used in the two rituals. It also serves to signal the larger narrative tradition around Jesus' death, as this remembrance is shaped in terms of the scriptures of Israel. Thus, the key phrase, "the *basileia* of Jesus is on the wood," indicates the definition of Jesus' *basileia* through his suffering. In other words, everything that has been said in *Barnabas* up to this point about the opposition between Jesus' rule and that of the evil ruler and about the identity of the community as rulers is here informed by the narrative traditions around Jesus' passion. The implications of this information for the present situation are spelled out in the next sentence:

> But why are the wool and the hyssop together? Because in this *basileia* there shall be wicked and vile days, in which we shall be saved. For the one whose flesh is pained is cured by means of the hyssop's vileness. (*Barn.* 8:6)

That is, the present situation of the community, as living in a time of eschatological conflict, is consonant with the understanding of Jesus' *basileia* as it is shaped by his suffering.

We observed already how the baptismal practices of the community constitute its members as the rulers. *Barnabas* 11 discusses baptismal practices in relation to Jesus' passion. *Barnabas* is especially concerned to show how the "water" and the "wood" belong together, and it does so through a series of psalm texts. This section thus connects the identity of the community, as enacted through baptism, with the traditions of Jesus' cross. Hence their baptismal status as rulers, already established in *Barn.* 6, is here defined further by association with Jesus' *basileia*, as that *basileia* has been established as "on the wood" in *Barn.* 8.

Barnabas 12 is also important in reinforcing this link between Jesus' cross and an ideology of rule. One of the "types" of the cross that *Barnabas* employs here is the story of Moses holding his hands up, so that the Israelites would prevail in the battle against the Amalekites (Exod 17). Exodus itself supplies a context of warfare, but *Barnabas* highlights this aspect in introducing the story, "When Israel was warred upon by strangers" (*Barn.* 12:2). It is important to note that it was Joshua who led the Israelites into this battle; later in this section *Barnabas* explicitly draws an onomastic and hence a typological relation between Joshua and Jesus (*Barn.* 12:10). *Barnabas* is thus able to use the victory over the Amalekites as a type of the eschatological victory over the enemy. According to *Barnabas*, when Moses instructs Joshua to go into the land as a spy, he tells him, "Take a book in your hands and write what the Lord says, that the Son of God[29] will cut off the entire house of Amalek by its roots at the

---

29. The Latin (L) manuscript here reads "Jesus."

end of days" (*Barn.* 12:9).³⁰ Kraft has described this mysterious book as "apocalyptic." Certainly what Joshua is to write concerns the last times and God's final victory.³¹

Barnabas takes this tradition of eschatological victory over the enemy and glosses it further in terms of kingship by following a quotation of Ps 110:1 with a quotation of Isa 45:1, "And again, Isaiah says as follows, 'The Lord said to my Lord, whose right hand I held, that nations would become obedient to him, and I will demolish the strength of kings" (*Barn.* 12:10–11). It is important to note that in the Septuagint Isa 45:1 begins, "The Lord said to Cyrus, my anointed." The similarity between Κῦρος (Cyrus) and κύριος (Lord) permits this interchange, which here emulates the opening of Ps 110:1. This shift is not, however, mere linguistic play. Rather, I would maintain that it serves to underscore the lordship of Jesus, particularly as the one who "will demolish the strength of kings" (*Barn.* 12:11). Thus, although *Barn.* 12 appears on its surface to present typologies of the cross, the deeper discourse concerns God's ultimate victory, through Jesus' cross, over the nations, Amalek, evildoers, and kings. This text indicates this victory as belonging to the last days, that is, to the present situation of the community.

It would be misleading, in my view, to characterize *Barnabas* as concealing its messages about ultimate victory over unjust rule and the true kingship of Jesus beneath the complexities of scriptural interpretation and christological interpretation or beneath a system of typologies. Rather, I would understand *Barnabas* as primarily concerned with the practices by which the community gains access to the *basileia* of Jesus, as well as to what the *basileia* of Jesus requires. Since the narrative practices concerning Jesus' passion serve to define Jesus' *basileia*, it is not surprising that the two—passion and *basileia*—combine in this passage to produce an understanding of the eschatological implications of Jesus' suffering and death. Apocalyptic notions about God's rule and governance, together with the passion traditions, infuse *Barnabas's* construction of the *basileia* of Jesus. At the same time, the statements about the cross in *Barnabas* are thoroughly defined by an ideology of conquest and rule.

---

30. This passage is dependent upon the LXX of Exod 17:16, "because with a hidden hand the Lord will make war upon Amalek from generation to generation"; see Prigent and Kraft, *Épître de Barnabé*, 172. The question of the "hidden hand" has a long exegetical history in midrashic tradition, into which *Barnabas* and Justin Martyr (*Dial.* 49.7) enter as they interpret this verse in terms of Jesus.

31. Kraft, *Barnabas and the Didache*, 120.

Concluding Observations about Wisdom and Apocalyptic

I have explored how *Barnabas* constructs both an ideology of rule and a set of ethical, interpretive, ritual, and narrative practices of rule. Portraying the community as the covenant people, the inheritors of the land, and the rulers of the earth, *Barnabas* advocates a set of practices for properly interpreting scripture. Out of this interpretive behavior emerges a set of ethical behaviors appropriate to this covenant identity. However, *Barnabas* also draws upon baptismal practices which serve to constitute the members of the community as rulers, as well as possessors of the covenant. The particular kind of baptism that we see in *Barnabas* is refracted through the narrative practices involved in speaking of Jesus' suffering and death. It is this narrative and interpretive activity that enables *Barnabas* to define Jesus' *basileia* as "on the wood." This understanding both of Jesus' *basileia* and of the identity of the community as rulers is set within a diagnosis of the present situation as "the last days" when "the worker of evil holds sway." Thus central to this ideology of rule is its setting amid eschatological conflict.

In *Barnabas* we may also note how traditions and practices that are usually parsed separately as either sapiential or apocalyptic work together. I have noted a number of instances of apocalyptic material, principally the apocalyptic chronologies in chapter 4 that enable *Barnabas*'s diagnosis of the present situation. *Barnabas,* however, also operates within an overall sapiential framework, inasmuch as the interpretive practices that the community is to adopt are summed up by the list, "wisdom, understanding, knowledge, and gnosis" (*Barn.* 2:3). In order for the members of the community to act properly and to participate in the *basileia* of Jesus, they need to adopt these sapiential practices of interpretation, principally, the interpretation of scripture. According to Barnabas's perspective, the inscribed community exercises its covenantally bestowed lordship in the last days by being wise and understanding, especially in its reading and enactment of the scriptures of Israel.

SELECT BIBLIOGRAPHY

Aitken, Ellen Bradshaw. *Jesus' Death in Early Christian Memory: The Poetics of the Passion.* NTOA/SUNT 53. Göttingen: Vandenhoeck & Ruprecht; Fribourg: Academic Press, 2004.
Argall, Randal A. *1 Enoch and Sirach: A Comparative Literary and Conceptual Analysis of the Themes of Revelation, Creation and Judgment.* SBLEJL 8. Atlanta: Scholars Press, 1995.
Atkinson, Kenneth. *I Cried to the Lord: A Study of the Psalms of Solomon's Historical Background and Social Setting.* JSJSup 84. Leiden: Brill, 2004.
———. "On the Herodian Origin of Militant Davidic Messianism at Qumran: New Light from *Psalms of Solomon* 17." *JBL* 118 (1999): 435–60.
Barnard, Leslie W. "The 'Epistle of Barnabas' and Its Contemporary Setting," *ANRW* 27.1:159–207.
Boccaccini, Gabriele. *Middle Judaism: Jewish Thought 300 B.C.E to 200 C.E.* Minneapolis: Fortress, 1991.
Carleton-Paget, James. *The Epistle of Barnabas: Outlook and Background.* WUNT 2/64. Tübingen: Mohr Siebeck, 1994.
Carr, David M. *Writing on the Tablet of the Heart.* Oxford: Oxford University Press, 2005.
Charles, R. H. *The Book of Enoch or 1 Enoch.* 2nd ed. Oxford: Clarendon, 1912.
Collins, Adela Yarbro. *Crisis and Catharsis: The Power of the Apocalypse.* Philadelphia: Westminster, 1984.
———. "The Political Perspective of the Revelation to John." *JBL* 96 (1977): 241–56.
Collins, John J. *The Apocalyptic Imagination.* New York: Crossroad, 1992.
———. "Apocalyptic Literature." Pages 345–70 in *Early Judaism and Its Modern Interpreters.* Edited by Robert A. Kraft and George W. E. Nickelsburg. SBLBMI 1. Philadelphia: Fortress, 1986.
———. "Cosmos and Salvation: Jewish Wisdom and Apocalyptic in the Hellenistic Age." *HR* 17 (1977): 121–42.
———. "Daniel and His Social World." *Int* 39 (1985): 131–43.
———. "Jewish Apocalypses." *Semeia* 14 (1979): 21–59.
———. "Was the Dead Sea Sect an Apocalyptic Movement?" Pages 25–52 in *Archaeology and History in the Dead Sea Scrolls: The New York*

University Conference in Memory of Yigael Yadin. Edited by Lawrence H. Schiffman. JSPSup 8. JSOT/ASOR Monograph Series 2. Sheffield: JSOT Press, 1990.

———. "Wisdom, Apocalypticism, and Generic Compatibility." Pages 131–43 in *In Search of Wisdom: Essays in Memory of John G. Gammie*. Edited by Leo G. Perdue, Bernard Brandon Scott, and William Johnston Wiseman. Louisville: Westminster John Knox, 1993. Repr. as pages 385–404 in Collins, *Seers, Sybils and Sages in Hellenistic-Roman Judaism*. JSJSup 54. Leiden: Brill, 1997.

Court, John. *Myth and History in the Book of Revelation*. Atlanta: John Knox, 1979.

Crenshaw, James L. *Education in Ancient Israel*. ABRL. New York: Doubleday, 1998.

———. *Old Testament Wisdom: An Introduction*. Revised ed. Atlanta: John Knox, 1998. [orig. 1981]

Davids, Peter H. *The Epistle of James: A Commentary on the Greek Text*. NIGTC. Grand Rapids: Eerdmans, 1982.

Davies, Philip R. "Reading Daniel Sociologically." Pages 345–61 in *The Book of Daniel in the Light of New Findings*. Edited by A. S. van der Woude. BETL 106. Leuven: Leuven University Press/Peeters, 1993.

———. "The Social World of Apocalyptic Writings." Pages 251–71 in *The World of Ancient Israel: Social, Anthropological, and Political Perspectives*. Edited by Ronald E. Clements. Cambridge: Cambridge University Press, 1989.

Dibelius, Martin. *James: A Commentary on the Epistle of James*. Revised by Heinrich Greeven. Hermeneia. Philadelphia: Fortress, 1976.

Goff, Matthew J. "The Mystery of Creation in 4QInstruction." *DSD* 10 (2003): 163–86.

———. *The Worldly and Heavenly Wisdom of 4QInstruction*. STDJ 50. Leiden: Brill, 2003.

Hanson, Paul D. "Apocalypticism." *IDBSup*, 28–34.

———. *The Dawn of Apocalyptic*. Philadelphia: Fortress, 1975.

Harrington, Daniel J. "The Raz Nihyeh in a Qumran Wisdom Text (1Q26, 4Q415–418, 423)." *RevQ* 17 (1996): 549–53.

———. *Wisdom Texts from Qumran*. London: Routledge, 1996.

Hartin, Patrick J. *James and the Q Sayings of Jesus*. JSNTSup 47. Sheffield: JSOT Press, 1991.

Himmelfarb, Martha. *Ascent to Heaven in Jewish and Christian Apocalypses*. New York: Oxford University Press, 1993.

Horsley, Richard A. "Empire, Temple, and Community—But No Bourgeoisie." Pages 163–74 in *Second Temple Studies I: Persian Period*. Edited by Philip R. Davies. JSOTSup 117. Sheffield: Sheffield Academic Press, 1991.

———. "Social Relations and Social Conflict in the Epistle of Enoch." Pages 100–115 in *For a Later Generation: The Transformation of Tradition in Israel, Early Judaism, and Early Christianity.* Edited by Randal A. Argall, Beverly A. Bow, and Rodney A. Werline. Harrisburg, Pa.: Trinity Press International, 2000.

———. "Wisdom Justified by All Her Children: Examining Allegedly Disparate Traditions in Q." Pages 733–51 in volume 2 of the *Society of Biblical Literature 1994 Seminar Papers.* 2 vols. SBLSP 33. Atlanta: Scholars Press, 1994.

Horsley, Richard A., and Patrick Tiller. "Ben Sira and the Sociology of the Second Temple." Pages 74–107 in *Second Temple Studies III: Studies in Politics, Class and Material Culture.* Edited by Philip R. Davies and John M. Halligan. JSOTSup 340. Sheffield: Sheffield Academic Press, 2002.

Johnson, Luke Timothy. *The Letter of James: A New Translation with Introduction and Commentary.* AB 37A. New York: Doubleday, 1995.

Koch, Klaus. *The Rediscovery of Apocalyptic.* SBT 2/22. Naperville, Ill.: Allenson, 1972.

Kraft, Robert A. *Barnabas and the Didache.* Vol. 3 of *The Apostolic Fathers: A New Translation and Commentary.* 5 vols. Edited by Robert M. Grant. New York: Nelson, 1964.

Kugler, Robert A. *From Patriarch to Priest: The Levi-Priestly Tradition from Aramaic Levi to Testament of Levi.* SBLEJL 9. Atlanta: Scholars Press, 1996.

Milik, J. T. *The Books of Enoch: Aramaic Fragments from Qumrân Cave 4.* Oxford: Clarendon, 1976.

Müller, Hans-Peter. "Mantische Weisheit und Apokalyptik." Pages 268–93 in *Congress Volume: Uppsala, 1971.* VTSup 22. Leiden: Brill, 1972.

Nickelsburg, George W. E. "The Apocalyptic Construction of Reality in *1 Enoch.*" Pages 51–64 in *Mysteries and Revelations: Apocalyptic Studies since the Uppsala Colloquium.* Edited by John J. Collins and James H. Charlesworth. JSPSup 9. Sheffield: Sheffield Academic Press, 1991.

———. "The Apocalyptic Message of *1 Enoch* 92–105." *CBQ* 39 (1977): 309–28.

———. "Enoch, Levi and Peter: Recipients of Revelation in Upper Galilee." *JBL* 100 (1981): 575–600.

———. "The Epistle of Enoch and the Qumran Literature." *JJS* 33 (1982): 333–48.

———. *1 Enoch: A Commentary on the Book of 1 Enoch Chapters 1–36; 81–108.* Hermeneia. Minneapolis: Fortress, 2001.

———. *Jewish Literature between the Bible and the Mishnah.* Philadelphia: Fortress, 1981. 2nd ed., Minneapolis: Fortress, 2005.

———. "The Nature and Function of Revelation in *1 Enoch, Jubilees,* and Some Qumran Documents." Pages 91–119 in *Pseudepigraphic Perspectives: The Apocrypha and Pseudepigrapha in Light of the Dead Sea Scrolls: Proceedings of the International Symposium of the Orion Center for the Study of the Dead Sea Scrolls and Associated Literature, 12–14 January, 1997.* Edited by Esther G. Chazon and Michael E. Stone. STDJ 31. Leiden: Brill, 1999.

———. "Social Aspects of Palestinian Jewish Apocalypticism." Pages 641–54 in *Apocalypticism in the Mediterranean World and the Near East: Proceedings of the International Colloquium on Apocalypticism, Uppsala, 1979.* Edited by David Hellholm. 2nd ed. Tübingen: Mohr Siebeck, 1989.

Olyan, Saul. "Ben Sira's Relationship to the Priesthood." *HTR* 80 (1987): 279–80.

Prigent, Pierre, and Robert A. Kraft. *Épître de Barnabé.* SC 172. Paris: Cerf, 1971.

Rad, Gerhard von. *Wisdom in Israel.* Translated by James D. Martin. London: SCM, 1972.

Rossing, Barbara R. *The Choice between Two Cities: Whore, Bride and Empire in the Apocalypse.* HTS 48. Harrisburg, Pa.: Trinity Press International, 1999.

Schüssler Fiorenza, Elisabeth. "The Phenomenon of Early Christian Apocalyptic: Some Reflections on Method." Pages 295–316 in *Apocalypticism in the Mediterranean World and the Near East: Proceedings of the International Colloquium on Apocalypticism, Uppsala, 1979.* Edited by David Hellholm. 2nd ed. Tübingen: Mohr Siebeck, 1989.

Smith, Jonathan Z. "Wisdom and Apocalyptic." Pages 67–87 in *Map Is Not Territory.* Chicago: University of Chicago Press, 1978.

Stone, Michael E. "The Book of Enoch and Judaism in the Third Century B.C.E." *CBQ* 40 (1978): 479–92.

———. "Enoch, Aramaic Levi and Sectarian Origins." *JSJ* 19 (1988): 159–70.

———. "Lists of Revealed Things in the Apocalyptic Literature." Pages 414–51 in *Magnalia Dei, the Mighty Acts of God: Essays on the Bible and Archaeology in Memory of G. Ernest Wright.* Edited by Frank Moore Cross, Werner E. Lemke, and Patrick D. Miller Jr. Garden City, N.Y.: Doubleday, 1976.

Suter, David. "Fallen Angel, Fallen Priest: The Problem of Family Purity in *1 Enoch* 6–16." *HUCA* 50 (1979): 115–35.

Thompson, Leonard. *The Book of Revelation: Apocalypse and Empire.* Oxford: Oxford University Press, 1990.

Tigchelaar, Eibert J. C. *To Increase Learning for the Understanding Ones: Reading and Reconstructing the Fragmentary Early Jewish Sapiential Text 4QInstruction.* STDJ 44. Leiden: Brill, 2001.
Tiller, Patrick A. *A Commentary on the Animal Apocalypse of 1 Enoch.* SBLEJL 4. Atlanta: Scholars Press, 1993.
VanderKam, James. *Enoch and the Growth of an Apocalyptic Tradition.* CBQMS 16. Washington, D.C.: Catholic Biblical Association of America, 1984.
———. "The Prophetic-Sapiential Origins of Apocalyptic Thought." Pages 241–54 in VanderKam, *From Revelation to Canon: Studies in Hebrew Bible and Second Temple Literature.* JSJSup 62. Leiden: Brill, 2000.
Werline, Rodney A. *Penitential Prayer in Early Judaism: The Development of a Religious Institution.* SBLEJL 13. Atlanta: Scholars Press, 1998.
Wright, Benjamin G. III. "Ben Sira and the Book of the Watchers on the Legitimate Priesthood." Pages 241–54 in *Intertextual Studies in Ben Sira and Tobit: Essays in Honor of A. Di Lella, O.F.M.* Edited by Jeremy Corley and Vincent Skemp. CBQMS 38. Washington, D.C.: Catholic Biblical Association of America, 2005.
———. "Fear the Lord and Honor the Priest: Ben Sira as Defender of the Jerusalem Priesthood." Pages 189–222 in *The Book of Ben Sira in Modern Research.* Edited by Pancratius C. Beentjes. BZAW 255. Berlin: de Gruyter, 1997.
———. "1 Enoch and Ben Sira: Wisdom and Apocalyptic in Relationship." In *The Early Enoch Tradition.* Edited by Gabriele Boccaccini and George W. E. Nickelsburg. Leiden: Brill, forthcoming.
———. "'Put the Nations in Fear of You:' Ben Sira and the Problem of Foreign Rule." Pages 77–93 in *Society of Biblical Literature 1999 Seminar Papers.* SBLSP 38. Atlanta: Scholars Press, 1999.
———. "Sirach and 1 Enoch: Some Further Considerations." Pages 179–87 in *The Origins of Enochic Judaism: Proceedings of the First Enoch Seminar.* Edited by Gabriele Boccaccini. Turin: Silvio Zamorani, 2002.
———. "Wisdom, Instruction and Social Location in Ben Sira and 1 Enoch." Pages 105–21 in *Things Revealed: Studies in Early Jewish and Christian Literature in Honor of Michael E. Stone.* Edited by Esther G. Chazon, David Satran, and Ruth A. Clements. JSJSup 89. Leiden: Brill, 2004.

Contributors

Ellen Bradshaw Aitken
Associate Professor of Early Christian History and Literature
McGill University
Montreal, Canada

Patrick J. Hartin
Professor of Religious Studies
Gonzaga University
Spokane, Washington

Richard A. Horsley
Distinguished Professor of Liberal Arts and the Study of Religion
University of Massachusetts Boston
Boston, Massachusetts

Matthew J. Goff
Assistant Professor of Religion
Florida State University
Tallahassee, Florida

George W. E. Nickelsburg
Professor Emeritus
University of Iowa
Iowa City, Iowa

Barbara R. Rossing
Associate Professor of New Testament
Lutheran School of Theology at Chicago
Chicago, Illinois

Sarah J. Tanzer
Professor of New Testament and Early Judaism
McCormick Theological Seminary
Chicago, Illinois

Patrick A. Tiller
Independent Scholar
Sharon, Massachusetts

Rodney A. Werline
Pastor
First Christian Church
Greensboro, North Carolina

Lawrence M. Wills
Professor of Biblical Studies
Episcopal Divinity School
Cambridge, Massachusetts

Benjamin G. Wright III
Professor of Religion Studies
Lehigh University
Bethlehem, Pennsylvania

Index of Ancient Literature

Biblical Literature (Including Deuterocanonical Literature)

Hebrew Bible

Genesis		2 Samuel	
1	96, 208	7:16	158
1:14–15	96, 159	**1 Kings**	
1:26	208	18:36–40	160
1:28	209	**2 Kings**	
39	28	22	21
39–45	29	**2 Chronicles**	
Exodus		36:20–21	143
17	211	**Ezra**	103
17:6	212	7:25–26	129
20:24	209	9-10	31
33:1	209	**Nehemiah**	
33:3	209	2:9	128
Leviticus		5:1–12	140
16	210	5:4	129
19	174	5:14	129
19:18	172	6	128
Numbers		10:26–29	129
19	210	10:40	129
21:24	210	13:28–30	128
32:22	209	**Job**	8, 24, 41, 44, 53, 57
32:29	209	4:12–21	57
Deuteronomy	8, 23	5:5–16	174
1:13	156	28	23
4:6	156	31:16–23	174
10:18–19	174	**Psalms**	
17:4–17	80	2:9	79
18:10–11	101	7:5	74
28–32	34	72:12–13	174
30:1–5	24	104:7	79
30:11–14	23	106:21	76
30:15–20	188	110:1	212
1 Samuel		**Proverbs**	24, 28, 41, 59, 62, 64, 65, 150
7	74	1–9	83, 185–88, 191

Proverbs (continued)

1:1–7	59
1:2–5	65
1:20	188
2:6	157
5:3	185
6:1–5	59
7:4–5	185
7:21	185
8	155
8:22–31	157
9:5–6	195
10–29	133
11:13	63
14:21	152
17:5	59
17:18	59
19:1	59
20:19	63
20:23	153
22:6	111
25:9	63
28:27	59
29:7	59
29:27	60
31	188
Qoheleth	28, 41, 44, 53, 150
3	57
Isaiah	23, 24, 25, 29, 33, 34, 37
6	21
10:5	75
10:19–19	75
11	80
11:2	80
11:2–3	30
11:2–4	79, 80
11:3–4	80
11:4	80
14	75
14:13	72
23:15–18	182
34:5–8	159
43:3	76
43:11	76
45:1	212
45:15	76
45:21	76
48:20	94
49:26	76
52–53	29, 33
52:11	194
52:13	32
53:10	32
55:1	195
56–66	128
60:16	76
61:10	183
65–66	37, 53
66:18–19	81
66:20	81
Jeremiah	23, 25, 28, 84
4:30	82, 183
25	6, 118, 191
46:10	159
50:8	194
51:6	194
51:9	194
51:34	76
51:45	194
51:50	194
Ezekiel	
1–2	21
16	182
16:13	182, 183
23	182
25–27	92
27:1–36	153
28	75
29:3	76
31–32	75
34	6, 117
34:8	120
34:16	117
Daniel	3, 5, 7, 20, 21, 22, 25, 26, 27, 28, 32, 35, 43, 46, 63, 64, 86, 123–45, 165, 167, 189
1	142
1–6	25, 32, 33, 141, 142
1:4	141, 156
1:5	141
1:8–16	141
1:17	32, 141–42
1:20	141–42
2	141, 142

INDEX OF ANCIENT LITERATURE 225

2:2	141–42	9:24	25
2:10	141–42	9:24–27	117
2:12	141–42	9:27	143
2:18	63	10–12	84, 141, 142
2:19	63, 141–42	11:3	85
2:27	141–42	11:31	143
2:27–29	63	11:33	60, 85
2:28	63, 141–42	11:34	72
2:29	63	11:35	143
2:30	63	11:40–45	75
2:47	63	11:40–12:3	58
3	29	12	142
4:6	63, 141–42	12:1	142, 143, 144
4:9	141–42	12:3	32, 33, 143
5	142	12:9	32
5:7	141–42	**Amos**	
5:8	141–42	2:6	140
5:11–12	141–42	6:4–6	139
5:12	141	8:4	175
6	29	8:4–6	153
7	21, 69, 76, 83, 84, 138, 141, 142	8:5	175
7–8	117	**Micah**	
7–11	25	2:1–2	140
7–12	6, 32, 84, 142	6:11	153
7:7–8	205	**Nahum**	
7:7–18	204	3:4	182
7:19–24	204	**Haggai**	128
7:27	142, 143	**Zechariah**	
8	141	1:12–17	143
8:13	143	9:9–10	80
9	26, 84, 142, 144	11	6, 117, 120
9:2	25, 141	**Malachi**	102, 128

Deuterocanonical literature

Tobit	22, 23, 24, 27, 42, 189	2:22–3:4	28
13	23	4:10–15	28
13–14	182	5	28, 29, 33, 58
14	23	6:12	91
Wisdom of Solomon	4, 18, 28, 29, 33, 41, 44, 49, 189	7:7	156
		7:24–27	157
1–5	53	8:21	156
2	28, 29, 33	9:2	159
2–5	28	9:4	156, 157
2:12	33	9:6	157
2:13	33	9:9–18	157
2:22	33	13:5	159

Wisdom of Solomon (continued)

14:11	159
Sirach 3, 6, 7, 8, 18, 22, 23, 24, 27, 30,	
31, 32, 35, 36, 41, 43, 45, 46, 48, 52, 53,	
54, 58, 89–112, 123–45, 150, 189	
Prologue 7–13	30
1	101
1:1	155–56
1:1–4	157
1:1–20	133
1:4–7	98
1:25–27	133
1:26	156
1:26–27	110
1:27	110
2	101
3	101
3:1–16	31
3:17	156
3:21	96, 97
3:21–24	96, 133
3:22	98, 100
3:23	100, 110, 111
3:30–4:10	125
4	101
4:1–10	136, 174–75
4:7	127, 134
4:8–10	127
4:11–19	133
4:15	134
4:17	110
5:1–8	58
6:18–31	133
6:20–21	110
6:22	110
6:32–37	65
6:33–34	134
6:34	126, 127
7	101
7:14	126, 127
7:29	135
7:29–30	106
7:29–31	106, 107, 126, 134
7:32	136
8:1–2	127, 134
8:8	127
8:8–9	134
8:14	127
10:1–3	126
11:1	134
11:4	97
11:7	96
13:3–4	127
13:9	82, 134
13:9–11	127
13:11	96
13:18–19	127
13:19	125
14:20–27	133
15:1	110
15:1–20	133
15:5–6	134
16:26–30	133
17:1–24	133
17:11	156
18:1–14	133
19:20–24	133
21:15	156
21:17	127, 134
23:14	134
23:16–21	58
24	23, 25, 100, 109, 133, 190
24–26	53
24:1–12	157, 178
24:2	156
24:10–12	107
24:19	195
24:19–21	195
24:23	110
24:27	30, 32
24:32	32
24:32–33	134
24:32–34	30
24:33	31, 107, 110
26:1	152
26:29	153
26:29–29:28	153
29:1–13	136
29:1–20	125
29:8–9	127
30:27	126
31:12–24	127
33:16–19	134
33:18	134

33:19	126, 134	43:2–8	95
34:1–8	32, 43, 133	43:3	95
34:1–9	100–1	43:4	95
34:3	102	43:24	97
34:5	102	43:32	100
34:6	102	43:32–33	98, 133
34:8	102	43:33	98
34:9–13	134	44–50	23, 135
34:12	127	45	106
34:21–22	174	45:6–7	126
34:21–27	127	45:7	106
34:21–35:13	107	45:15	106
35:1–12	126	45:15–16	126
35:1–13	135	45:17	107
36	138	45:20–21	126
36:11–16	23	45:20–22	126
36:13	158	45:25	106
36:20	159	48:25	98
37:22–24	134	49:12	107
37:23	134	50	106
38:1–3	52	50:1–4	132
38:24	30, 52	50:1–21	126
38:24–39:11	125, 127, 134	50:5–15	126
38:27–34	125	50:13	106
38:32–33	134	50:16	106
38:33	134	51:21–29	30
38:34–39:1	127	51:23	109
39:1	52	**Baruch**	22, 23, 24, 27, 42, 189
39:1–3	30	1:1–3:8	72
39:1–11	30, 107, 141	2:28	23
39:2–3	141	3	23
39:3	52	3:29–30	23
39:4	30, 32, 126, 134	4:1–9	23
39:5–8	26	4:1	25
39:6	134, 156	4:–5:9	24
39:8	32	**1 Maccabees**	
39:10	134	8:23	77
39:16–35	133	12:6	127
42	98	**2 Maccabees**	
42:2	136	7:28	53
42:15	97	**4 Ezra**	20, 21, 26, 27, 33, 53, 189
42:15–25	133	3:1–2	182
42:15–43:33	97	3:28–31	182
42:16	98, 133	9–10	182
42:19	98, 133	14:1–26	26
43	98	14:13	60
43:1–33	133	14:37–48	26

New Testament

Matthew		1:18	157, 158–59
3:1–2	158	1:19	151
5–7	170	1:19–27	151
5:3	171	1:21	156
5:5	171	1:22	155
5:5–12	152	1:23–24	155
7:13–14	188	1:25	152, 153, 161
7:26–30	53	1:27	161, 165, 167
11:28–29	195	2	176
15:24	158	2:1	162
Luke		2:1–7	167, 172
6	170	2:1–12	168
6:20	152, 171	2:5	160, 161, 170, 172
6:20–23	152	2:6	172
12:24–31	53	2:6–7	173
Q	8, 18, 19, 20, 53	2:7	174
Acts		2:8	167, 172
16:19	173	2:8–9	163
19:24	173	2:8–19	163
1 Corinthians		2:12	167
1:27	171	2:13	150
Galatians		2:19	166
4:26	182	2:24	161
6:1	156	2:26	151
Ephesians		3	151
4:2	156	3:1	156, 160
2 Timothy		3:1–12	156
2:25	156	3:5–10	160
Titus		3:13	149, 156
3:2	156	3:13–18	155, 156–57, 167
Hebrews		3:13–4:10	177
12:22	182	3:14–16	157
James	3, 7, 8, 18, 19, 149–78	3:15	176, 178
1:1	157, 167, 172–73	3:16	151
1:2	151, 162	3:17	157
1:4	151	3:17–18	157
1:5	151, 155, 157	3:18	150–51, 157
1:5–8	155	4	151
1:6	151, 156	4:1	151
1:9–10	177	4:1–4	176
1:10	155, 160	4:3	178
1:11	155, 160	4:4	155, 176, 178
1:12	152, 153, 160, 161, 162, 166	4:6	178
1:14–18	176	4:7	176, 178
1:17	157, 159, 178	4:7–10	151

INDEX OF ANCIENT LITERATURE 229

4:10	178	17–18	183
4:12	160	17–21	190
4:13–17	153, 173	17:1	182
5:1	154	17:4	182, 190, 191
5:1–6	153, 154, 159, 168, 173, 174, 175	17:5	191
		17:9	190
5:1–11	166	18	181, 192, 193
5:3	154, 159	18:3	192, 194
5:5	154–55, 159, 163	18:4	182, 183, 3–94, 195
5:7–11	159	18:9–19	193
5:8	159, 176	18:11–13	154
5:9	159, 161, 165	18:12	192
5:12	160	18:16	192
5:16	156	18:19	192
5:17	160	19:7	182, 183
5:20	161	19:7–9	191
1 Peter		19:8	182, 183
3:16	156	19:9	190, 194
5:13	82	19:10	182
Revelation	3, 8, 20, 165, 167, 181–96	20:6	190
1:3	190	21–22	191, 195
1:9	161	21:8	190, 195
2–3	192, 193	21:9	182
2:9	192	21:27	182, 190, 195
3:17–18	192	22:7	190
9:21	190	22:9	182
13:18	190	22:14	182, 190, 195
14:15	190	22:15	190
16:15	190	22:17	195
17	181		

DEAD SEA SCROLLS AND RELATED LITERATURE

Dead Sea Scrolls	49, 58, 81, 202		
Aramaic Levi	6, 48, 90, 91, 93, 94, 95, 96, 99, 100, 102, 105, 108, 110, 111	**1 QpHab**	72
		6:1–5	33
		12.2–6	176
4QLevi^aar	101, 102	**1QS (*Community Rule*)**	29, 46, 188
13–60	105	3:13	33
65–72	94	3:13–4:26	29, 33, 62, 187, 189
82–106	99	4:18–26	29
102–106	99–100	4:25–26	66
106	100	5:7–9	33
1QH (*Hodayot*)	46	6:6	52
12[4]:5–6	32	8:12–16	33
12[4]:5–5:4	33	8:14–15	52
12[4]:27	32	9(1)	33

1QS (*Community Rule*) (*continued*)		4Q417	
11	33	1 i 3	61, 65
11:3–4	61	1 i 3–4	61
11:3–9	29	1 i 6	61, 65
11:19	65	1 i 6–8	62, 65, 66
1Q26 (see also 4Q415–418, 423)		1 i 8	61
1 1	61	1 i 8–9	66
1 4	61	1 i 10–12	62
2 2	62	1 i 12–13	66
1Q27		1 i 18	61, 65
1 i 3–4	61	1 i 18–19	62
4QEn^c		1 i 21	61
1 iv 5	64	1 ii 3	61
5 ii 26–27	64	2 i 10	65
4QpPs37		2 i 10–11	61, 62
2.9–11	176	2 i 17–20	59
4Q161	79	4Q418	
4Q174	79	9 8	61, 65
4Q184	85–87	9 15	61
1–7	86	10 1	61
4Q185	85–87	10 3	61
4Q213b		43 2	61, 65
3–4	99	43 2–3	61
4Q245	79	43 4	61, 65
4Q252	79	43 6	61
4Q285	79	43 14	61, 65
1 9–10	173	43 16	61
4Q415–418, 423 (see also 1Q26)		69 ii	61
(4QInstruction)	3, 5, 46, 57–67	77 2	61, 62
4Q415		77 4	61, 65
6 4	61	81 65	
24 1	61	81 i 12	173
4Q416		81 4–5	61
1	61, 65	81 17	59
2 i 5	61, 65	88 3	59
2 ii 6–7	59	103 ii	62
2 ii 17–18	59	123 ii 3–4	61
2 ii 18–20	60	123 ii 4	61, 64
2 iii 9	61, 65	123 ii 5	65
2 iii 14	61	172 1	61
2 iii 14–15	59	179 3	61
2 iii 15–16	59	184 2	61
2 iii 15–19	60	190 2–3	61
2 iii 18	61	201 1	61
2 iii 18–19	62	219 2	66
2 iii 20–21	62	4Q418c	
2 iii 21	61	8	61

INDEX OF ANCIENT LITERATURE 231

4Q423		CD (*Damascus Document*)	33, 103,
3 2	61, 62	104	
4 1	61	1	35
4 4	61	1:10–12	33
5 2	61	5:6–8	73
7 7	61	6:2–11	33
4Q424			
1 10	60		

OTHER NONCANONICAL JEWISH LITERATURE

Apocalypse of Abraham	20, 21	Parables	69
2 Baruch 20, 21, 25, 26, 27, 33, 52, 53,		1–5	25
189		1–36	137, 164
1:1	25	1:2	137
4	182	2:1–5:4	24, 53
10:1	25, 182	3	28
11:1	182	5:6	24
38:1–4	26	5:8	32, 139
41–42	26	6	28
44–45	60	6–11	103
51:1–10	25	6–16	103, 104, 108
54:1	26	6–36	6, 90
54:13	26	8:3	64
55	26	9	116
67:7	182	9–10	116
76:5	60	10:4–5	115
77 34		10:9	115
3 Baruch	20, 27	10:11–11:2	29
1 Enoch 3, 5, 6, 7, 8, 20, 21, 22, 23, 24,		12–16	21, 24, 103
25, 26, 27, 28, 31, 32, 35, 36, 43, 45, 46,		12:3	31
48, 52, 53, 63, 64, 69, 90, 91, 92, 94, 95,		12:3–13:7	31
99, 100, 103, 104, 105, 108, 109, 110,		12:4	31, 137
111, 113–21, 123–45, 162, 202		13	101
Animal Apocalypse	6, 7, 24,	13:3–7	137
25, 113–21, 137, 138, 140, 145		13:8	137
Apocalypse of Weeks	23, 137,	14	99, 101
138, 145, 164		14:2	137
Astronomical Book 6, 64, 86, 90, 92,		14:8	137
93, 94, 95, 99, 102, 104, 109, 137		14:18–23	137
Book of Watchers	6, 64, 90, 92,	15:1	31, 105, 137
93, 94, 95, 99, 102, 104–5, 108, 115–		15:2	103
21, 137, 138		15:2–4	103
Dream Visions	137, 140	15:34	103
Epistle of Enoch 60, 65, 85, 87, 92,		16:3	64
137, 139, 140, 143, 149, 162–65,		17–19	32
166, 168, 175		17–36	27, 32

1 Enoch (continued)

Reference	Page
19:3	137
20	115
20-36	32
26–27	37
33–36	94
33:2–4	94
34–36	94
37:1	24
41:3	64
42	57
42:1–2	178
52:2	64
62–63	28
72–82	6, 90, 137
72:1	64
75:2	94, 95, 109
80:2–8	94, 95
81:1–2	137
81:1–82:4	24
81:2	64
81:5	115
81:6–82:3	31
82	60
82:1	137
82:1–4	31
82:2–3	139
82:4–7	94, 95, 109
83–90	6, 137
85–90	138
87:2	115
88:1–3	115
89:28–35	24
89:39	138
89:50	138
89:51	114
89:51–53	25
89:59–60	114
89:59–90:27	138
89:61	115
89:66	138
89:67	138
89:73	92
89:73–74	138
89:74	118
90:2	116
90:6	121
90:6–14	141
90:7	118
90:14	115
90:17	115, 116
90:22	115, 116
90:24–25	115
91	24
91:3–4	24
91:4	60
91:11–17	164
91:18–19	24
92–104	85
92–105	24, 25, 27, 92, 137, 149, 154, 162–65, 166, 168
92:1	24, 137, 162
93:1–10	164
93:2	64
93:7	138
93:8	138
93:9	138
93:10	24
93:13	138
94–103	31
94–105	24, 31
94:1	60, 154, 162–63
94:1–4	24
94:6	163
94:6–7	140
94:7	140
94:8	154
94:8–9	163, 175
94:9	160
95:1	154
95:2	154
95:3	154
95:4–7	154
95:6	140
95:7	175
96:1	163
96:1–3	154
96:4–5	175
96:4–8	154
96:5–6	139
96:8	139
97:2	139
97:2–10	154
97:5–6	164

INDEX OF ANCIENT LITERATURE 233

97:6	140, 164	1.7	71
97:8	140	1.17–18	71
97:8–10	160	**Josephus, *Life***	
97:10	140	2	111
98:4	139–40	***Jubilees***	28
98:7–8	140	23:17	35, 52
98:8–99:10	33	30 99	
98:9	31, 139	30:7	99
98:12	140	***Letter of Aristeas***	
98:15	31	96–98	129
99:2	31, 140	**Odes of Solomon**	202
99:10	24, 25, 31	19:1–4	208
99:13	140	40:1	208
99:15	160	**Philo**	185–87, 189
100:5	139	**Philo, *On the Sacrifices of Cain and***	
100:6	31	***Abel***	
100:8	140	20–21	185–86
101:1	53	20–35	184
102:1	164	***Psalms of Solomon***	3, 5, 6, 8, 69–87,
102:4–104:8	28		176
102:9	140	1	70, 72, 73, 83
103:1	64	2	70, 71, 72, 73, 75, 76, 83
103:1–3	164	2:1–2	71
103:3	139–40	2:1–3	71
103:9	139–40	2:4	72
103:11–12	139–40	2:4–8	72
104:12–13	31	2:6	78
105	60	2:7	72
105:2	24	2:7–8	72
106	63	2:8	72
106:19	64	2:11–14	73
2 Enoch	27	2:12	78
Josephus, *Against Apion*		2:15	73
1.187–189	130	2:16	78
Josephus, *Antiquities*		2:18	73
12.138–44	132	2:25	75, 78
12.142	127	2:26	77
12.157–236	130	2:26–27	75
12.158–161	131	2:27	71
12.163	131	2:28–29	75
12.184	131	2:29	77
12.224	132	2:29–30	75
14.3–4	70	2:32	76
14.4	71, 77	2:33	80
14.16	71	2:34	79
Josephus, *Jewish War*		2:36	79
1.6–7	70	3	70

Psalms of Solomon (continued)

3:3	79	14:4	78
3:4	79, 80	15	70
3:5	79	15:1	176
3:8	79	15:6	78
3:12	80	15:13	80
4	70, 80	16	70
4:1	79	16:11	80
4:6	79	17	6, 69, 70, 77–81, 83, 84
4:8	79	17:1	76, 78
4:9–13	78	17:3	76, 78, 80
4:20–22	78	17:5	74, 77
4:21	78	17:6	74, 80
4:23	80	17:6–10	74
4:24	78, 80	17:7	71
5:1–4	78	17:9	71
5:5	78	17:11	71
5:18	80	17:12	71
6	70	17:13	80
7:3	80	17:14	71
7:9	80	17:15	78
8	70, 73, 83	17:16	79
8:1–6	73	17:17	78
8:7	73	17:18	78
8:9	73	17:19	78
8:9–13	73	17:20	78
8:10	73	17:21	78, 85
8:11	73	17:22–27	78
8:12	73	17:23	80
8:16–17	71	17:26	79
8:18–20	71	17:28	80
8:23	79	17:29	80
8:23–24	73	17:30	80
8:33	76	17:30–31	81
9	70	17:32	79
9:3	79	17:33	80
10	70	17:34	76, 78, 81
10:2	80	17:37	80
10:6	79, 176	17:39	80
12	70	17:40	80
12:1	78	17:41	78, 80
12:4	78, 80	17:42	80
13	70	17:43	79, 81
13:7	80	17:46	76, 78
13:8	80	17:51	78
13:12	80	17:23	78
14	70	18:2	176

Sibylline Oracles		13:1–9	105
3.562	153	14:4	105
5.420–27	182	*Testament of Moses*	28, 69
5.143	182	*Testament of Reuben*	
5.159	182	3.13	191
Testament of Judah		*Testaments of the Twelve Patriarchs*	
13.4–5	191	188, 190	
Testament of Levi	90, 92, 99		
8:17	105		

Noncanonical Christian Literature

Epistle of Barnabas	3, 9, 188, 197–213	8:5	210
1–17	197	8:6	211
1:11	203	10	206
2–16	205	11	211
2:1	197, 203, 204	12	211, 212
2:1–3	205	12:2	211
2:2–3	204	12:9	211–12
2:3	205, 213	12:10	211
2:10	203	12:10–11	212
4	204–8, 213	12:11	212
4:1	204	13:1	206
4:3	202, 204	14	206
4:3–5	198–99	16:1–4	198–99
4:5	206	16:4	201
4:6–8	206, 207	18–20	197
4:9	205	18:1	203
4:13	203, 205	Clement of Alexandria	185, 189, 191, 202
5	207		
5–8	207	Clement of Alexandria, *Paedagogus*	
5:1	207	2.10.110	184
5:3	203	*Didache*	**188**
5:6	208	3.7	171
6	211	*Gospel of Thomas*	
6:8	208	54	171
6:11	208	**Justin Martyr**	**202**
6:12	208	Justin Martyr, *Second Apology*	
6:13	203	11	184
6:13–14	209	Justin Martyr, *Dialogue with Trypho*	
6:16–17	209	49:7	212
6:18	209	Polycarp, *To the Philippians*	
6:19	210	2:3	171
7	210	*Shepherd of Hermas*	188
7:11	210		
8	210, 211		

Greek, Roman, and Ancient Near Eastern Literature

Aelius Aristides	184, 189	Lucian, *Hermotimus*	184
Story of Ahikar	23	Lucian, *On Salaried Posts*	184
105	59	Lucian, *Professor of Public*	
137	59	*Speaking*	184
Athenaeus, *Deipnosophistae*		Maximus of Tyre	184
12.510	184	Maximus of Tyre, *Orations*	
Cicero, *On the Offices*		14.1	184
1.32.118	184, 185	Oracles of Hystaspes	202
Dio Chrysostom	185, 191	Philostratus	89
Dio Chrysostom, *Orations*		Philostratus, *Life of Apollonius*	
1.66–84	184	6.10	184, 190
1.79	190	Philostratus, *Lives of the Sophists*	
Diodorus Siculus		482–83	184
40.3	129	496	184
Epictetus		Pseudo-Hecataeus	130
1.2.20	153	Silius Italicus	184
1.6.37	153	Silius Italicus, *On Punishments*	
3.24.40	153	15.1–132	184
Hecataeus of Abdera	129	15.25	190
Julian, *Orations*		Tabula of Cebes	184, 190–91
2.57	184	Xenophon of Athens	191
Lucian	184–85	Xenophon of Athens, *Memorabilia*	
Lucian, *Double Indictment*		2.1.21–22	184, 187
21	184		
Lucian, *The Dream*			
6	184		

INDEX OF MODERN AUTHORS

Aarde, A. van 149
Aitken, E. B.   9, 12, 13, 202, 208, 215
Alexander, L. 193
Allegro, J. 186
Argall, R. A.   10, 11, 12, 22, 24, 25, 31, 32, 43, 45, 48, 58, 82, 91, 92, 94, 96, 97, 100, 101, 110, 111, 121, 139, 188, 215, 217
Atkinson, K.   70, 71, 78, 79, 81, 215
Avery-Peck, A. J.   4, 9, 11, 37
Bagnall, R. 130
Baltzer, K. 202
Barnard, L. W.   199, 201, 202, 215
Bauckham, R. 193
Baumgartner, W. 23
Bedenbender, A. 57
Beentjes, P. C.   90, 97, 134, 219
Berger, K. 187, 189
Berquist, J. L.   11, 43, 44, 47, 128
Bettenson, H. 194
Black, M.   94, 95, 109, 175
Blenkinsopp, J.   128, 129
Boccaccini, G.   90, 92, 93, 110, 215, 219
Bockmuehl, M. 63
Boer, M. C. de 13
Boismard, M.-E. 182
Bow, B. A. 217
Brown, R. E. 63
Bruce, I. A. F. 200
Bryan, D. 118
Burkes, S. 58
Camp, C. V.   11, 14, 188
Caquot, A. 70
Carleton Paget, J.   200, 201, 215
Carr, D. M.   14, 60, 215
Charles, R. H.   17, 114, 115, 215
Charlesworth, J. H.   27, 41, 162, 217
Chazon, E. G.   13, 54, 90, 218, 219

Clements, R. A. 219
Clements, R. E.   123, 216
Clifford, R. 195
Collins, A. Y.   12, 14, 194, 215
Collins, J. J.   5, 9, 11, 17, 19, 20, 22, 27, 28, 40, 41, 42, 43, 44, 45, 57, 58, 59, 60, 78, 83, 142, 143, 149, 162, 165, 166, 169, 187, 189, 190, 215, 216, 217
Corley, J.   90, 219
Coughenour, R. A.   22, 24
Court, J.   182, 183, 216
Crenshaw, J. L.   18, 41, 42, 44, 51, 60, 63, 150, 216
Crim, K. R. 83
Cross, F. M.   21, 57, 218
Crossan, J. D. 69
Cryer, F. L. 62
Dahl, N. A. 208
Davids, P. H.   156, 157, 158, 159, 170, 178, 216
Davies, P. R.   91, 123, 125, 128, 129, 144, 216, 217
Dibelius, M.   150, 151, 156, 158, 172, 173, 177, 178, 216
Di Lella, A. A.   90, 96, 97, 98, 101, 106, 110
Doran, R.   10, 12, 14, 37
Draper, J. A. 13
Dupont-Somer, A. 81
Eissfeldt, O. 81
Elgvin, T.   10, 58, 60, 61, 62, 65
Elliot, N. 12
Eshel, E. 94
Falk, D. 59
Fekkes, J. 183
Flannery, F. 52
Flint, P. W. 58
Foerster, W. 76

Fox, M. V.	42, 47	Johnson, L. T.	73, 158, 170, 172, 173, 178, 217
Frerichs, E. S.	92		
Friesen, S. J.	12	Johnson, T. J.	14
Gammie, J. G.	19, 57, 149, 169	Jonge, M. de	70, 75, 80, 90
García Martínez, F.	37, 63, 73, 176	Kampen, J.	11, 12, 14, 58, 202
Gebhardt, O.	115	Kloppenborg, J. S.	11
Gera, D.	130	Knibb, M. A.	11, 64
Gillihan, Y. M.	13	Knight, D. A.	17, 18
Ginsberg, H. L.	25	Koch, K.	17, 20, 217
Gitin, S.	10	Koester, H.	170
Goff, M. J.	5, 13, 58, 61, 66, 216	Kraft, R. A.	11, 17, 18, 188, 189, 199, 201, 202, 203, 204, 205, 212, 215, 217, 218
Goodman, M.	201		
Gottwald, N.	129		
Grabbe, L. L.	10, 43	Kraybill, J. N.	194
Grant, R. M.	199, 217	Kugler, R. A.	90, 94, 99, 217
Green, D. E.	202	Kurtz, M. R.	12, 130
Greenfield, J. C.	94, 99, 102	Lange, A.	58, 62
Greeven, H.	172, 216	LaPorte, J.	185
Gruen, E. S.	12	Larcher, C.	28
Gunkel, H.	17	Larsen, K. B.	59
Gunther, J. J.	199	Laws, S.	158, 161
Habel, N.	188	Leeuwen, R. Van	188
Halligan, J. M.	10, 91, 125, 217	Lemke, W. E.	218
Hann, R. R.	81, 82	Lenski, G.	91, 107, 124
Hanson, P. D.	17, 20, 216	Lewis, N.	101
Harrington, D. J.	10, 12, 43, 58, 59, 61, 62, 64, 66, 186, 187, 216	Lieu, J.	91
		Mack, B. L.	18, 135
Hartin, P. J.	5, 7, 8, 10, 169, 170, 216	Magness, J.	10
Hauck, F.	152, 153	Martin, F.	115
Hellholm, D.	92, 195, 218	Martin, J. D.	1, 18, 58, 218
Hempel, C.	58, 91	Meyers, C. L.	195
Hengel, M.	34, 97, 101	Milavec, A.	13
Henze, M.	12	Milik, J. T.	90, 94, 217
Himmelfarb, M.	102, 103, 105, 108, 216	Miller, P. C.	101
Hofmann, J. Chr. K. von	115	Miller, P. D.	105, 218
Hoglund, K.	188	Moore, R.	186
Hollander, H. W.	90	Muilenberg, J.	195
Horsley, R. A.	7, 9, 12, 13, 19, 39, 43, 48, 69, 76, 79, 82, 85, 86, 89, 91, 107, 108, 111, 125, 129, 139, 216, 217	Müller, H.-P.	5, 57, 217
		Murphy, C. M.	11, 59, 61
		Murphy, R. E.	18
Hvalvik, R.	202, 206	Murphy-O'Connor, J.	195
Inowlocki, S.	14	Mussner, F.	156, 158, 159
Isaac, E.	162	Najman, H.	61
Jackson-McCabe, M. A.	11, 169	Neugebauer, O.	95
Jacobson, A.	10	Neusner, J.	4, 9, 11, 32, 37, 92, 96
Jewett, R.	10	Newman, J. H.	61
Johnson, E. E.	10, 13	Newsom, C.	11, 13, 117, 118

INDEX OF MODERN AUTHORS

Nickelsburg, G. W. E. 3, 4, 5, 9, 10, 11, 12, 13, 14, 17, 18, 23, 25, 27, 28, 32, 33, 35, 37, 39, 40, 41, 42, 44, 46, 49, 54, 57, 64, 70, 72, 83, 90, 91, 92, 95, 99, 102, 103, 105, 108, 109, 119, 123, 149, 162, 163, 164, 165, 167, 189, 215, 217, 219
Olyan, S. M. 92, 96, 104, 106, 107, 135, 136, 218
Parry, D. W. 58, 60
Pearson, B. A. 22
Penner, T. C. 170
Perdue, L. G. 19, 42, 149, 169, 189, 216
Pickett, R. 13
Piper, R. A. 12
Pleins, J. D. 59
Porter, P. 117
Price, S. F. R. 12, 76
Prigent, P. 190, 191, 199, 201, 202, 203, 212, 218
Prostmeier, F. R. 199, 200, 202
Puech, É. 37
Rad, G. von 1, 18, 21, 57, 58, 73
Rahlfs, A. 69
Ramsaran, R. A. 13, 14
Reeves, J. C. 202
Richard, P. 194
Richardson, P. 199, 200, 201
Ricks, S. D. 60
Rigaux, B. 63
Robinson, J. A. T. 200
Rofé, A. 96
Rossing, B. R. 8, 9, 12, 218
Ruiz, J.-P. 182
Russell, D. S. 86
Saldarini A. J. 11
Sanders, J. T. 10
Satran, D. 219
Sayler, G. B. 34
Schaper, J. 128
Schiffman, L. H. 58, 187, 216
Schlier, H. 161
Schürer, E. 72, 74
Schüssler Fiorenza, E. 190, 195, 218
Schwartz, S. 131
Scott, B. B. 216
Scott, J. M. 13
Segal, A. F. 60
Shils, E. 104
Shiner, W. 14
Shukster, M. B. 199, 200, 201
Skehan, P. W. 90, 96, 97, 98, 101, 106, 110
Skemp, V. 90, 219
Smallwood, E. M. 200
Smith, J. Z. 22, 34, 57, 218
Soulen, R. N. 83
Stadelmann, H. 106
Stalker, D. M. G. 58
Stone, M. E. 17, 21, 24, 26, 32, 57, 90, 93, 94, 99, 102, 104, 105, 108, 218
Strugnell, J. 58, 59, 61, 62, 64, 66
Suter, D. 99, 102, 103, 104, 105, 218
Talmon, S. 93
Tanzer, S. J. 4, 5, 9, 11, 14, 51, 53
Tcherikover, V. 92, 130
Thomas, C. M. 13
Thompson, L. 193, 218
Thompson, T. L. 62
Tigchelaar, E. J. C. 14, 58, 59, 61, 62, 73, 219
Tiller, P. A. 6, 8, 10, 12, 14, 48, 91, 107, 108, 111, 113, 115, 118, 121, 125, 132, 217, 219
Tov, E. 58
Trafton, J. L. 81
Tromp, J. 77
Tucker, G. M. 17, 18
VanderKam, J. C. 57, 58, 95, 118, 219
Vanhoye, A. 182
Vermes, G. 32, 72, 186
Vogt, E. 63
Volz, P. 17
Vouga, F. 172, 173, 178
Ward, R. B. 172
Watson, W. G. E. 176
Wellhausen, J. 81
Wengst, K. 202
Werline, R. A. 5, 12, 52, 73, 85, 217, 219
Westermann, C. 83
Wettstein, J. 190, 191
White, J. L. 76
Wilken, R. L. 185

Williams, D. K.	13	Woude, A. S. van der	144, 216
Williams, M. A.	150, 172	Wright, B. G.	6, 10, 11, 12, 13, 43, 48, 134, 135, 137, 219
Wills, L. M.	13, 14, 141, 143, 202		
Wiseman, W. J.	216	Wright, R. B.	69, 72, 74, 76, 79, 81, 84, 85, 176
Wolfson, E. R.	61		
Wooden, R. G.	14	Wright, W. C.	184

www.ingramcontent.com/pod-product-compliance
Lightning Source LLC
Chambersburg PA
CBHW030341240426
43661CB00052B/1700